ALSO BY DAVE ZIRIN

A People's History of Sports in the United States

Welcome to the Terrordome: The Pain, Politics, and Promise of Sports

Muhammad Ali Handbook

What's My Name, Fool? Sports and Resistance in the United States

BAD SPORTS

How Owners Are Ruining the Games We Love

Dave Zirin

Scribner

NEW YORK   LONDON   TORONTO   SYDNEY

SCRIBNER

A Division of Simon & Schuster, Inc.
1230 Avenue of the Americas
New York, NY 10020

First Scribner hardcover edition July 2010

SCRIBNER and design are registered trademarks of The Gale Group, Inc.,
used under license by Simon & Schuster, Inc., the publisher of this work.

For information about special discounts for bulk purchases, please contact
Simon & Schuster Special Sales at 1-866-506-1949
or business@simonandschuster.com.

The Simon & Schuster Speakers Bureau can bring authors to your
live event. For more information or to book an event contact
the Simon & Schuster Speakers Bureau at 1-866-248-3049
or visit our website at www.simonspeakers.com.

Text designed by Paul Dippolito

Manufactured in the United States of America

1   3   5   7   9   10   8   6   4   2

Library of Congress Cataloging-in-Publication Data

Zirin, Dave.
Bad sports : how owners are ruining the games we love / Dave Zirin.
p.   cm.
1. Sports—Management. 2. Sports—Economic aspects—United States.
3. Stadiums—United States—Finance. 4. Sports facilities—United States—Finance.
5. Sports and state—United States. I. Title.
GV713.Z57 2010
796.06'9—dc22   2009049920

ISBN 978-1-4165-5475-2
ISBN 978-1-4391-7574-3 (ebook)

To Izzy and Jacob. Little brothers unite!
And to the memory of Dennis Brutus,
Andrea Lewis, Lester Rodney, and Howard Zinn.

I'd rather own than be owned.

—STEPHON MARBURY, BASKETBALL PLAYER,
WANDERING SEEKER OF TRUTH

Contents

BAD SPORTS

Intro: Diogenes in High Tops

In a rich man's house there is no place to spit but his face.

—DIOGENES

I once had a coach who could spit tobacco hard enough to break a window. He smelled like a hamper and only wore pants that came with a drawstring. And every last person on the team loved the guy. He always said to us, "Sports is like a hammer, gents. And you can use a hammer for all kinds of things. You can use it to build a house, or you can use it to bash somebody's head. Choose wisely."

In the twenty-first century, far too many sports fans have a headache that is rapidly entering migraine territory. It's not just the 1,440 minutes a day of televised sports coverage causing the damage. It's not even the sports talk radio blabbocracy that is making people reach for the Extra Strength Tylenol. The headache comes from the idea that we are loving something that simply doesn't love us in return. If sports was once like a playful puppy you would wrestle on the floor, it's now like a house cat demanding to be stroked and giving nothing back. It's the way it gets harder to sit through a full game, or the way you go a year without making it to the ballpark and fail to even notice. It's the extra commercials tacked on to a broadcast, as companies attempt to use the games to "brand" our subconscious. It's when you decide to finally take the trip to the park, look up the ticket prices, and decide immediately to do something, anything, else with your time. It's the way you don't feel the same urgency to watch every second of every game for fear you might miss something magical. As economic times get tougher, the question of what to trim out of the budget doesn't become a question at all.

Fun has become pain, and sports have become expendable. Ask a junior high classroom whether they know or even care about sports, and the answer should send a chill up the spine of all league commissioners. In my mind, this is a tragic state of affairs. How did sports become so overbearing in our culture, and yet so distant from our personal embrace? When, as fans, did we develop the equivalent of battered spouse's syndrome? And who is at fault for this state of affairs? There are certainly fans who blame the players for being too wealthy and too aloof. If only they didn't live in gated communities, only emerging to charge for autographs. There also are nonfans who blame the fans themselves. If only they would stop buying tickets and merchandise, the game would change. But the days of pointing the finger at players and fans have to end. If a car's brakes failed, you wouldn't blame the driver. All eyes would be on the manufacturer. If professional sports have been beating us over the head with their hammer, it's the owners who need to answer for this sorry state of affairs. Players play. Fans watch. Owners are uniquely charged with being the stewards of the game. It's a task that they have failed to perform in spectacular fashion.

These are the caretakers, and yet, with barely a sliver of scrutiny, they are wrecking the world of sports. The old model of the paternalistic owner caring for a community has become as outdated as the Model T. Because of publicly funded stadium construction, luxury box licenses, sweetheart cable deals, globalized merchandizing plans, and other "revenue streams," the need for owners to cater to a local working- and middle-class fan base has shrunk dramatically. Fans have become scenery for television broadcasts.

The fastest-growing sector of fans? People who love sports, but hate what they are becoming. I interviewed a focus group of more than three thousand fans for this book and this feeling of resentment was the common denominator. As one person said, "I still check out the games but I feel no connection. It's like sex that I feel dirty about afterward."

Yes, people watch but, with rare exceptions, no longer see sports as a linchpin of community cohesion. Because owners believe that they don't need the fans, they do more than put the interests of those who don the foam finger last: they have also, in a novel and unprecedented manner, used the ballpark as a showcase for their politics, which tend to be of the right-of-center persuasion. We have seen a hyperpatriotism and even a religious program being brought to the often publicly funded playing field. They seem to be saying that it's their world and we just live in it even if our taxes pay for their stadiums with every unfilled pothole and underfunded library. It's time to upset the setup.

Whether you are a sports fan or not, sports affects the national discussion and economy like never before. It shapes how we understand our cultural landscape and is a prime economic player in the game of urban politics. It also rests under a dizzying maze of government antitrust exemptions and secrecy like no other business of comparable size. The reason why the bulk of owners are unknown, hiding in the darkness, is that the light is kind neither to them nor their spreadsheets. Like the fey Blanche DuBois, they are favored by shadows, and certainly financially they deeply "depend on the kindness of strangers"—us.

This book is going to argue that every last shred of absolute power they possess should be stripped from their hands. The sports fan, Joe Twelve-Pack, Plain Jane, Mario Marginalized, needs to have a seat at the table, particularly if our teams get even one solitary dollar of public money. If a team owner is particularly abusive to a community, local fans should be able to divvy up the shares and buy the team back. This is not just about tax justice. It's about a project of reclamation: a grand adventure to change the game.

I didn't feel that way before starting this project. I wanted to speak to every last owner who would talk to me. I wanted them to defend the way our modern athletic industrial complex is run. I wanted to see if they felt their teams were still the vital cogs to our communities that they once were.

I spent the last year trying to land an interview with any one of them. The goals of the interview were straightforward: to find an owner who believes in the good of sports before the good of their pocketbooks; someone who cares about the long-term health of the product over short-term gain; someone who thinks players don't sign away their humanity just because they sign a contract; someone who doesn't see publicly funded stadiums as a divine right; someone who sees his team's health as a community political trust instead of an individual political opportunity. I was searching for an owner who would openly address why, despite the unprecedented popularity of sports, so many fans are down on the games themselves. I wanted to ask how ownership can be so at odds with the pulse of fans. Like Diogenes, I was just searching for an honest person.

In Ancient Greece, Diogenes the Cynic carried a lamp in daylight, engaged in his quest for an honest man. I was ready to be proudly cynical as I went about my task. Cynicism, in the classical sense, isn't about rudely doubting the best intentions of others like some flannel-wearing, grunge-era slacker. It's about the search for truth. As Simon Critchley, author of *The Book of Dead Philosophers,* wrote, "Cynicism is basically a moral protest against hypocrisy and cant in politics and excess and thoughtless self-indulgence in the conduct of life. In a world like ours, which is slowly trying to rouse itself from the dogmatic slumbers of boundless self-interest, corruption, lazy cronyism and greed, it is Diogenes' lamp that we need to light our path."[1]

I was ready to shine the lamp, to be skeptical, to actually rejoice in the face of good intentions but recoil at hypocrisy. But not one owner took the bait. We sent out a hundred letters. We made a thousand phone calls. I even dropped in on an office or five. I was very polite. I didn't have a camera. I wasn't trying to be a somewhat-more-svelte Michael Moore. I just wanted to chat. And yet their lips were sewed tighter than a mob boss in front of a congressional inquiry. I contacted all the appropriate offices, set up appointments, but as soon as questions were submitted in advance, I was done.

One owner actually did get back to me, and for that I am grateful. I almost dedicated this book to him. His name is Ed Snider, and he is the CEO of Comcast Spectacor and the power behind the Philadelphia 76ers and Flyers. I learned from Mr. Snider that he believes the best thing about being an owner is that "you never get bored." The worst thing is that "the salaries are entirely out of whack." I learned that he has "never had the problem" of a player with objectionable political beliefs. I learned that he believes owners need to be "visible to the fans. The fans should be able to identify with the owner, and the owner should be able to identify with the fans."[2] I learned little else. After a few more aphorisms, the dial tone was in my ear and I was yesterday's reporter.

Why does the taciturn Snider, in the pantheon of owners, qualify as loquacious? Maybe they just don't like talking to sportswriters. When it comes to some of my brethren, I could not be more sympathetic. As the late Hunter S. Thompson put it, with his delicate sensibility, "Sportswriters are a rude and brainless subculture of fascist drunks, a gang of vicious monkeys jerking off in a zoo cage . . . more disgusting by nature than maggots oozing out the carcass of a dead animal."[3] Not exactly someone any sane person would want to join for a cup of coffee.

Maybe owners have just written off the media as irrelevant to their grand plans. As the Napoleonic Daniel Snyder, owner of the Washington Redskins, has shown, if you don't like the press you're getting, one option is just to buy your own. Or maybe their lips were sealed because of my own minor, low-frequency reputation as something of a muckraker who has opposed the public funding of stadiums, the crackdown on players for political outspokenness, and the general ham-handedness of ownership. Either way, it's that inscrutable voice of ownership that is missing from this book. But their silence is, in its own way, a powerful commentary.

It's not that all sports owners are venal, snacking on baby seal quesadillas with Goldman Sachs executives before going to their publicly financed dog fight. The issue is that evil or not, accountability and accessibility do not rank high on their to-do list.

We shouldn't expect sports owners to reform out of the goodness of their hearts. They represent corporations trying to max out every last cent. But it's one thing when we pay insane ticket prices and then also shell out money for both parking at the stadium and then the shuttle to get from the parking lot to the stadium entrance. That can be enraging, but it's still our choice. It's another thing altogether when the owners both call for and receive public funds and taxpayer dollars. We need to insist that by taking our money, they are entering into an unspoken agreement not just with the various mayors, governors, or political lackeys eager to lick some sweet salt off the rim, but also the citizens themselves. One theme we will return to over and over in the following pages is that if our dollars are to be used, we must have some say in the way the teams are operated. One of the fans I interviewed, James Generic, said to me, "I can't stand how the owners extort money from the public on the stadiums and then charge freaking seven bucks for a beer at a game!"

We have every right to demand to be treated like humans. And there is no human who should have to suffer a plastic bottle of Coors Light for seven dollars.

By looking at a series of the more high-profile and nefarious owners, I hope to make a simple case: well-intentioned or otherwise, owners in the twenty-first century are destroying what took more than a hundred years to build. Some simply aren't fit to lead. Throughout this book we will hear other voices: those of the fans I spoke to. Sports fans at times are presented as being just a step up on the evolutionary scale from a feces-tossing baboon. But their words here are of people sick and tired of feeling like going to a game is an expensive exercise in masochism. Sports fan Harvey Bender said to me bluntly, "The only connection owners have to their communities any longer is profit extraction."

I will start by looking at the man who set the mold and then didn't have the good grace to break it: New York Yankees boss George Steinbrenner. The press now speaks of the wheelchair-bound eighty-year-old patriarch with a very understandable and reverential nostalgia. This was a man of his time, the larger-than-life paternalistic owner. But while Steinbrenner may be a throwback to a different style of ownership, he is also a "throw forward" whose style and persona have spawned a series of crude clones, as little Boys from the Bronx populate the owners' boxes of the sports world. Big Stein copyrighted the patent on the idea of repeatedly threatening to move your team and squeezing the taxpayer to the point of wheezing. He may have invented this method of business, but others have perfected it. I will look at how Oklahoma City Thunder owner Clay Bennett, like Steinbrenner on steroids, took the hoops team of Shawn Kemp, Gary Payton, and Slick Watts, the Seattle SuperSonics, and tore them from their roots, implanting them in his hometown of Oklahoma City.

But they are just the beginning. I will also look at the way politics and the right-wing edge of the evangelical movement are starting to use sports as a soapbox. This fusing of politics and religion spans from former sports owner and former president George W. Bush and his stint as head of Major League Baseball's Texas Rangers, to examining Colorado Rockies owner Charlie Monfort and Orlando Magic boss Dick DeVos.

Then there are the "death-grip" owners, whose presence has been so toxic to their organization and community that they could run the baseball team of All-Star ghosts from *Field of Dreams* and still lose: Dan

Snyder and Peter Angelos of the NFL's Washington Redskins and Major League Baseball's Baltimore Orioles, respectively, have destroyed two of the proudest teams in sports. I also look at Donald Sterling of the Los Angeles Clippers, David Glass of the Kansas City Royals, and James Dolan of the New York Knicks. Three different teams and three different markets but all crippled by ownership incompetence. (Apologies to all Oakland residents that Raiders boss Al Davis was not included on this list.) I also examine how mismanagement is destroying the National Hockey League and how the son of former secretary of the Treasury Hank Paulson, he of the $700 billion in bank bailout funds, is attempting to extract funds for a public stadium in the liberal enclave of Portland, Oregon.[4] The stories are different, but I hope that they weave together a picture about the many offensive heads on this chimerical creature called ownership. To be clear, there are without question owners who by any objective measure fulfill their responsibilities to their community, owners who treat both players and fans with a measure of respect. My argument here is that owners who pillage their communities should face consequences, and we need to start thinking of ways to remove teams from the clutches of "death-grip" owners. One way is to build movements of fans. In chapter 15, I examine the situation in England where Texas Rangers owner Tom Hicks bought the beloved soccer team Liverpool FC and how fans have refused to be financial roadkill. We also need to start a discussion about alternatives to private ownership.

One possible alternative could be the team in the small city of Green Bay, Wisconsin. The Green Bay Packers, a team owned for decades lock, stock, and cracker barrel by fans, is woven into the tapestry of that city in a way that makes you think you're traveling back to a perhaps fictional time when fans came first. Although rarely discussed in detail, the Green Bay ownership structure could be the living, breathing, successful alternative we have been waiting for.

Mike Lupica of the *New York Daily News* once wrote, "You are owed nothing in sports, no matter how much you care. You are owed nothing no matter how long you've rooted or how much you've paid to do it."[5] I couldn't disagree more. We are owed plenty by the athletic industrial complex. We are owed loyalty. We are owed accessibility. We are owed a return on our massive civic investment. And more than anything, we should raise our fists to the owner's box and say that we are owed a little bit of goddamn respect. We aren't owed this respect because it's the kind or the human thing to do. We aren't owed any love because we cheered ourselves hoarse and passed the precious rooting tradition down to our children. We are owed it because the teams are ours as much as they are theirs. Literally. By calling for and receiving public funds, owners have sacrificed their moral, if not financial claim, of ownership. It's unrealistic to expect owners to behave better on their own recognizance, but cities and city councils that hand over funds to the sports plutocracy should in turn have some say in the way the teams are operated. As Jesse Barton, a former assistant city manager in Coos Bay, Oregon, said to me, "If the teams truly are a public good, government should acquire appropriate equity stakes in the teams in which they invest. But the owners virtually always resist that. The reason they resist is that the owners know that fundamentally, their teams aren't a type of public good. They know that instead, their teams are a business that serves a particular segment of society, and not the society in general."[6]

The last goal of this book is to ask the question: whose games are these, anyway? Are they the property of owners who let us watch for a price, or are they ours, and owners should merely play the role of caretaker for the generations of fans who animate their games? And if the games are ours, then who should own the teams? Dare we imagine a world without Steinbrenners? It's not like we haven't paid for the privilege.

The classic Coen brothers' film *Miller's Crossing* includes a line where the world-weary Tom says to the crime boss Leo, "You only run this town because people think you run it. The minute they stop thinking it, you stop running it."[7] The first step is bringing these titans of the luxury box down to earth. Up close the flaws become craters, and the steps we need to take crystallize as we conceive of reclaiming the games we love.

This question affects all of us whether we see ourselves as sports fans or not and the cost of not holding ownership accountable can prove deadly.

1. When Domes Attack

I n August 2005, when Hurricane Katrina flattened New Orleans and the world saw the levees rupture, the only safe harbor for poor residents was in the Louisiana Superdome. When the Mississippi River bridge collapsed in Minneapolis, Minnesota, the new Twins stadium was to break ground that very week. In spring of 2009, when a Washington, D.C., Metro train went off the tracks, a publicly funded $1 billion stadium had just opened its doors the previous year.

There is no Montgomery Burns or Bond villain celebrating this state of affairs. No one in the owner's box is maniacally chortling as our cities rot (at least I hope not). There are finite resources in a given city budget in the best of times, and these are anything but the salad days and these are the results when stadiums come first.

The landscape is made worse by the fact that during the economic boom of the 1990s, the longest period of economic expansion in U.S. history, publicly funded stadiums became the substitute for anything resembling an urban policy in this country. These stadiums, ballparks, arenas, and domes were presented as a microwave-instant solution to the problems of crumbling schools, urban decay, and suburban flight. They are now the excrement of the urban neoliberalism of the 1990s, sporting shrines to the dogma of trickle-down economics. In the past twenty-five years, more than $30 billion of the public's money has been spent for stadium construction and upkeep from coast to coast.[1] Though many cities now resist paying the full tab, any kind of subsidy is a fool's investment, ending up being little more than monuments to corporate greed: $500 million welfare hotels for America's billionaires built with funds that could have been spent more wisely on just about anything else.

And the dollar amount keeps growing. We are perhaps extorted from most visibly when our communities cover a stadium's price tag. But this isn't the only method the sports bosses use to stick us with the bill. A college football bowl game might be brought to us by GMAC, but the only reason GMAC still has a pulse is the more than $10 billion it has received in the taxpayer bailout funds. Last year, a proposed ban on federal stimulus dollars going to stadiums was also dropped.

As Neil deMause, coauthor of the book *Field of Schemes,* said to me, "The history of the stadium game is the story of how, by slowly refining their blackmail skills, sports owners learned how to turn their industry from one based on selling tickets to one based on extracting public subsidies. It's been a bit like watching a four-year-old learn how to manipulate his parents into buying him the new toy that he saw on TV; the question now is how long it takes our elected officials to learn to say 'no.' "[2]

But our elected officials have been more like the children in this scenario, as sports owners tousle their hair and set the budget agendas for municipalities around the country with a simple credo: stadiums first and people last.

Polls show that consistent majorities don't want public funds spent on stadiums.[3] That means a bulk of sports fans oppose the stadium glut as well. We may love baseball. We may love football. We may bleed our team's colors on game day. But that doesn't mean we should have to pay a billionaire millions of dollars for the privilege to watch. The counterargument is job creation. But employment opportunities created by the domes are the kinds of irregular poverty wage jobs that expand the gap between rich and poor. "They're parking garage attendants, they are hot dog salespeople, they are waiters and waitresses, sometimes cooks, people who do maintenance work and repair work and cleaning," said Cleveland union activist John Ryan during that city's stadium battles. "And none of them are jobs that the mayor hugs his kids and says, 'I hope you can get one of those jobs someday.' "[4]

We've now seen the extreme results of these kinds of priorities. In cities as politically, ethnically, and geographically diverse as New Orleans, Minneapolis, and Washington, D.C., the results are like a horror movie: *When Domes Attack.*

NOLA

After Hurricane Katrina flattened the Gulf Coast, the Louisiana Super-dome morphed into a homeless shelter from hell, inhabited yet uninhabit-able for an estimated thirty thousand of New Orleans's poorest residents.[5]

It took Hurricane Katrina for them to actually see the inside of the Superdome, a stadium whose ticket prices make entry an exclusive affair. At the time of the hurricane, game tickets cost $90, season seats went for $1,300, and luxury boxes for eight home games ran more than $100,000 a year. But the Katrina refugees' tickets were courtesy of the federal and local government's malignant neglect.

It was only fitting, because these thirty thousand people helped pay for the stadium in the first place. The Superdome was built entirely on the public dime in 1975, as a part of efforts to create a "New New Orleans" business district.[6] New Orleans leaders have a history of elevating politi-cal graft to a finely honed art, and in this case they did not disappoint. Much of jazz legend Louis Armstrong's historic old neighborhood was ripped up for extra stadium parking,[7] and, in an instance of brutal fore-shadowing that would shame Wes Craven, an old, aboveground cemetery was eradicated to make space for the end zones.[8] As a Saints fan said to me, "New Orleans's football team is nicknamed 'the Saints,' their brand is the fleur-de-lis, and the owner, Tom Benson, makes no bones about dancing on other people's graves. Oh, yeah, the fleur-de-lis was also the emblem viciously branded on enslaved Africans to identify them as being from Louisiana. Talk about ownership."[9]

New Orleans officials decided that building the largest domed sta-dium on the planet was in everyone's best interests. Even coming in years late, and at triple the expected budget, the Superdome was ready for busi-ness in August 1975.[10] And business it has brought. It has been the site of six Super Bowls, four Final Fours, and the 1988 Republican National Con-vention.[11] It is now the home of the 2010 Super Bowl champion Saints. It also launched a thirty-year path toward destruction for the Big Easy: a path that has seen investment for the tourist industry and the accom-panying minimum-wage jobs, but no stable industry; a path that's seen money for the stadium but not for levees; money for the stadium but not for relief following an all-too-predictable disaster.

The tragedy of Katrina then became a farce when the Superdome's inhabitants were finally moved: not to government housing, public shelters, or even another location in the area, but to the Houston Astrodome. Ladies and gentlemen, in a moment when charity and irony collided, we had the March of Domes. Houston was a fitting destination. This was a place that stood up to the NFL's Houston Oilers when they demanded a new stadium. The mayor, Bob Lanier, said at the time, "The subsidy they get is totally disproportionate to the economic benefit they bring. . . . It would shame Jay Gould and his fellow robber barons of the nineteenth century. Even Genghis Khan got sated after a while."[12] Lanier, it should be pointed out, then caved, in 1998, when a new baseball stadium was demanded by Houston Astros' owner Drayton McLane. The city then funded the infamously named Enron Field. Lanier said, "The result [of not using public funds] is that we won't have any pro sports in Houston. Things might change someday, but the reality is that if you say [no to public subsidies] in today's market, you're below any market."[13] And if nothing else, you get an extra mass shelter for the next natural disaster.

Houston is now a city that suffers in silence, with two new stadiums (the expansion NFL team, the Houston Texans, also found a home), and according to 2007 data, more than a third of children living below the poverty line.[14] If Houston suffers in silence from these priorities, New Orleans, even four years after Katrina, still makes a sane person want to holler.

When the city was ready to begin the rebuilding, it was as if nothing had been learned. The first major renovation in New Orleans, the symbol of deliverance, was the $185 million overhaul of the Louisiana Superdome,[15] $94 million of which came from FEMA.[16] Never mind that the Dome's adjoining mall and hotel were still shuttered or that the city hasn't seen that kind of money spent on low-income housing destroyed by Hurricane Katrina. The road back for the Big Easy began in the Dome. As one ESPN talking head solemnly told us, "The most daunting task is to scrub away memories of the Superdome as a cesspool of human misery."[17]

These memories shouldn't be scrubbed away but remembered, so we don't repeat the same damn mistakes. The stadium was overhauled and rehabilitated. Public housing wasn't. If you move beyond Bourbon Street, you can still witness the houses of worship that are still half sunk in the water or see homes with marks on them to show where dead bodies were found. You can also see the locations where the B. W. Cooper, C. J. Peete, Lafitte, and St. Bernard housing projects used to rest.

These four "developments," which housed 4,584 families, have been demolished.[18] Many of these families haven't even come back since the levees broke, unable to reclaim their homes and advocate for their communities.

New Orleans is crying out for grand acts of daring and leadership. Nothing grand is coming from Washington, D.C. When the Super Bowl–winning Saints visit the White House, it might be the first time President Barack Obama says the words "New Orleans" in a public setting. The answer begins not with "scrub[bing] away memories of the Superdome" but in amplifying those memories so they fuel a movement to bring back not only the city but also every last resident who wants to return.

As New Orleans resident and commentator Harry Shearer wrote in 2009, "The farther we get into [the Obama] administration, the clearer it becomes that New Orleans is now enjoying its second consecutive federal administration which, far from offering to fix what it broke, far from offering a hand of support, is merely offering one finger."[19] This is particularly poignant as quarterback Drew Brees and the New Orleans Saints hold the Lombardi trophy. Team success is not an express train ride to solvency or recovery.

Minnesota

For too many years stadiums were exalted as the difference between a cutting-edge city ready for the globalized world of tomorrow, and a sleepy town left behind in the dust. The stadium pushers ask the question with the aggressive posture of a corner evangelist. Do you want your city left behind? Do you want to be trapped in a Thornton Wilder play or be featured in *Condé Nast Traveller*?

When the late Minnesota Twins' owner Carl Pohlad failed to fleece the locals in a stadium referendum, one of his minions bemoaned that the Twin Cities—the birthplace of Prince, Morris Day, and Hüsker Dü—would become (heaven forbid) "another Bismarck, North Dakota." Pohlad died at age ninety-three in January 2009 with the title "the richest owner in baseball."[20] He first made his money by foreclosing on the land of Minnesota farmers during the Great Depression.[21] As an owner, he is perhaps best known for trying to contract his own team.[22] He's the only sports boss who could be comfortably profiled by both John Steinbeck and John Feinstein.

Pohlad found himself repeatedly frustrated in his quest for stadium manna. The multibillionaire spent the last two decades of his life trying to get the taxpayers of his home state to give him $522 million for a state-of-the-art megadome.[23] It seemed that Minneapolis–St. Paul, with its social democratic traditions, wouldn't go the way of Houston, Texas. This is a state where the Democrats call themselves Democrat Farm and Labor (DFL) and Republicans are in fact named the Independent Republicans (IR). Of course, it's also the state that gave us Governor Jesse Ventura, so anything is possible.

Granted, the old home of the Twins, the Hubert H. Humphrey Metrodome, isn't the most attractive of stadiums. It's like watching a game inside a condom. The late, great Billy Martin, who managed the Twins in 1969, once said, "How could Hubert Humphrey's parents name him after this dump?"[24] The solution seemed obvious. Either continue to enjoy the latex charms of the Metrodome or have the billionaire Pohlad finance and build his own stadium. Pohlad, however, insisted that the state pick up at least half the tab.[25] The people in numerous referendums were polite and firm that the Pohlad way was not the Minnesota way.[26]

They even voted it down when the Minnesota Twins ran a TV commercial featuring a ballplayer visiting a boy in the hospital. A voice-over solemnly announced, "If the Twins leave Minnesota, an eight-year-old from Wilmer [Minnesota] undergoing chemotherapy will never get a visit from [Twins infielder] Marty Cordova."[27]

It turned out that the boy had already died by the time the commercial aired.

Pohlad was undeterred, saying, "Sports is a way of life, like eating. People say, 'You should pay to feed the homeless.' But the world doesn't work that way."[28]

He couldn't win even with then governor Arne Carlson in his pocket. Carlson described himself as "the state's number one booster" for the team.[29] When he was asked why the multibillionaire Pohlad couldn't buy his own stadium, Carlson said, "That's irrelevant," and lashed out at stadium critics, saying that they were fomenting "class warfare."[30] Carlson, that old honeydripper, then tried a romantic tack, saying, "When you call up a hot tootsie for a date, you're not going to go to the water treatment plant."[31] It still didn't work. Carlson's stadium scheme for Pohlad was opposed by 69 percent of the electorate.[32] Even a majority of self-identified Twins fans opposed the deal.[33]

But you don't get to be ninety-three without some serious stubbornness pulsing through your veins. Pohlad continued to fight for his fair share of the public trough. "I don't know if you'd call me evil," he said. "I've been put into an impossible situation."[34] The impossible situation was that no matter how many politicians were in his pocket, no matter how many commercials he funded, no matter how many times he sent former players—such as team icon Kirby Puckett—to shill around the state, a significant majority of the people simply opposed the stadium.

Eventually he came around to the puckish wisdom of former New York mayor Rudolph Giuliani. Giuliani once said that the problem with stadium referendums is that people won't vote for them. Pohlad took the Giuliani gospel to heart. His people worked it behind the scenes, giving hundreds of thousands of dollars to politicians in both parties, eventually making a mockery of the Farm and Labor label on the Democrats and the Independence label on the Republicans.[35, 36] Governor and presidential aspirant Tim Pawlenty, who has vetoed every effort to raise taxes to refurbish the state's infrastructure, became a born-again stadium supporter. Others also got religion and began to worship at the altar of "revenue streams," "naming rights," and "luxury boxes." As the Minnesota-based *City Pages* put it, "After a long string of public relations disasters that have entrenched his reputation as a miserly, something-for-nothing businessman, Carl Pohlad—the richest owner in major league baseball—has finally learned his political lesson. This time all the hardball haggling occurred behind closed doors."[37]

Groundbreaking for Pohlad's monument to corporate greed and political graft was supposed to be on Thursday, August 2, 2007. Unfortunately for all concerned parties, earlier that week, the I-35W Mississippi River bridge (officially known as Bridge 9340) collapsed, killing 13 and injuring 145.[38] Celebrations, complete with ceremonial shovels, were hastily scuttled. The irony was simply too much: to celebrate the fleecing of the public to the tune of half a billion dollars—more than $300 out of the pockets of every taxpayer—while bodies had still yet to be recovered from the river, would have been monstrous, even for the congenitally shameless Pawlenty.[39]

Washington, D.C.

The U.S. capital is more than a tale of two cities; it's also a tale of two worlds. First we have Washington, home of the White House, the Capitol Building, and the Washington Monument. This city is the province of fat-cat power brokers and slick-talking lobbyists oozing from one five-star steak house to the next. Then we have D.C., a majority African-American city with some of the highest poverty, infant mortality, and HIV rates in the nation. This city is where residents taste a cold reality where services have been cut to the bone and 50 percent of young black men are in prison or on parole.[40] The only public hospital was shut down, the schools creak in buildings that predate Prohibition, and the roads have potholes cavernous enough to provide safe harbor for the rats that contend for power after dusk.

Former mayor Anthony Williams looked at this urban environment in desperate need of reinvestment and saw the answer as clear as his ubiquitous bow tie in the mirror: a new baseball stadium. A $611 million tax hike was jammed through the D.C. City Council to build the new park.[41] Cost overruns would take the project to more than $1 billion.[42] The park was built even though the team, the Washington Nationals—having just made the journey from being the Montreal Expos—didn't have an owner. They were the foster child of Major League Baseball, run by the office of Commissioner Bud Selig. But after D.C. put together this "ultimate sweetheart deal," it was only a matter of time before prospective owners began to line up. The wretched Montreal Expos got to move from a decrepit near-empty stadium built in celebration of the 1976 Summer Olympics, to a brand-spanking-new near-empty stadium in Southeast Washington, D.C.

How a couple dozen of the richest men in the United States—major league owners—got one of the most impoverished cities in the Western Hemisphere to give them $1 billion is still a mystery. It was a heist so audacious that all the Sopranos still must be shaking their heads in admiration. Just to compare, the St. Louis Cardinals' franchise paid for 77 percent of their new $387 million stadium.[43] The Detroit Tigers paid for 62 percent of their $327 million stadium, Comerica Park.[44] In D.C., the city picked up every penny.[45]

Williams gurgled with glee at the press conference announcing this exercise in corporate welfare. He boasted that because the stadium would be funded by business taxes, and "the people in D.C. won't pay one dime."[46]

But Mayor Williams didn't mention the rise in the cost of living, as businesses pass on these new taxes to consumers. (Numerous D.C. neighborhoods have since become case studies of gentrification.) He didn't mention that cost overruns have nowhere to hide except in regressive taxes on the backs of D.C. residents. He didn't mention the city's willingness to take people's homes and bulldoze them to the ground if they live on the proposed stadium site and don't want to sell. (This they call "eminent domain.") He also said that the stadium would create jobs. He didn't say that this could be a case of robbing Peter to kill Paul.

Roger Noll, coauthor of the book *Sports, Jobs, and Taxes: The Economic Impact of Sports Teams and Stadiums,* wrote, "Any independent study shows that as an investment, it's silly. If they're trying to sell it on the grounds of actually contributing to economic growth and employment in D.C., that's wrong. There's never been a publicly subsidized stadium anywhere in the United States that had the effect of increasing employment and economic growth in the city in which it was built."[47]

In the end, Mayor Williams's plan was pushed through without the pretense of referendum, even though the great majority of the people of D.C. wanted no part of it. A poll released by the Service Employees International Union found that 70 percent of the city opposed public funding, and more than half strongly opposed it.[48] These numbers crossed all ethnic and racial lines. But the mayor insisted on giving D.C. a new baseball stadium the same way a dog gets medicine at the vet: held down, pried open, and force-fed. But still, as residents squirmed, Williams had his media-offensive line drive-blocking ahead.

Tom Boswel of the *Washington Post* played his part selling the stadium by expounding about how "revitalized" stadium-blessed cities such as Cleveland are in the wake of Major League Baseball's noblesse oblige.[49] He neglected to mention that Cleveland had just been named the poorest city in the United States, with the poverty rate hitting 30 percent.[50]

Sally Jenkins, also of the *Post,* captured the true dynamic perfectly, writing, "If we strip away all the pastoral nonsense, and the nostalgia, and the exuberant projections about urban redevelopment, doesn't it look like the nation's capital is being extorted by Commissioner Bud Selig?"[51]

But Mayor Williams wasn't done. Proving once again that inflicting injury is no fun without a sweet insult, he wanted the team to be named the Grays. "Grays" is neither a self-aggrandizing nod toward the former mayor's less than sparkling personality nor his favorite color. It was, in Williams's words, "a tribute" to the area's old Negro National League team the Homestead Grays, which featured Hall of Fame legends Josh Gibson and Buck Leonard. (The name Grays was eventually passed over for the Nationals.)

The mayor's nostalgia for the Negro Leagues and his touching olive branch to this majority African-American city was somewhat dulled by his battle plan to build this $1 billion lemon in the overwhelmingly black Southeast neighborhood of Anacostia.

It was a stunning act of chutzpah. Williams wanted to gentrify the most historic black neighborhood in the city in the name of honoring the Negro Leagues. Not since the production of the 1992 pornographic film *Malcolm XXX* has a symbol of African-American pride been so abused. But the stadium was pushed through with fawning help from the local press. Rarely has the coverage of an event been so pandering, so utterly absent of objectivity than the *Washington Post's* coverage of the debut of the Washington Nationals' new stadium.

The *Post* reported on the ballpark's grand opening with hard-hitting articles such as "Lapping Up a Major Victory, and Luxuries, at New Stadium."[52] Without even a raised eyebrow, the article quoted people from the suburbs of Maryland and Virginia about how much fun they were having on stadium grounds playing *Guitar Hero* and eating authentic D.C. half smokes from Ben's Chili Bowl before the big game. The column should have come with coupons for the Make Your Own Teddy Bear booth.

But that was nothing compared to Tom Boswell. Some Boswell gems from opening night included, "Imagine 25,000 people all smiling at once. Not for a few seconds, but continuously for hours. You won't see it at a tense World Series. But when a brand-new ballpark opens, especially in a city that hasn't had such an experience for 46 years, people can't help themselves."[53]

In a nod to actual journalism, Boswell did manage to raise a few questions. "Are they worth the money? Has MLB mastered civic extortion, playing one city against another?" But have no fear. He had no answers. "That's a different story, a different day."[54] Unfortunately, it's a story over the past three years he has never written. He did quote another suburban game-tripper making the trek into the big bad city who said, "Sometimes you got to spend money to make money." Of course, it's not his money, but why quibble?

Boswell was actually a model of restraint compared to *Post* city columnist Marc Fisher. In a piece titled "The City Opens the Ballpark, and the Fans Come Up Winner," Fisher wrote, "An investment in granite, concrete and steel buys a new retail, residential and office neighborhood. It buys the president of the United States throwing out the first ball. And it buys a son showing his father what his boy has become."[55] (I don't even understand that last line. A son shows his father . . . his boy? So the father is a grandfather? Is this some sort of southern Gothic goes to the ballpark? Maybe Fisher was just blissed out on $8 beers and making his own teddy bears.)

While Boswell and Fisher were given prime column real estate to gush, columnist Sally Jenkins didn't even get a corner of the comics page. Her absence was conspicuous, but it's very understandable why Jenkins, the 2002 Associated Press sports columnist of the year, didn't get to play. Four years ago, she refused to gush over prospects for a new stadium. "While you're celebrating the deal to bring baseball back to Washington, understand just what it is you're getting: a large publicly financed stadium and potential sinkhole to house a team that's not very good, both of which may cost you more than you bargained for and be of questionable benefit to anybody except the wealthy owners and players. But tell that to baseball romantics, or the mayor and his people, and they act like you just called their baby ugly. It's lovely to have baseball in Washington again. But the deal that brings the Montreal Expos to Washington is an ugly baby."[56]

Jenkins's words have come to pass. But this isn't just an "ugly baby," it's Rosemary's baby. It's $1 billion of taxpayer money in a city that has become a ground zero of economic segregation and gentrification; $1 billion in a city set to close down a staggering twenty-four public schools. That's $1 billion, rammed through a mere five months after a mayor-commissioned study found that the district's poverty rate was the highest it had been in a decade and African-American unemployment was 51 percent.

That's $1 billion in a city where the libraries shut down early and the Metro rusts over. That's a living, throbbing reminder that the vote-deprived District of Columbia doesn't even rest on the pretense of democracy. This isn't just taxation without representation. This is sports as ethnic and economic cleansing. Fittingly, when the stadium opened, President George W. Bush came out to throw the first pitch. Fittingly, he was roundly booed. He stood on the mound, proudly oblivious, taking center stage yet again in what can only be described as occupied territory.

Many in D.C. were relieved when after a seventeen-month search, the Nationals finally found ownership in the Lerner family. The Lerners are a clan of real estate tycoons building the grandest minimalls in the D.C. area. They have one-stop-shopped their way to a fortune estimated at $3.5 billion.[57]

The family's eighty-year-old patriarch, Theodore Lerner, gushed in an interview, "We're delighted to receive the opportunity to own this franchise. It's something I've been thinking about all my life, from the time I used to pay 25 cents to sit in the bleachers at Griffith Stadium," the former home of the Washington Senators.[58] He also said, "I plan on doing everything I can do to make sure this franchise becomes an international jewel for Major League Baseball, the nation, D.C., and its wonderful fans." But unless Lerner was referring to that prized jewel known as "the cubic zirconium," this simply has not been the case. Last-place finishes, meager attendance (even in that new stadium), and boredom have been the hallmarks of the club under the Lerners. There is a very good reason why the Washington Nationals are referred to as "the Gnats."

In addition to putting out a product that has stymied any goodwill the city was feeling about the return of baseball, the Lerners stonewalled for months on the $3.5 million they owed the city in back rent on the taxpayer-funded stadium.[59] In October 2008, the Lerners finally announced that they would happily pay the millions, but only in exchange for $4 million more in taxpayer-funded concessions.[60] This was the move that put the public cost of the stadium at more than $1 billion.

As Dave McKenna, sports columnist for the *Washington City Paper,* wrote, "All year, they hit more wrong notes than a grade-school cellist. The Lerners, after all, had responded to the initial reports about the unpaid rent not by apologizing but by threatening to dock the city $100,000 a day until the stadium they'd been using for months was, to their way of thinking, 'finished.' The Nationals had played nearly 50 home games in the allegedly unfinished stadium by that point."[61]

The Lerners also held two large fan events at hotels outside Washington, D.C., in the Maryland suburbs. It probably shouldn't surprise us that the midwives of the area's minimalls were more comfortable in the 'burbs. But while the local politicians were furious, they were all bark and no bite. The attitude of the Lerner family should have emboldened the city to take the team and the stadium back and run it in the public interest. Instead, the City Council howled a bit and then rolled over, hoping for a tummy scratch. Not surprisingly, the expected economic development hasn't been there, either.

Fan Steve Guzowski said to me, "As a current D.C. resident, I (along with every other district citizen) have a daily reminder about our great civic investment that is Nationals Park. A year and half after the stadium's opening, Half Street still remains a giant bowl of mud, while the Lerner family reaps the in-stadium markup on concessions without any up-front investment on the facility they call home."[62]

Meanwhile, as the city has fallen further and further into disrepair, the chickens of corporate welfare came home to roost. On June 22, 2009, two Washington, D.C., Metro trains collided, killing nine and sending more than seventy-five to the hospital.[63] The accident took place a ten-minute walk from my house, and, like many others, I spent most of that day on the phone, either assuring people that my family was safe, or checking on friends to make sure no one was in the hospital or worse. Everyone I knew was fine, although several had been on the trains involved, shaken but not grievously injured. The relief was palpable, even physical. But then the stories started to be released in small doses, and relief turned to horror.

There were the families of the dead on television: the inconsolable loved ones of train operator Jeanice McMillan, forty-two; David and Ann Wherley, both sixty-two; Mary Doolittle, fifty-nine; LaVonda King, twenty-three; Veronica DuBose, twenty-nine; Cameron Williams, thirty-seven; Dennis Hawkins, sixty-four; and Ana Fernandez, forty. A teacher, a young mother, a retired National Guard major general, a woman who cleaned office buildings while raising six children—all gone.

The wreckage near my house was not an accident site. Essentially, it was a crime scene. The subsequent investigation revealed that the trains and the tracks were rife with problems—the lead train car was one of the original 1000-Series, which dates back to the Carter administration. Train maintenance was overdue. Metro's crash avoidance system had experienced repeated problems and failures. Safety recommendations had gone ignored.

The Metro became our broken levee: an utterly preventable tragedy if only people in government had the will to do the public good.

Our current D.C. mayor, Adrian Fenty, stepped up to the cameras after the crash, ready to have his "Giuliani moment" of a mayor in control of a crisis. But he didn't have to explain why the District of Columbia is on the hook for a $1 billion ballpark, where the city's last-place team toils in front of their dozen or so biggest fans. No one asked, "Why, under your watch, does the D.C. government own sky boxes at all sporting venues? Why are you in discussion for more stadium spending—on soccer, hoops, and the mother of all stadium deals, the possible return of the Washington Redskins from suburban Maryland to the district?"

Every billionaire sports owner has his hand out because Fenty has shown that he will turn his pockets inside out for them—this despite the fact that Fenty became mayor on the strength of standing up to the Nationals' stadium deal when he was on the City Council.

It is a question of priorities, plain and simple.

I spoke to former Major League Baseball All-Star and *Ball Four* author Jim Bouton about the publicly financed "doming" of America. He said:

> It's such a misapplication of the public's money. . . . You've got towns turning out streetlights, they're closing firehouses, they're

cutting back on school supplies, they're having classrooms in stairwells, and we've got a nation full of kids who don't have any health insurance. I mean, it's disgraceful. The limited things that our government does for the people with the people's money, to spend even a dime or a penny of it on ballparks is just a crime.

It's going to be seen historically as an awful folly, and it's starting to be seen that way now, but historically that will go down as one of the real crimes of American government, national and local, to allow the funneling of people's money directly into the pockets of a handful of very wealthy individuals who could build these stadiums on their own if it made financial sense. If they don't make financial sense, then they shouldn't be building them.[64]

Bouton went on to say, "If I was a team owner today, asking for public money, I'd be ashamed of myself. But we've gone beyond shame. There's no such thing as shame anymore. People aren't embarrassed to take—to do these awful things."[65]

Bouton is absolutely correct. When it comes to fleecing our cities, some of the richest people in this country have shown a complete absence of shame. The question is whether we are going to finally stand up and impose our priorities on them, instead of continually taking it on the chin. Every time a publicly funded stadium is considered in your hometown, New Orleans, Minneapolis, and Washington, D.C., need to be part of the conversation and debate. Stadiums aren't built out of thin air. They're built on our backs.

2. Business, Never Personal

Everybody needs money; that's why they call it money.
—DANNY DEVITO, *HEIST*

O ther cities may not have suffered as openly as New Orleans, Minneapolis, and D.C., but almost every major sports town knows
what it feels like to be held up for that sweet stadium cash.

For much of the past twenty years, sports have relied on public subsidies to a degree that would shame the automobile industry and agribusi-
nesses paid not to grow corn. Two-thirds of baseball teams alone have
gotten new stadiums—including the New York Yankees, whose $1.3 bil-
lion park opened in 2009,[1] and the New York Mets, who also inaugurated
their own $1 billion stadium, called Citi Field.[2] Yes, a city with rotting in-
frastructure now has a stadium whose naming rights have been bought
by a bank that's been given billions in bailout funds.

There was a time when being a sports owner was a license to print
money. But today it's an industry resting on a rickety, arthritic foundation.
Owners lord over a business awash in secrecy, that sees its profits come not
through its product but cable television, global merchandise, and above all
else, public subsidies. This is why former Cleveland Browns and Baltimore
Ravens owner Art Modell called NFL owners "twenty-six Republicans that
vote socialist."[3] They are the true welfare kings. No industry receives as high
a percentage of corporate welfare while keeping its books hidden in shadows. But the party may be coming to a close. After cars, banks, houses, and
retail centers, sports may be the next industry to find itself flattened by the
broader financial crisis. There was a time when sports was thought to be
absolutely recession-proof. Those days belong on a newsreel.

The best evidence of this is not at the bottom of the sports food chain but at the top: the league that was supposed to be crisis-free, the National Football League. Football is a blue-collar game at white-collar prices in the best of times. But today we are seeing fans "blacked out" by the league. The NFL has what they call a "blackout policy," where the teams that don't sell out home games "black out" the television broadcasts to local communities. In 2008, only nine games were off the air in local markets.[4] In recessionary 2009, Jacksonville preemptively announced that they would have to black out all eight of their home games.[5] Detroit, a city with 29 percent unemployment,[6] blacked out their sorry team's first win in more than a year.[7] First you lose your job, then your team. It's not just deindustrialized cities living in hard times such as Detroit or tiny burgs like Jacksonville. The 2009 Super Bowl saw the city of Tampa, Florida, taking in 20 percent less profits than projected and $45 million less than in the two previous years.[8] That's a $30 million loss, as companies chose to host far fewer parties during a week that's usually like Mardi Gras for multimillionaires. Even the Victoria's Secret and *Playboy* VIP parties were canceled, leaving sportswriters an entire year with no one to tell them how handsome they are.[9] Tampa Bay's financial blow doesn't harm only the legal economy. The downturn also harmed professional escorts, recreational drug dealers, and illegal gambling opportunities, all of which makes a typical Super Bowl Party something that would make Caligula blush.

Super Bowl commercials reflected the new economic reality as well, with the usual frat-house sexism (partially) surrendered for ads that reflected the concerns of working-class Americans. There was an Avon cosmetics saleswoman—Daryn from Texas—saying, "If someone asks me how they can make money right now, I say do what I'm doing, sell Avon."[10] There were those creepy talking babies from e-Trade grousing about how the "economy is a little rough."[11]

A Budweiser ad put corporate types in a boardroom, wondering where all the profits had gone, with not one of their trademark farting horses in sight. Even General Motors and FedEx, longtime Super Bowl advertisers, didn't have their game faces on, choosing to sit it out entirely. But it wasn't just the ads. Production budgets were set to low all around. Matt Lauer's pregame interview with Barack Obama suffered from audio malfunctions (far less exciting than a wardrobe malfunction). There was even a representative of the healthiest growth industry in the United States right now—the U.S. military—as four-star General David Petraeus was honored with the coin toss before the big game. Even the halftime show was recession-oriented, featuring our troubadour of hard times, Bruce Springsteen. The Boss unfortunately didn't fulfill the wishes of *New York Times* sports columnist Harvey Araton to "[go] rogue and rail against . . . those corporate fat cats."[12]

If the strongest link in the economic food chain, the Super Bowl, is rotting, imagine the stench as you travel down the chain. The sports world is leaking money like the U.S. Treasury. The National Football League's redheaded stepchild, the Arena Football League, had to cancel its last season. In 2009, twenty-two of the thirty Major League Baseball teams saw attendance drops.[13] The Ladies' Professional Golf Association has canceled three tournaments and dropped millions in prize money.[14] The NFL and the National Basketball Association had to lay off sizable percentages of their corporate workforces.[15, 16]

The NBA in particular has looked vulnerable in the current climate. The league took out a $200 million line of credit to aid failing teams, even though Commissioner David Stern tried to spin this as a sign of the league's health (which holds the logic of the pope saying that condoms spread AIDS).[17] The situation has in truth been broadly recognized as dire. ESPN.com columnist "The Sports Guy" Bill Simmons called the league the No Benjamins Association ("benjamins" being mid-1990s vernacular for $100 bills).[18]

Musty slang aside, Simmons wrote about his experience at the 2009 NBA All-Star Game, effectively capturing the mood: "Everyone is scared. Money hangs over everything. That's what I ended up discussing for four solid days in Phoenix. Hands down, it was the most depressing All-Star Weekend I've ever attended. Celebrities were scarce. The parties weren't as good or plentiful. Even the number of groupies seemed lower than usual. It's not as if everyone was drinking Natural Light and eating Hamburger Helper, but still, when you're celebrating a weekend with the No Benjamins Association, you know it. . . . Here's a little game to play during your next NBA outing: Look around for how many suites are dark."[19]

As grave as the situation may be in hoops, it's baseball, the American pastime, that saw a season-long bleed at the turnstiles. "Historically, baseball has been recession-resistant," Donald Fehr, executive director of the Major League Baseball Players' Association, told the *New York Times* in November 2008.[20] But Fehr is looking at a historical model far different from the current economic sporting landscape. He's comparing a jalopy to a Hummer. This isn't the 1930s, or even the 1970s. Gone are the days when fans continued to support baseball—or any of the major sports—during tough times as an entertaining and affordable escape for the family.

This is not to say that pro sports commissioners will be appearing anytime soon before Congress, hats in hand begging for a bailout, at least not if they have even the slightest sense of self-preservation. But there are harsh similarities between the path followed by Major League Baseball owners and investment banking execs that bet short on the present at the expense of the future. The sports business has become as inflated and volatile as the insurance, auto, and housing markets, and any of the familiar industries that focused on short-term gain over long-term health. Sports owners have spent the past fifteen years gorging themselves, seeing the value of franchises explode at the expense of middle- and working-class fans. The revenue streams became floods, but the floods presaged drought.

Just look at the three main revenue streams of the last generation, the trinity of the great sports bubble: public funds for stadium construction, corporate boxes and their offspring "personal seat licenses," and television megadeals alongside twenty-four-hour sports media. Except for television, these revenue sources are feeling about as relevant as your McCain/Palin bumper stickers.

What hasn't changed is that even with budgets strained to the gills, team owners still come hat in hand and demand their park or else.

What has changed, however, is the anger that such a request can incur. When Chicago bid for the 2016 Olympics and city aldermen voted unanimously to cover any cost overruns on the games, public opinion shifted against it: 84 percent of the city opposed holding the Olympics if they would mean even one solitary dime coming out of their pockets.[21] Organizations sprouted up to dog city officials. When the Yankees demanded and received $370 million more in city bonds the same month that they paid $400 million for two high-end free agents, New Yorkers seethed.[22] In the Bay Area, the San Francisco 49ers look poised to become the Santa Clara 49ers as the city by the bay couldn't abide the funding demands of team ownership.

In addition to publicly financed stadiums, sports owners also have been filling the financial gaps by spiking season ticket prices, building more luxury boxes, and spreading the pernicious plague of what's known as "personal seat licenses," which effectively reserve the same high-end seat for the well-heeled all season. They have been able to make even more money with fewer fans in attendance. Some teams have tried to adjust to the thorny times. The Cincinnati Bengals, in economically masticated Ohio, have had to drop their seat license fees from $2,783 to $536.[23] The Yankees started the 2009 season in their new stadium with bloated $2,000 game tickets. They had to slash those prices dramatically as a ring of empty seats in the front rows didn't exactly look great on camera.[24]

The true artist of finding revenue streams where none existed is Dallas Cowboys' owner Jerry Jones. In 2009, Jones opened his new $1.5 billion stadium in Arlington, Texas, that stands as a proud monument to excess.[25] The City of Arlington provided more than $933 million (including interest) in bonds as funding.[26] But in this economic climate, they have yet to sell the corporate naming rights.[27] Residents have taken to calling it "Jones-Town," "Jones-Mahal," the "Death Star," and my personal favorite, the "Boss Hog Bowl." Hog is right. It is the largest domed stadium in the world and contains a titanic flat-screen television that hangs from twenty-yard line to twenty-yard line and is known as "Jerry Vision." After attending a game, one fan, Harper Caron, said to me, "I wanted so badly to watch the game. But the television just drew my eyes and I couldn't look away."[28] The screen also is in constant danger of being hit by punts. When NFL commissioner Roger Goodell asked if it could be raised, Jones simply said "no" because it would not be "aesthetic." The stadium aesthetic includes having cheerleaders as cage dancers throughout the upper decks and the players having to run through a sports bar to enter the field. Fun for the whole family . . . if your family is on the brink of group therapy. But Jones defends every last trapping, saying that unlike other owners, he knows "how to grow the pie."[29]

No one really knows what it means to "grow the pie," but Jones does know how to make money. He charges $100,000 for two of his deluxe personal seat licenses—for tickets that would normally be $129 a game.[30] Jones also charged fans to tour the new facility, and broke new ground when he sold tickets to a standing-room-only area outside the stadium known as "party pass" tickets. One fan who was there described it thusly: "Absolute disaster. That's it. Concession lines were way too long, bathrooms were overcrowded, it reminded me of the Superdome after Hurricane Katrina."[31]

It's no exaggeration, and even a cliché, to point out that working-class people have been priced out of attending sporting events; it's no longer possible for kids to trade in some milk bottles for a ticket to the game. They would need an entire herd of cattle. One fan, Allan Classen, said to me, "It is a shame that second mortgages have to be obtained in order to take a family out to a ball game these days. Three figures are spent just to buy hot dogs, chips, and pop for a family of four."[32]

The need for revenue streams trumps all other concerns. This need, coupled with these economic hard times, puts a barrier between fans and their aspirations to connect with the team. Randy, an "avid—some might describe it as insane—N.Y. Giants fan," said to me, "I put my name on the season ticket holder waiting list in their 2007 Super Bowl run with the expectation that I wouldn't be called for another twenty years. However, due to the personal seat license (PSL) policy costing in some cases as much as $7,500 a seat—a price that few people ever, let alone now, can afford—my name was moved to the front of the list. It pains me to think that not only can I not afford to purchase these seats now, but I will likely never have another opportunity, since the PSLs allow an owner to pass the seat along through inheritance or resale."[33]

But there is a bigger problem at play. Sports, which once was a welcome diversion from economic crisis, now, at best, highlights the crisis and, at worst, exacerbates it. ESPN baseball expert Jayson Stark said at the start of the 2009 baseball season, "Enough already. No more talk about the economy. Please. No more charts showing attendance during previous recessions. Please . . . has baseball been affected by the economy? Sure. Obviously. Now let's move on. At times like these, we don't need baseball to remind us we barely have enough money left in our life savings to buy a hot dog and popcorn. We need baseball to remind us it's guaranteed to bring us seven consecutive months of uninterrupted fun."[34]

It's just not that easy anymore. Of course, the hard-core fanatics will always be there, but whether the casual fans will return to throw pennies in the jars of owners who so clearly mismanaged the game for the past generation is an open question. Another fan, Roger Hanigan, said to me, "The owners are the main people reaping a profit from new stadiums yet insist on handouts from cities to build stadiums with as many luxury boxes as they can fit. Luxury boxes that most taxpayers will never even get close enough to smell. Somehow, this is all blamed on high player salaries and agreements with unions, and not a poor business model, which is the owners' responsibility."[35]

Considering the price of tickets, the use of public subsidies, and the economic climate, it seems that it would be a no-brainer to make sure tickets would be made affordable for fans. Major League Baseball has held several promotions, such as "Messin' with Recession" night in Toronto. The Atlanta Braves and the Milwaukee Brewers sold buck-a-game seats. The Braves even took the shocking step of telling fans that they could actually bring in outside food and beverages to Turner Field. But on the whole, baseball raised their average ticket prices during the past off-season.

Maybe bankers, auto execs, and others also mismanaged their affairs, but we don't go to our local Bank of America branch to escape. We didn't grow up collecting cards of various mortgage officers. We don't play "fantasy assembly line." The most dangerous portent is that the growth in popularity of everything from interactive video games to mixed martial arts shows that major sports leagues don't have a personal license on people's attention spans. The flood of money that seems the most secure right now is banked in the television deals and the hype machine of twenty-four-hour sports television. As long as there are games, there will be people with megawatt smiles and surgically created dimples telling us to watch. The question, though, is whether people, in searching for escape, will be hesitant to return to entertainment that for too long has taken them for granted. Owners better hope not. The model of dependence on publicly funded stadiums and luxury boxes is unsustainable, and professional sports will need a radical economic reconstruction to survive the coming period, or risk losing a generation of fans to Xbox, Facebook, and other pastimes that don't cost an arm and a leg.

Of course, ticket prices can be lower, but as you will read, the argument here will be to actually put some teams in the hands of fans to turn them into community-based entities. If taxpayers are already putting money into stadiums, shouldn't they get a piece of the franchise? Imagine if every time you saw a Raiders hat or an A's jersey, you knew the profit on the sale was going back into the public till instead of Al Davis's pocket. Imagine if a portion of concession costs, a small drop of that $8 beer, went to local charities? Now, that's what we can all agree meets the definition of "shared sacrifice." This can make devastating economic sense, as we will see from the example in Green Bay. But here is where the political proclivities of the owner's box gum up the works.

3. The Keyser Soze Principle

I'm telling you this guy is protected from up on high by the Prince of Darkness.

—THE USUAL SUSPECTS

Howard Cosell called it "rule number one of the jockocracy": the idea, against all evidence of history, that "sports and politics don't mix."[1] That maxim has unfortunately been applied exclusively to socially conscious athletes and not the people who run the show. There is a reason why not one baseball owner was called to testify during the congressional inquisition on steroids: the owner's checkbook is one place where sports and politics truly do collide.

Owners believe in the politics of the publicly funded stadium, or the million-dollar fund-raiser for friendly members of Congress. They also prefer to practice their politics in the shadows. Call it the Keyser Soze principle. In the film *The Usual Suspects,* Kevin Spacey's character, Verbal Kint, references the poet Charles Baudelaire and says, "The greatest trick the devil ever pulled was convincing the world he didn't exist." Sports owners maraud our communities, but most sports fans have no idea who they are. There is probably no greater example of the Keyser Soze principle than Phil Anschutz. Anschutz is worth $7.8 billion.[2] He also is a minority owner of the Los Angeles Lakers, Kings, and Sparks.

Despite his prominent perch, the sixty-nine-year-old Anschutz has given only three interviews in the past forty years. His spokesperson Jim Monaghan says that Anschutz sees this as "three interviews too many."[3]

You might think that means Anschutz is shy about his views. Hardly. He is only shy about speaking them. Called the "stealth media mogul" by *Forbes* magazine, Anschutz owns the *Weekly Standard* and the daily tabloid the *Washington Examiner*.[4] Both are hard-line conservative publications. Both lose money. The *Weekly Standard* is a $5 million per year failure, and the *Examiner* is a "free tabloid throwaway."[5] He has them print hundreds of thousands of free copies with an editorial page that proudly projects Anschutz's political program.[6] He "wanted nothing but conservative columns and conservative op-ed writers," said one former employee.[7] Despite Anschutz's conservative prescription for the rest of us, he is a personal devotee of socialism for the rich. Through his stakes in the Los Angeles teams Anschutz has benefited from millions in state and federal money for stadium ventures. He takes tax money with one hand and with the other funds his conservative publications as well as his other extracurricular political projects. Anschutz's hobbies include underwriting the right-wing edge of the evangelical movement. He helped to fund Colorado's Amendment 2, a ballot initiative that would have made it legal to fire someone on the basis of his or her sexual orientation.[8] He also has given millions to promote intelligent-design theory and advance critiques of evolution.[9]

Anschutz isn't alone.

Sports owners are some of the most politically well-connected people in the United States, buying access on the Hill with cold cash wrapped up in luxury box tickets, memorabilia, and other sports cachet.

As sports economist Andrew Zimbalist has written, "Today, a guy who owns a sport team is somebody who has generated a big pile of money in some other industry, and it's very likely that their primordial financial interests and instincts are rooted in that other industry."[10]

Owners as a whole also stand with ideas set squarely to the right of the mainstream. That is certainly their right and their business, but when we see how the power of sports ownership intersects with public funds, the question of whether a stadium should be a right-wing pulpit becomes particularly pressing. An owner who abuses this trust should be seen as unfit to steward a team.

Philadelphia Flyers and 76ers owner Ed Snider demonstrated this dynamic with brazen cool, going out of his way to use his teams as platforms for Sarah Palin during the 2008 presidential election. This act of political public relations cannot be understood without knowing what makes Ed Snider tick. When I spoke with him, he said to me that he believed owners should be, as he put it, "visible to the fans. The fans should be able to identify with their owner. If you don't really know who the owner is, then you don't have one."[11] But who is Ed Snider?

In addition to his day job as the CEO of Comcast Spectacor, managing two sports franchises in a sports-mad town, and being a benefactor for the arts, Snider is an acolyte of sleep-inducing author Ayn Rand. It's certainly understandable why Snider and other Rand disciples, such as former Federal Reserve chair Alan Greenspan, love Rand. She tells them that they achieve success because they are exceptional and others fail because they are failures. Snider was particularly aroused by Rand's genius, taking the time to cofound the Ayn Rand Institute in 1985.[12] (You can even find Snider on YouTube reading a speech with his musings about Rand's *Atlas Shrugged*.)

Snider has largely kept his politics to the level of donations and support for the Ayn Rand Institute. But that changed in the post-9/11 world. He became a leading donor to Freedom's Watch, an organization built around supporting the foreign policy of George W. Bush.[13] The organization launched a $15 million public relations campaign to support the troop "surge" in Iraq and perpetuate the fiction that there was a connection between the war in Iraq and 9/11. In the ad, a military veteran, over shots of the World Trade Center, says solemnly, "They attacked us, and they will again. They won't stop in Iraq."[14] The dream was also to support candidates in 2008 who would take the Bush agenda onward and upward.

Snider, clearly still on Freedom's Watch, then abused his ownership to push his politics during the heat of the 2008 presidential race. He decided that his Philadelphia Flyers and their fans would make the perfect October backdrop for the McCain/Palin campaign. He invited "America's Number 1 Hockey Mom" for a ream of free advertising by bringing her out on the ice at the Wachovia Center.[15] In making this decision, he answered, unequivocally, the following question: what do you get when you cross a failing candidate, a failing team, and a failed bank? You get Alaska governor Sarah Palin at the Wachovia Center dropping the puck on opening night for the Flyers.

But you also had a vivid, living example of the risks taken when an owner assumes that he owns both the team and the fans as well. For when Sarah Palin walked onto the ice, the boos could be heard in Pittsburgh.

The classic Broad Street Bully welcome was described by *New York Times* hockey blogger Lynn Zinser as "resounding (almost deafening) boos."[16] Sports blogs reported a similar response. Curiously, when this was picked up by CNN and other "fair and balanced" news services, the response was described as "a mix of cheers and boos." Believe the sportswriters. There was a mix, all right: a mix of boos and piped-in rock music desperate to cover the catcalls. But while music could muffle some of the boos, they couldn't cover up the anti-Palin signs spread throughout the crowd.

You might excuse Governor Palin for thinking this appearance would be a public relations "gimme." It was opening night, and the hockey faithful would be in well-lubricated good spirits. The JumboTron, our twenty-first-century altar of truth, sent forth a simple request: "Flyers fans, show Philadelphia's class and welcome America's number-one hockey mom, Sarah Palin!"

But Palin, the former sportscaster, knew what she was walking into. As added insurance, the governor strode on the ice with her adorable seven-year-old daughter, Piper, who wore a Flyers jersey. Politics aside, considering that this was Philly, Palin's decision to put her daughter in front of this crowd could have been justification to call child protective services. Palin acknowledged this strategy beforehand, saying, "I've been warned that Flyers fans, they get so enthused, that they boo everybody at the drop of the puck. But what I thought I'd do is I'd put Piper in a Flyers jersey, bring her out with me. How dare they boo Piper!"[17] Well, they dared.

Granted, Philadelphia fans are a breed apart. At an Eagles game in 1968, they booed Santa Claus on Christmas weekend. That's not just an urban legend. They actually booed Santa. ("He had it coming!" said one fan). They once jeered at Dallas Cowboys wide receiver Michael Irvin when he was motionless on the stadium turf with a neck injury. The following week, Eagles fans showed up at the game in neck braces. The stadium where the Eagles play has its own courthouse to quickly process unruly fans. But it's clearly not just football and hockey. Philadelphia baseball fans booed the children of the Phillies players who couldn't find eggs in a team-sponsored Easter egg hunt that took place on the field. Couple that with the extra-strength unpopularity of Palin in the Philadelphia area and we had a political situation that quickly unraveled out of Snider's control.

Responsibility for this failed political charade starts and ends with Snider, who, along with the execs of the National Hockey League, defended this egregious act by saying that this wasn't about political kabuki, but an effort to promote the league. NHL deputy commissioner Bill Daly reinforced the point that this was not about politics but marketing by saying: "Governor Palin is a supporter of the sport, which she has proclaimed publicly. As a public figure who has a very public connection with hockey, her recent associations with the Flyers and other NHL franchises is not surprising and, in our view, not inappropriate."[18]

And as Snider commented to the press, "Because of the tremendous amount of publicity she has brought to our sport, we invited the most popular hockey mom in North America to our home opener to help us get our season started. We are very excited she has accepted our offer and we are very proud of the publicity she is generating for hockey moms and the sport of hockey."[19]

Flyers fans in Philly were not nearly so giving, but you can understand why Palin chose this venue. As *Philadelphia Weekly* executive editor Liz Spikol said, "Of all the sporting events that could appeal to conservative voters in Philly, hockey would be the Republicans' best bet. But the electorate is changing and not even hockey fans are easy pickings."[20] This was certainly proved in practice. Palin's presence sparked an organization, modeled mockingly after the GOP's Swift Boat Veterans for Truth, called Hockey Moms against Palin.

Palin's popularizing of the term "hockey mom" holds a symbolic value that contrasts with two other types of mom in the American imagination: urban black mothers, whose children rarely play hockey, and the latte-drinking, suburban, Democratic-voting soccer moms. But there are hockey moms—and dads—in Philadelphia, far from the American heartland, and on that Saturday night, they weren't having any of it.

Commenting on the debacle, Pennsylvania governor Ed Rendell observed, "This is why I say that sports and politics don't mix."[21] But it's not sports and politics that don't mix. The problem is when owners use the platform handed to them by taxpayers to play propagandist.

This constitutes the hijacking of sports by wealthy owners and their political puppeteers. Snider said to me that he has never had any conflicts with political players, saying, "We've never had that issue. We've never dealt with it. It would depend on what words were used. If someone said Bush should be impeached, we'd have a problem."[22] It boggles the mind that calling for a Bush impeachment is a problem, but using your sway as owner to promote candidates who want to continue Bush's policies is just plain old freedom of speech. This is the politics of a bizarro world where up is down, black is white, and an owner is granted political prerogatives that players lack.

This is the way that most political owners on the whole like to operate. Use the symbols of your sport and the money you've banked to make your impact with a stealthy silent touch. When a certain prospective owner came onto the scene who had made his money precisely by marketing conservative politics as loudly as is humanly possible, he was quickly dispatched. That is why the owners flushed Rush Limbaugh.

Limbaugh came within a hairbreadth of owning an NFL team. A man with a history of ugly commentary rich in both its diversity and scope attempted to become the overlord of the St. Louis Rams. It was almost too good to be true. It would have been like putting Jon & Kate in charge of a day-care center. We could have just sat back and watched the hijinks ensue.

They almost had an owner who once said, "The NFL all too often looks like a game between the Bloods and the Crips without any weapons. There, I said it."[23] He also criticized all-pro quarterback Donovan McNabb for owing his success to the "media's social concern" to see a successful black quarterback.[24]

In a league that has practiced historic partnerships with the NAACP, they almost had an owner who said, "The NAACP should have riot rehearsal. They should get a liquor store and practice robberies."[25]

In a league that has long had a mutually beneficial interaction with whoever was occupying the Oval Office, they almost had an owner who said that "in Obama's America . . . the white kids now get beat up with the black kids cheering, 'Yay, right on, right on, right on, right on.' "[26]

In a league that features a team called the Redskins, they would have had an owner who said, "Holocaust? Ninety million Indians, only four million left? They all have casinos . . . what's to complain about?"[27] (In retrospect, maybe he should have tried to buy the Redskins instead.)

You might think that NFL players with their nonguaranteed contracts and short shelf life would be hesitant to speak out against Limbaugh. But you'd be wrong.

New York Giant Mathias Kiwanuka said in the *New York Daily News*, "I don't want anything to do with a team that he has any part of. He can do whatever he wants; it is a free country. But if it goes through, I can tell you where I am not going to play."[28]

McNabb said at his weekly press conference, "If he's rewarded to buy them, congratulations to him. But I won't be in St. Louis anytime soon."[29]

New York Jets linebacker Bart Scott said, "I can only imagine how his players would feel. . . . He could offer me whatever he wanted; I wouldn't play for him."[30]

In the NFL there has always been one code of conduct for players and another for ownership. Retired player Roman Oben called out the hypocrisy perfectly: "Character is a constant point of emphasis for NFL and team officials when it comes to the players; potential owners should be held to the same level of scrutiny and accountability."[31]

Following the lead of the players, NFL Players' Association president DeMaurice Smith said, "I've spoken to the commissioner [Roger Goodell] and I understand that this ownership consideration is in the early stages. But sport in America is at its best when it unifies, gives all of us reason to cheer, and when it transcends. Our sport does exactly that when it overcomes division and rejects discrimination and hatred. . . . I have asked our players to embrace their roles not only in the game of football but also as players and partners in the business of the NFL."

All it took was the looming specter of Limbaugh, and all of a sudden players, the union, and even sportswriters were speaking out.

NFL commissioner Roger Goodell finally had enough. He effectively nixed the deal, saying that Limbaugh's "divisive comments" had no place in the NFL. "I've said many times before, we're all held to a high standard here," Goodell said to reporters. "I would not want to see those comments coming from people who are in a responsible position in the NFL—absolutely not."[32]

Goodell's statement was complemented by Colts owner Jim Irsay, who said, "I myself couldn't even think of voting for him. . . . I'm very sensitive to know there are scars out there. I think as a nation we need to stop it. Our words do damage, and it's something that we don't need. We need to get to a higher level of humanity and we have."[33]

Only Rush could give an Irsay, whose family moved the Baltimore Colts to Indianapolis in the dead of night, the higher ground. Other owners issued decidedly lukewarm comments about the possibility of sharing space with Rush. Rush's existence among this exclusive fraternity of billionaires would violate the number one rule of ownership: protect the bottom line. He was simply too toxic for their billion-dollar brand.

If Rush became an owner, he would immediately become the face of ownership. With rare exceptions, they don't want a face.

The owners like their politics to reside in the land of the financial or symbolic. An athlete who opposes the war needs to "shut up and play." A potential owner such as Rush who makes his living with his mouth is a gauche, embarrassing slob. But an owner who uses his publicly funded stadium as a political pulpit is a pillar of his community.

To know the politics of ownership, as the saying goes, you follow the money. In the last presidential election, they broke hard for John McCain. According to an analysis by politico.com, the collective owners in baseball, basketball, football, and hockey handed over more than $3.2 million for McCain and a meager $615,000 for Barack Obama, a nearly 6 to 1 differential.[34]

This is a different universe from the rest of the country where Obama raised several hundred million dollars more than McCain, who resorted to public funding to stay financially competitive. In this world of power and influence backed by 50 cc's of sporting testosterone, McCain even raised 600 percent more from team owners in Obama's backyard of Chicago.[35]

In Arizona, McCain's home field, it was even worse for Obama, with

$550,000 going to McCain and a grand total of zero dollars for the man who would be president (McCain and his wife, it should be noted, in addition to those seven homes, own a piece of Major League Baseball's Arizona Diamondbacks).[36]

In other words, McCain, who offered an economic plan of billions in corporate and stock market tax breaks, was a very attractive candidate to someone such as New York Jets owner Robert Wood Johnson IV, an heir to the Johnson & Johnson fortune, who bundled more than $500,000 for McCain.[37]

McCain, who took a journey from calling the religious right "agents of intolerance" to embracing Governor Palin, also attracted owners who see the ballpark as a proper place for religious political expression.

Take former Arizona Diamondbacks majority owner Jerry Colangelo. A longtime friend of McCain, Colangelo launched a group along with other baseball executives and ex-players called Battin' 1000: a national campaign that uses baseball memorabilia to raise funds for Campus for Life, the largest antichoice student network in the country.[38] The group stands against all abortions, even in the case of incest or rape. Their motto: "Prolife—without exception, without compromise, without apology."[39]

Colangelo also was deputy chair of Bush/Cheney 2004 in Arizona, and his deep pockets created what was called the Presidential Prayer Team—a private evangelical group that claimed to have signed up more than a million people to drop to their knees and pray daily for Bush.[40] During the summer of 2004, Colangelo bought ads on twelve hundred radio stations urging listeners to drop to their knees and pray for the president to win reelection.[41]

But the sharpest example of how ownership and right-wing politics collide was when George W. Bush was almost made the commissioner of Major League Baseball. If the offer had been formally made, and the job had been the answer to Bush's midlife crisis instead of the presidency of the United States, the world might be an altogether different place. But instead, owners in the early 1990s went with a car salesman from Milwaukee named Allen "Bud" Selig. They just didn't believe that Bush had the chops to follow in the immortal footsteps of people such as Bowie Kuhn and Ford Frick. While owners didn't believe Bush could run the major leagues, they felt very confident he could run the country, with a majority of them pouring millions into his 2000 and 2004 campaigns.[42] This alone should encourage us to examine alternatives to traditional ownership.

From 1989 to 1998 Bush was the general managing partner of the Texas Rangers. Because of his famous name, he often was referred to in the press as the "owner" of the team. Bush actually was the figurehead of a Rangers ownership group made up of his father's friends and allies. It was a necessary move for the politically ambitious Bush, whose previous life experience involved little more than a string of business and political failures and a bionic liver. Before finding his niche in the owner's box, Bush had a series of youthful indiscretions that lasted until he was forty, which, it's safe to say, stretches our definition of youth. In 1989 he told *Time* magazine why he was buying the team. "My biggest liability in Texas is the question 'What's the boy ever done? He could be riding on Daddy's name.' "[43]

Baseball was seen as an ideal vehicle for his financial and political aspirations. For the son of the president, getting a piece of the action took an initial investment of $600,000, 1.8 percent of the franchise. The $600,000 was borrowed, of course.[44]

The person who encouraged Bush to look at sports as an easy way to get in the public eye was his idolatrous adviser Karl Rove. Rove, who years later described the starbursts he felt upon meeting Bush in 1973 ("Huge amounts of charisma, swagger, cowboy boots, flight jacket, wonderful smile, just charisma—you know, wow."[45]), said in 1994 that he believed owning the team "gives him . . . exposure and gives him something that will be easily recalled by people."[46] Major League Baseball commissioner and GOP donor Peter Ueberroth greased through the deal with astonishing speed in 1990. It also was heartily approved by outgoing Rangers owner Eddie Chiles, who knew Bush when Dubya was a child and used to call him "Young Pup."

After buying the team, any trace of humility in Bush was gone. In baseball parlance, he truly acted like the man who was born on third base but acted like he hit a triple.

"I was like a pit bull on the pant leg of opportunity," Bush said in an interview with *New York Times* in July 2000. "And I just grabbed on to it. I was going to put the deal together. And I did."[47]

After the franchise changed hands, the financiers gave Bush an extra

10 percent stake on the grounds that "his name" offered a measure of "celebrity" to the purchase. This bonus would make Bush's eventual take exponentially larger.

But it was his political connections that allowed Bush to set the absolute standard for a large-scale, often imitated land extortion. When his ownership group tried to coerce the state of Texas to pay for a brand-spanking-new facility called the Ballpark in Arlington, Bush and his team of owners threatened to uproot the team if the city did not foot the bill. The local government caved, and in the fall of 1990, they guaranteed that the city would pay $135 million of an estimated cost of $190 million.[48] The remainder was raised through a ticket surcharge. In other words, local taxpayers and baseball fans footed the entire bill. There also was a sales tax to help handle the debt. This passed in a referendum with a 65 percent vote,[49] sold to Arlington voters with Bush's glad-handing help. In solid economic times, it seemed to make sense. But in 2009 it would be curious to know if the people of Arlington might want a do-over.

At the end of the day, the owners of the Rangers, including Bush, got a stadium worth nearly $200 million without putting down a penny of their own money.[50] But the scam did not end there. As part of the deal, the Rangers' ownership was granted, in addition to the stadium, a chunk of land that was acquired with the aim of creating a "sports entertainment destination," including the Coca-Cola Sports Park, which the Rangers organization says is fun "for children of all ages."[51] Other parts of the land gift were left to just sit and accrue value. All of the undeveloped acreage, of course, increased in value as a result of the stadium's construction. To make this happen, the late Democratic governor Ann Richards, who once said that Bush's father was born with a "silver foot in his mouth" and who referred to Dubya in their 1994 gubernatorial race as "some jerk,"[52] shamefully signed into law an extraordinary measure that established the Arlington Sports Facilities Development Authority (ASFDA), which had the power to seize privately owned land deemed necessary for stadium construction.[53] As journalist Joe Conason has written, "Never before had a municipal authority in Texas been given license to seize the property of a private citizen for the benefit of other private citizens." Eminent domain—for the wealthy—had struck again. On November 8, 1993, with the stadium ready to open in the spring, Bush went public with his plans to run for governor. Conason commented, "He didn't blush when he proclaimed that his campaign theme would demand self-reliance and personal responsibility rather than dependence on government.[54]

Bush held on to his investment in the team as governor, and by the time he cashed out in 1998, the return on his original $600,000 investment in the Rangers was 2,400 percent, upping his takeaway to a cool $14.4 million.[55] Even by the standards of the dot-com era, that's a sweet return. Somewhere Jim Cramer is palpitating. While the money made Bush independently wealthy for the first time in his life, the stadium had an even greater impact on his political fortunes. So just to recap: Son of a U.S. president is loaned $600,000. He fronts an effort to get a $190 million stadium built almost entirely with public taxpayer money. That stadium is then used as the launching pad for a political career that otherwise may never have existed. Then taxes are cut for the rich, and we invade Afghanistan and Iraq, wrecking the economy in the process. But at least Arlington has a sweet ballpark.

It's this history that ensconced Bush as a leader in the burgeoning effort to see pubic subsidies as the new economic cornerstone of ownership. In turn, ownership began to shovel contributions toward both his campaigns for the presidency. A 2004 Associated Press review found that the former Texas Rangers owner received significant contributions from owners of more than half of the thirty major league teams.[56] Seven owners even held the distinction of being "Bush Rangers," meaning they raised at least $200,000 each, and six were "Bush Pioneers," signifying $100,000 apiece.[57]

Bush's most ardent supporters in the owners' boxes were a rogues' gallery of right-wing ideologues with the bucks to back it up. There was the Detroit Tigers' owner with his own Republican electoral ambitions, Michael Ilitch; San Francisco Giants' owner Peter Magowan; and a fellow Yankee imperial figurehead, George Steinbrenner.

Owners loved Bush as much for his prowess at securing that peach of a stadium deal as they did for being their tax cutter in chief. No one ever fronted a stadium swindle better than George W. Bush.

Why does all of this matter? Surely the fact that wealthy owners tilt right is hardly news. But it does show that even by the standards of business leaders, owners are particularly conservative and, as we will see in great detail, conspicuously connected to the religious right. Rush Limbaugh joining their ranks would only have made it all the more obvious. The problem is that they can't seem to just show us the games without all the shenanigans. If we are going to foot the bill for their stadiums, there is no need to underwrite their political adventures as well.

4. The Boss: George Steinbrenner as Throwback and Role Model

To the rich go the spoils. George Steinbrenner built an empire. He really did. He deserves to build a great stadium. He deserves to have the best team money can buy.

—MARK TEIXEIRA

Young baseball fans, if the breed does in fact still exist, have no idea how powerful a presence George Steinbrenner could be. If anyone ever seemed too big for New York, for better and certainly for worse, it was the man who has been the principal owner of the New York Yankees for more than a quarter of a century. He took a once-proud franchise that had become a miserable shell of itself and turned it into an international brand. He also terrorized the city that was the home of the Bronx Bombers, with threats to move the team to New Jersey, Connecticut, and most jarringly, next to Manhattan's West Side Highway. Despite, or because of, the threats, Steinbrenner got his stadium: conservatively, more than $850 million in public bonds went toward the $1.3 billion structure that was completed for the 2009 season.[1] That $1.3 billion, in true Yankee tradition, was the priciest park in the country. Top tickets tripled in cost. ESPN did stories about CEOs who had to make choices between laying off employees or keeping their season tickets. While the rest of country sweated out the financial future, Yankee Stadium was all about "mission accomplished."

But responsibility for the new stadium ticket prices perhaps falls more squarely on the shoulders of Steinbrenner's sons Hank and Hal, who appeared, seemingly out of nowhere, two years ago to take up the reins. The Boss no longer lords over his Yankee empire. The eighty-year-old Steinbrenner, a man who once weighed whether he preferred more to "inflict joy" or "inflict pain," is a shell of himself.[2] He sits in a wheelchair, sunglasses on his face, and is largely infirm. The change has taken place rapidly over the past three years, and like an ancient monarch kept out of sight, this is a Steinbrenner few now get to see. Especially in the wake of the Yankees coasting to the 2009 World Series, nostalgia is quickly replacing honest assessment. Commissioner Bud Selig said right before the start of the Series, "He renovated the stadium, and then he set about rebuilding that Yankee image. I know he was controversial and all of that, but what he accomplished with that franchise is one of the most remarkable stories in sports. He has created a remarkable legacy, not just in New York but in all of baseball. The great popularity the sport now enjoys is due to people like George Steinbrenner."[3]

But before we start wiping our eyes in remembrance of days of yore, we should remember that Steinbrenner, while being a bridge to the past with his larger-than-life personality, also was a bridge to the future. This was the kind of man who was the model for owners from coast to coast on how to hold cities hostage for an endless flow of municipal funds. He was the kind of man who demanded costly stadium renovations in the 1970s, when the city was already enduring a fiscal nightmare. He claimed that he needed just $48 million to bring the stadium up to code. It ended up, according to *Baseball Statistics,* costing $160 million.[4] He developed an unassailable financial advantage over other teams by helping launch the Yankee Entertainment and Sports (YES) Network, which requires fans to buy premium cable services if they want the games. The team's $486 million deal allows them to exist in a financial universe different from every other team in baseball.

Even the YES Network is not free of scandal. Former MSG Network president Bob Gutkowski is as of this writing suing Steinbrenner for $23 million, saying that he laid out the whole plan for YES over the course of multiple meetings. Then he was treated like the oft-fired Billy Martin after a five-game losing streak.

"[T]heir position was to stall me, string me along and, in the end, block the meeting," said Gutkowski. "Their actions made it clear that the only way for me to be fairly compensated for the idea that I brought to George and the work that I performed was to sue him."[5]

Steinbrenner's remarkable ability to make money is intertwined with an unblinking and highly militaristic brand of patriotism. As Robert Elias writes in his book *The Empire Strikes Out*, "Addicted to the movie *Patton*, Steinbrenner wrote the preface to *Patton Leadership: Strategic Lessons for Corporate Warfare*, praising the general as the 'ultimate warrior'—the phrase he also uses to describe his favorite Yankee ballplayers."[6]

Yankee Stadium has been Steinbrenner's stage for his own personal George M. Cohan extravaganza. His patriotic fervor erupted after 9/11, and even in Bush's America of legal torture, the Patriot Act, and Abu Ghraib, the news from the stadium made you do a triple take. Steinbrenner decided that Yankee fans weren't patriotic enough for his tastes. During the playing of "God Bless America," the second national anthem played during the seventh-inning stretch, too many fans in his view weren't standing at attention. He decided there was only one solution: he had stadium workers put chains along the aisles to keep people out of the aisles during the playing of the song. Off-duty police officers and other assorted stadium security paid handsomely by Big Stein were there to make sure the chains were respected by the rabble.

This should really have sparked a rallying cry: "Fans of the world, unite! You have nothing to lose but your chains on the bleachers!" Most complaints from fans were less focused on the importance of civil liberties and more on the distended state of their bladders. This was a disaster waiting to happen, and it did.

One fine day in August 2008, a man named Bradley Campeau-Laurion just wanted to leave his seat and use the bathroom at the old Yankee Stadium. The thirty-year-old New York resident had no idea that nature's call would lead him down a road to perdition where he would be accused of challenging God, country, and the joys of compulsory patriotism at the ballpark.

All Campeau-Laurion did was try to go to the men's room during the seventh-inning stretch. In swooped two New York Police Department officers working security detail, who reportedly roughed him up and threw him out of the ballpark. Campeau-Laurion then filed a civil suit against the city, the cops, and the team for violating his rights.[7]

"New York's finest have no business arresting someone for trying to go to the bathroom at a politically incorrect moment," said Donna Lieberman, executive director of the New York Civil Liberties Union, which represented Campeau-Laurion in the lawsuit.[8] According to the complaint, Campeau-Laurion drank two beers and took the seventh-inning stretch to mean he could actually go stretch away from his aisle.

"As he walked toward the tunnel leading to the concourse, a uniformed New York City police officer put up his hands and mumbled something to Mr. Campeau-Laurion," according to the complaint, blocking his way to the bathroom during the "God Bless America" sing-along. As Campeau-Laurion tried to move past the officer, the policeman grabbed his arm and said, "He's out" to another officer, who twisted his left arm behind his back, hustling him down the ramp and out of the stadium.[9]

Campeau-Laurion said, "I don't care about 'God Bless America.' I don't believe that's grounds constitutionally for being dragged out of a baseball game . . . I simply don't have any religious beliefs. . . . It devalues patriotism as a whole when you force people to participate in patriotic acts. It devalues the freedom we fought for in the first place."[10]

But this was never just about Steinbrenner's patriotism. It was about control. It was about a reckless arrogance and ambition that made him perfect for a New York Yankee franchise that had dominated Major League Baseball before falling on hard times in the 1960s. The author Gay Talese wrote in 1958, years before Steinbrenner's ascension, "God, Brooks Brothers, and United States Steel are believed to be solidly in the Yankees' corner. . . . The efficiently triumphant Yankee machine is a great institution, but, as they say, who can fall in love with U.S. Steel?"[11] Columnist Jimmy Cannon put it more bluntly: "I imagine rooting for the Yankees is like owning a yacht."[12] Cannon wrote that line years before the Ohio shipbuilder with the Williams College pedigree bought the club.

There is certainly an old-school belligerence that Steinbrenner cultivated. He would be a man's man, from an age before smoke-free bars and baby carrots. You can see him in a *Mad Men* scenario drinking scotch for breakfast, secretaries at his beck and call. But while Steinbrenner represents the past, he is a bridge to the future: a template for every modern owner who sees carefully controlled media attention as a holy grail and publicly funded stadiums as the ends of competition. His tenure has spanned and even defined our modern athletic industrial complex.

Sports today is a trillion-dollar globalized business, even bigger than Talese's vaunted U.S. Steel. The Yankees now are the ultimate baseball global brand, but Steinbrenner purchased the billion-dollar franchise in 1972 for $10 million. That's less than scrappy, middle-aged former Yankee outfielder Johnny Damon made in 2009. It's also $3 million less than the previous owner, CBS, paid for it.[13] As owner, he gleefully and immediately assumed the character of the Boss.

The Yankees under Steinbrenner won their first world championship in 1977. Laid out beautifully by Jonathan Mahler in his book *Ladies and Gentlemen, the Bronx Is Burning,* that season of 1977 was the summer when Queens's own Archie Bunker exploded out of his lounge chair, ready to lash back. As a citywide blackout, combative strikes by city workers, and Son of Sam competed for headlines, the *New York Post* was bought by Rupert Murdoch and Ed Koch became mayor on an anticrime, pro–death penalty platform. Steinbrenner stood astride this fever dream, an absolute colossus. Somehow, by 1976, he had pushed through a complete overhaul of Yankee Stadium on the public dime. Amid public housing projects going up in flames and the near bankrupting of the city, the House That Ruth Built got a home makeover courtesy of the New York taxpayer.[14] This fed his confidence, ego, and belief that he could deliver this team to the promised land through the force of his volcanic will. When the Yankees made the World Series in 1976 and then won it in 1977 and 1978, it seemed to Steinbrenner and the media around him that his might made right.

Steinbrenner had become, in the words of one writer, "every worker's nightmare, the satanic CEO, a fanatically controlling overlord who borrows his warmed-over rhetoric from Vince Lombardi and his managerial style from Stalin."[15] And as former Yankee general manager Bob Watson said, "If things go right, they're his team. If things go wrong, they're your team. His favorite line is, 'I will never have a heart attack. I give them.'"[16] But this arrogance brought by early success did not serve him or his beloved team well. The Yankees went eighteen years without winning another World Series title. Through it all, Steinbrenner never stopped trying to change managers: he did it twenty times in his first twenty-three seasons. Five times he hired and jettisoned Billy Martin. He canned the beloved Yogi Berra just sixteen games into the 1985 season. "Winning is the most important thing in my life, after breathing," Steinbrenner said. "Breathing first, winning next."[17]

There's another side to the Boss as well, a side that even his detractors acknowledge. It's a side I had the good fortune to see. When I was a kid, Dick Young, the legendary columnist from the *New York Post,* passed away. Young wore his prejudices on his sleeve, and wrote in a pugnacious style that made you gnash your teeth. As the *New York Times* wrote in Young's obituary, "With all the subtlety of a knee in the groin, Dick Young made people gasp. . . . He could be vicious, ignorant, trivial and callous, but for many years he was the epitome of the brash, unyielding yet sentimental Damon Runyon sportswriter."[18]

When Young died, it was announced in the *Post* that the service would be open to the public. I couldn't help but notice that the Manhattan-based funeral home was a mere ten-minute bus ride from my house. Like any normal preteen in New York City, I dressed up in a blue blazer and tie and went to Dick Young's funeral. As soon as I walked through the door, I felt like Bill O'Reilly at the Apollo Theater. I just had no business there. Everyone from the New York sports scene was present, from St. Johns hoops coach Lou Carnesecca to the local sports anchors, perhaps straight from the television studios, the pancake makeup still streaked on their cheeks. This was not my tribe. Also for an open service, there were no fans there that I saw, and certainly no unaccompanied minors, both of which made people's stares feel like daggers, and the room's soft, recessed lighting feel like spotlights.

As I shuffled my feet, feeling more like a voyeur than a mourner, unsure whether I should make a break for the exit, a meaty hand clamped on my shoulder and started to rub the back of my head. "This guy's here. Now we can get started," he said as he guided me inside. I looked up and it was George Steinbrenner. My first thought was, "Holy shit! The owner of the Yankees, the freakin' Boss, has his hand on my neck!" My second thought was, "What the hell is wrong with his hair?" The back of his head looked like it had been chopped up with gardening shears. Steinbrenner then pushed me inside roughly and turned his back to me, resuming his conversation with a big smile and a laugh. Several people then asked me, "Who are you?" Just a social New York City Park Avenue funeral. I was more than grateful. Steinbrenner was doing what he told sportswriter Ira Berkow he loved most, "inflicting some joy." As the late sportswriter Dick Schaap noted, that is a "neat, and curious phrase, I *inflict* joy."[19] But that day, upon me, he inflicted a little bit of mercy, if not joy.

Researching Steinbrenner, it's remarkable how seamlessly this story fits with the Steinbrenner some people remember: the kind of guy who would reach out to an awkward kid like some kind of Daddy Warbucks, and then shove him inside. He may have been the model for the new breed of ownership we are afflicted with today, but he also was a part of that last group of the paternalistic owners, the people who felt like it was their duty in ownership to plow profits back into the team, creating a brand that the city could be proud of.

The 1980s in so many ways make up the heart of the Steinbrenner era. The Yankees were the winningest team in baseball over the course of the decade and after 1981 didn't win one division title or take home one pennant during the decade. It was all about George. As Mark Puma wrote, "The managerial carousel was on high speed. Among the casualties was popular Yogi Berra, whom Steinbrenner fired in 1985. Berra responded by shunning the Yankees for fourteen years. Lou Piniella was hired and fired twice by Steinbrenner. Dallas Green, canned in 1989, dubbed Steinbrenner 'Manager George.' "[20]

As Steinbrenner bragged of dishing out coronaries and drove his team into the ground, a prominent adult magazine named him "one of the ten sexiest men in sports."[21] He epitomized his times. The Reagan 1980s were made for people who could combine an elite pedigree with a bullying posture. The only difference between Donald Trump and Steinbrenner was that Trump got the front page of the *New York Post* and Steinbrenner the back.

Steinbrenner once said, "This country was built on people with guts who wanted more than they had—like the people in those little covered wagons who went West and fought the weather and the Indians."[22] In Steinbrenner's mind, the Indians were always his employees, fit to be trampled. In addition to firing twelve secretaries during his first five years, and an endless parade of managers, Steinbrenner would chart the length of his players' hair like a barber with OCD. He once took the opportunity during his precious national anthem to chart the hair length on every player's head and sent a memo to then manager Ralph Houk on who in fact would need a trim.[23]

He is someone who said, "A boss can be totally wrong, you know, but he is the boss, and he worked to get there. Discipline is the most necessary condition for success, corporate and sports. No leader, whether in the army or in a school or in a company or on a team, can let one of his employees say to him, 'Get off my ass or fire me.' "[24] What makes Steinbrenner exceptional is not that he believes the above. All owners do. It's that he articulated it for the media. Would that he only had a blog. This was Steinbrenner's American Way.

Part of the American Way meant not only having a relationship with Richard Nixon but also befriending liberal icons such as Ted Kennedy and Tip O'Neill. It meant hiring Mayor Rudolph Giuliani's former deputy mayor for economic development as team president while Steinbrenner was lobbying for a publicly funded stadium.

Steinbrenner may have enforced a strict dress code and gone on a mission against the sin of sideburns, but that strong emphasis on appearance was never backed up by demanding that conduct off the field match the clean-cut exterior. If he never demanded that his players be role models, it was largely because he wasn't one himself. On that score, he was no hypocrite.

Steinbrenner was the first person convicted of a felony in connection with the Watergate scandal, a conviction that led to his being suspended from Major League Baseball. He was then issued a pardon by Ronald Reagan in 1989, two days before Reagan left the White House.[25] But Steinbrenner was suspended again, in 1990, for paying Howie Spira, a twenty-one-year-old clubhouse gofer with gambling issues, to dig up dirt on the Boss's star slugger Dave Winfield. As Dick Heller wrote, this "remains one of the less savory episodes in recent sports history."[26]

Only after Steinbrenner was suspended by Major League Baseball and was firmly out of Yankees' operations did the team replenish their farm system, stop signing shiny, high-priced free agents, and lay the groundwork for a remarkable string of success, winning four World Series in five years. Backed by farm system products such as Derek Jeter, Jorge Posada,

Andy Pettitte, and the immortal Mariano Rivera, alongside overachieving calloused veterans such as Scott Brosius and Tino Martinez, the team found its way into the hearts of the city.

Likewise, only after Steinbrenner decided to once again take an active role in the team, after 2003, were they mired in what for the Yankees had been—until 2009—a terrible slump. In a replay of the 1980s, high-priced geriatric pitchers such as Kevin Brown and Randy Johnson arrived just in time to look terrible. This is the great Steinbrenner contradiction: for all of his Vince Lombardi via Williams College bombast, the team perhaps would have had more success if the baseball people just could have done their jobs in peace.

This is why, as Bob Costas said in an interview with Larry David (who mimicked Steinbrenner to perfection on *Seinfeld*), "George Steinbrenner is a ready-made comedic character." But he only became funny with age. This is why he inspires such vivid memories when we abandon the nostalgia. No one hugs a grizzly bear. But we all laugh and point once they're in a cage. This was all on display at the end of the 2008 season, when the House That Ruth Built, the home of Murderers Row, the eighty-eight-year-old Yankee Stadium, finally shut its doors.

Like owners who come to resemble their dogs, Steinbrenner in many ways became Yankee Stadium: respected, even feared, but never loved. Contrast the razing of the stadium and the attendant reaction with any other of the classic stadiums. Imagine, for a moment, if the city political leaders and team owners of the Chicago Cubs and the Boston Red Sox tried to bulldoze Wrigley Field or Fenway Park. Fans in those cities would be chaining themselves to the wrecking balls. Armed with only a beer and a bratwurst, they would be doing their best impression of Tiananmen Square.

But there was nary a whimper for Yankee Stadium. From ex- and current players, to the rabid fans that make the pilgrimage to the Bronx, to the tweedy, misty-eyed baseball cognoscenti, the collective sentiment was summed up simply by Yankee captain Derek Jeter with an answer that also could have been said about Steinbrenner himself: "It's time."

Some of this speaks to fatigue over the soap operatic politics that surrounded the efforts to get the stadium built.

The absence of sentiment also speaks to the psychology of a ball club and fan base developed by Steinbrenner. It's an approach to the game that's been mercenary in its pursuit of success and pitiless relative to other concerns. If a new stadium means new revenue streams, which would mean an even more crushing financial advantage over their opponents, then so be it. In the 2008 off-season, while the city—and the country—were reeling from the stock market and housing plunge, the Yankees signed two marquee players—CC Sabathia and Mark Teixeira—to nine-figure contracts while demanding $380 million more in public funds from the city.[27]

And yet even the Yankee faithful—in a frenzy to return to a world championship—may balk once they step back and look at what their new stadium will mean for that pesky real world that acts as backdrop to all their history and success. If the old stadium was the House That Ruth Built, the new park is the House That Steinbrenner and Bloomberg Fleeced. Mayor-for-life Michael Bloomberg, the only non-Alaskan politician on the planet to come out in September in defense of John McCain's asinine statement that "the fundamentals of our economy are strong," said, "We want these kinds of facilities here. Having new stadiums is as important as other things in terms of, not just the spirit for the people who live here, but our economy."[28] He said this despite the ample evidence that publicly funded stadiums are little more than sporting "shock doctrines": privatizing profits and socializing debt.[29]

Bloomberg made this statement on Capitol Hill testifying about global warming, for some reason. In a different room on the Hill, other hearings were taking place where Representative Dennis Kucinich declared he found "waste and abuse of public dollars" in construction of the new stadium. Kucinich's panel investigation found "substantial evidence of improprieties and possible fraud by the financial architects of the new Yankee Stadium."[30]

"Not only have we found waste and abuse of public dollars subsidizing a project that is for the exclusive benefit of a private entity, the Yankees, but also we have discovered serious questions about the accuracy of certain representations made by the City of New York to the federal government," Kucinich said.[31]

Representative Diane Watson, Democrat of California, took it even further, arguing that in the context of economic crisis, the idea of funding these monuments to corporate greed is immoral. "In this country we have allowed the upper class to destroy the middle class," she said.[32]

Anyone who has been to New York City knows how correct this is. The airports look like dilapidated, old Hollywood movie sets. The roads are broken. And the South Bronx, where the new stadium is located, has been picked apart.

When members of the local community board objected several years ago to giving the richest team in baseball a few hundred million bucks to build a brand-new stadium in their borough, they were purged by then Bronx borough president Adolfo Carrion.[33] Carrion also pushed for the removal of one of the South Bronx's few public parks, to be replaced by an Alamo of gentrification. Carrion was well rewarded. He was tapped by Barack Obama to be director of the White House Office of Urban Affairs.

The idea that a new Yankee Stadium would be a rebuilding priority in a crumbling city is more than just fodder for ironic musings in the *Village Voice*. It becomes symbolic of everything that's wrong with the athletic industrial complex. But Steinbrenner, in his current infirmity, seems to be enjoying what can only be described as a modest renaissance.

At the 2008 All-Star Game, a frail version of Big Stein arrived and took a lap in a Yankee golf cart. His old nemesis *Daily News* columnist Mike Lupica was even moved to write a testament to the old bear, writing, "Finally came George Steinbrenner. The field at Yankee Stadium was still for the players, the way it always has been, the way it will be across 161st St. There were louder cheers for those players than for him Tuesday night, much louder, all night long and into the morning. They still treated him like an All-Star at the Stadium. One last time, everybody sure knew the old man was in town."[34] They knew. They paid respect. But there wasn't a wet eye in the house.

If Lupica tried to pen a sober assessment, the announcers went for full treacle. Fox lead announcer Joe Buck insisted with passion that Steinbrenner be inducted into the Hall of Fame. While reveling in the sheer spectacle of this self-created Yankee Stadium moment, Buck glowingly cited Steinbrenner's dedication to doing "whatever it takes" to win and making the Yankees such a successful franchise.[35] No one would doubt that he did "whatever it takes," but it looks pale when we see that they achieved greatness in the 1990s only when he was locked out of his offices. He also inflated the idea of owner like no one else. He showed that availability and accessibility for the cameras are not the same as account-ability to the fans.

We should remember Steinbrenner, the man who bridged eras, with-out nostalgia. He justified all his misdeeds by saying, "The reason baseball has its problems is that owners weren't involved twenty years ago. They treated the sports as a hobby, as a toy. . . . I'm an involved owner. I'm like Archie Bunker. I get mad as hell when we blow one."[36] But Archie Bun-ker never went to Williams. He never fired secretaries by the carload. He felt tossed around by a world changing too fast for its own good. George Steinbrenner created that world. Now, throughout our cities, we live with the results.

5. Clay Bennett, the Seattle SuperSonics, and the Question of Ownership

There is something that happens to this city when the Sonics are making a run. The winter seems warmer. The cold weeks go by faster. The coffee and microbrews just taste better. This is something our community has grown with for the past forty-one years. Please bring back our team and restore our collective dreams.

—FROM THE WEBSITE IHATECLAY.COM[1]

I n a just universe, there would be a constitutional amendment preventing sports franchises from moving to other cities. Sports teams operate on an entirely different emotional, or even spiritual, plane than any other corporate entity. There is no question about who owns General Motors. Even if you drive your GM truck for years, even if the government pours billions of bailout dollars into its coffers, you don't think that you have some sort of ownership claim to the company. Just because your hands are permanently glued to your MacBook, you don't confuse yourself with Steve Jobs. A local team is different.

When a pro sports squad resides in a city for decades, when its triumphs, failures, and even uniform colors become part of how citizens define themselves, then the question of ownership becomes a contested concept. The owner's name is in the papers, but the community feels a separate sense of possession. A team can feel as much an organic part of a city as the firehouse, the library, or a distinct monument. Fans assume they will have the opportunity to bestow the team on to their children. Stories of heroes past will be passed down like heirlooms. No one expects the team to move any more than we would expect a person to buy the St. Louis Gateway Arch and place it in Reno.

This can be a powerful, even magical connection. When an owner severs the connection, the wounds can become jagged scars, commented upon with resentment and regret for generations. I was raised with stories from my Brooklyn-born-and-raised father of Walter O'Malley's 1958 heist of the Brooklyn Dodgers to Los Angeles and the shattered hearts across the borough. An old joke in Brooklyn is, "What do you do if you have Hitler, Stalin, and Walter O'Malley in a room and only two bullets? Answer: you shoot O'Malley twice." As anyone raised in postwar Brooklyn will attest, O'Malley's 1958 move to Los Angeles ranks as something beyond diabolical. But O'Malley saw the writing on the wall: the massive migration to the West Coast that was reshaping the nation. The exploding Cold War defense industry had taken root, and L.A. had supplanted New York as the undisputed media capital of the world. Moving the Dodgers was just business, not personal. But you couldn't tell that to the people of Brooklyn. As Brooklyn-born journalist Pete Hamill wrote, "After 1957, it seemed like we would never laugh again. Of course, we did. It's just that we were never young again." Fans demonstrated at Borough Hall, Ebbets Field, and the Dodgers' main office, at 215 Montague Street. Their signs read, "Brooklyn is the Dodgers. The Dodgers are Brooklyn." Even though the team had brought two million fans to the park, it wasn't enough. There had to be a new stadium, perhaps a newfangled thing called a *domed* stadium, to protect the team from inclement weather. O'Malley said that without this "dome" he would be seeking sanctuary elsewhere, and when the people of Brooklyn said no, that's exactly what O'Malley did.[2]

O'Malley was once quoted as saying, "Baseball isn't a business. It's a disease."[3] True enough, he was the Typhoid Mary of ownership, who spread his virus to the City of Angels, for Brooklyn wasn't the only place gutted by O'Malley's far-seeing avarice. As Ebbets Field became the Ebbets Field Apartments, O'Malley made Los Angeles ground zero for the first modern stadium landgrab. There was another community out west seen by O'Malley and Major League Baseball as merely "the future site of Dodger Stadium." It was known as Chavez Ravine.

Called "a poor man's Shangri-la" by its residents, Chavez Ravine had been home to generations of Mexican Americans living in a tightly knit valley community. But to the L.A. city government, the area was seen as a savage, lawless landscape outside of their immediate control. The people of Chavez Ravine ran their own schools and churches and even grew their own food. It was the center of the Zoot Suit Riots, the epic 1943 battles between white sailors and the sharply dressed *pachucos*. It was seen as over-ripe for development. In 1949, the National Housing Act, which offered federal money to construct public housing projects, was passed. The Los Angeles Housing Authority used the seizure provided by the NHA to bulldoze Shangri-la.[4]

Chavez Ravine residents were informed that their homes were going to be leveled for "public housing." Some departed willingly with meager compensation. The ones who stood firm had their homes bulldozed and received nothing.[5] This is known as eminent domain. There was a protest movement that stood with the people of Chavez Ravine, but it wasn't strong enough to beat back the leveling of the land.

It's here where the story starts to twist in that pulpy, left coast way. Another organization appeared out of nowhere to step up against the public housing proponents. They were called Citizens Against Socialist Housing (CASH). They had no symathy for the Mexican Americans sent out of their homes. Instead, their target was both the public housing plan and the assistant director of the Los Angeles City Housing Authority, Frank Wilkinson. Wilkinson was subsequently called before the House Un-American Activities Committee for being a Communist. He was fired from his job and sentenced to one year in jail.[6]

As Wilkinson said years later, "It's the tragedy of my life, absolutely. I was responsible for uprooting I don't know how many hundreds of people from their own little valley and having the whole thing destroyed."[7]

This is what set the stage for O'Malley to swoop in and grab the land for little more than peanuts and Cracker Jacks. As Wilkinson said, "We'd spent millions of dollars getting ready for [public housing], and the Dodgers picked it up for just a fraction of that. It was just a tragedy for the people, and from the city it was the most hypocritical thing that could possibly happen."[8]

Yet another protest struggle, the first anti-stadium movement, arose to challenge O'Malley's shady shenanigans. Violent clashes took place as pro- and anti-stadium forces squared off. Debates flared across the city. An actor and professional anti-Communist making a transition to politics named Ronald Reagan stepped in to call opponents of the stadium plan "baseball haters."[9] He might as well have argued that they were eating borscht with Khrushchev. A public referendum was forced on the issue, and stadium proponents won with 51.5 percent of the vote, allowing O'Malley to move forward. (Of course, the refugees of Chavez Ravine, many of them immigrants, could not vote.) In 1959 the city began clearing the land for the stadium after removing the last few families who had held out. On April 10, 1962, the 56,000-seat Dodger Stadium officially opened, but the period of 1951 to 1961 is still whispered among older Angelenos as the "Battle of Chavez Ravine."[10]

While O'Malley may occupy a special place in the Callous Owners' Hall of Fame, he has competition in the "most hated" category.

In Baltimore, the name Bob Irsay, who hustled away the beloved Baltimore Colts to Indianapolis under a cloud of darkness in 1983, is as reviled as O'Malley is in Brooklyn. Charm City fans carry themselves as scarred as their Brooklyn brethren. Since their loss was football and not baseball, because they were Baltimore and not Brooklyn, far less poetry and prose has been spilled in their memory. But in an unglamorous, hardscrabble city such as Baltimore, the Colts belonged to the community in a fierce fashion. There is the famous scene in Barry Levinson's film *Diner* when the character Eddie, played by Steve Guttenberg, won't marry his longtime girlfriend unless she can pass a Baltimore Colts trivia test. (As his friend comments, "We all know most marriages depend on a firm grasp of football trivia.")

The bestselling book *Johnny U*, about Colts legendary quarterback Johnny Unitas, also goes through, in terrific detail, how the team lived among the fans. They weren't isolated by fame and fortune. Instead, they made relatively modest wages and were the neighbors and off-season coworkers of the people in Charm City. They were Baltimore as much as they were the Colts. The entire sense of connectivity and continuity meant nothing to Bob Irsay and he wanted a new stadium or he wanted out. In a state of profound inebriation, Irsay even appeared on television to threaten city and state government officials, not to mention Colts fans.

In his alcoholic stupor, he spoke the truth as he saw it, saying to the press, "What are you all doing here? I don't know what in the hell this is all about. I have no intention of moving the goddamn team."[11]

Maryland state senator Julian Lapides captured the intensity of the moment, saying, "It is simply unconscionable that cities are forced to succumb to blackmail by pro football and baseball. You should not capitulate to blackmailers. You don't deal with hostage situations. You don't deal with terrorists. I put these teams in the same category."[12] The Maryland House of Delegates even passed a bill to forcibly purchase the Colts from Irsay, threatening to seize the team under the same eminent domain laws used for stadium landgrabs.[13]

But it was too late. Irsay had already packed his football operations into fifteen infamous green-and-yellow Mayflower moving trucks. Under the watchful eye of Pinkerton guards, the team's equipment made that fateful journey from Baltimore to Indianapolis. His own mother told *Sports Illustrated* that her son was a "devil on earth."[14] The *Baltimore Sun* dubbed him "football's most reviled figure."[15] But Indianapolis had a domed stadium ready and waiting for the highest bidder. Indianapolis mayor William C. Hudnut III was jubilant when he spoke to the *New York Times* right after the Colts arrived, saying, "It's a wonderful thing for our community. It's a boost to the city's image nationally and to local morale as a symbol of major league status."[16]

The ascension of the Baltimore Ravens—brought to Baltimore after being torn from Cleveland—has certainly eased the sting among Baltimoreans. Those old enough to remember 1983, however, still wince.

Whether it's O'Malley or Irsay or countless other owners, the men in charge have been crystal clear: it doesn't matter how beloved, how treasured, or how rooted a team may be. Greener pastures, not to mention a publicly funded stadium, will necessitate a change. Even when teams don't move, the threats to cut and run, the Steinbrenner special, have been exercised in markets both big and small. Today the City of Los Angeles, without an NFL team, has an $800 million plan to build a stadium if a team in another city wants to move. Already, owners in San Diego and Minnesota are making noise that if they don't get more subsidies, they might view the City of Angels favorably. Let's hope Los Angeles doesn't get another notch on its bedpost and break another city's heart.

But beneath the superficial drama, the fact that an owner from outside a community can lay claim to a franchise and move it across the country is one of the most loathsome features of contemporary sports.

That's exactly what happened in 2008, when two Oklahoma rustlers named Clay Bennett and Aubrey McClendon bought the National Basketball Association's Seattle SuperSonics, gutted a fifty-win team of all its stars, demoralized a city, and moved to their hometown of Oklahoma City. The people of Seattle committed a grave sin in the eyes of NBA commissioner David Stern and the new owners. They loved their team, but refused to give the Bennett/McClendon duo a new $300 million stadium. Seattle citizens turned back referendums and pressured politicians and argued that the team was housed in a perfectly good building called the Key Arena.[17] Plans for a new facility were protested from the streets to the statehouse. They wouldn't roll over, so Stern, Bennett, and McClendon made an example of them and now the Seattle SuperSonics are the Oklahoma City Thunder, a very promising young team with a name that sounds like they should be playing roller derby.

The mere idea of the SuperSonics in Oklahoma still feels out of whack, like Sir Mix-A-Lot cutting a country/western album. In Clay Bennett, the city had a villain straight from central casting. As one writer observed, "With his brush cut and beefy build, his lifelong Republicanism, and partners made rich by fossil fuels, Bennett pushed all the wrong buttons in liberal, urbane, health-conscious, ecologically sensitive Seattle."[18] Peter von Reichbauer, a council member in King County, which includes Seattle, said, "Decisions were made instantly, both in the media and in the bars and taverns, 'This is a guy from out of state who wants to take this team out of state.' "[19] They had reason to believe it, since Bennett had spent about as much time in Seattle as the sun. But at first he said all the right things. When Bennett bought the team, he said to great applause, "The Sonics, Storm [the WNBA franchise], and Seattle are synonymous. And we take our history seriously."[20]

Clearly not seriously enough. Seattle holds a profoundly rich basketball tradition that rests deeply in the marrow of the community. It's a history that included utterly unique players such as "The Glove" Gary Payton (who spoke at the Save Our Sonics rallies), Slick Watts, "the Reign Man" Shawn Kemp, and "the X-Man" Xavier McDaniel, who had a classic cameo in the Seattle-based film *Singles*. The SuperSonics name was from the Seattle-based Boeing's supersonic transport planes. More than football or baseball, this was first and foremost a hoops town. As former Sonics coach George Karl said, "There's a soul and a history to basketball in Seattle. I know owners want to make more money, but is the way to do it really by making the sport more business-oriented?"[21]

Seattle schoolteacher Jesse Hagopian said to me in the aftermath of the move, "The pain is real. My wife's stomach is larger than an NBA regulation ball and we are expecting our first kid any day—which makes Seattle's loss of the Sonics weigh heavier than when the news was originally announced. The SuperSonics, as they were known in the glory days, were part of a maturation process—both stimulating and stunting my intellectual growth—that I won't be able to share with my child."[22]

Clay Bennett and Aubrey McClendon, along with their minority partners, decided that the team wasn't Jesse's to share and were Oklahoma bound. They undertook this project with the blessing, encouragement, and some would say prodding of NBA commissioner David Stern. Stern has been the most powerful commissioner in sports for decades, a man compared to Vito Corleone, and someone with a sense of grandiosity that would shame a Latin American dictator.

Stern lacks only the epaulets on his blue blazers, at least in public. In recent years the man they call "Money" has issued a series of bizarre decrees about player comportment, changing the ball, and demanding a dress code among players. He is like the revolutionary leader in Woody Allen's *Bananas* who declares, "I am your new president. From this day on, the official language of San Marcos will be Swedish. In addition to that, all citizens will be required to change their underwear every half hour. Underwear will be worn on the outside, so we can check."

Stern, a political liberal, met with Bush 2004 campaign strategist Matthew Dowd to figure out how to spread the league's appeal to "nontraditional" NBA states. Owners love Stern's efforts to give the league what Stern calls "red state appeal."[23] Arguably, there is no state redder than Oklahoma. And it's no wonder that Bennett—a serious GOP money man—sent what was supposed to be a private e-mail to Stern where he gushed, "You are just one of my favorite people on earth."[24] Their bipartisan love is built on a foundation of passion for our tax dollars.

It should be the right of citizens to refuse to publicly fund a stadium, especially during economically troubled times. Sometimes stadiums are funded without a public referendum. But even when a referendum does occur, grassroots opposition can be silenced by intimidation and big-money public relations campaigns. This was the background to the stadium hostility in Seattle, where a rash of school closings and the formation of modern-day Hoovervilles, tent cities for the homeless, now define the once chic urban landscape.

During the salad days of the 1990s, the people of Seattle drank the Kool-Aid of public stadium funding for a decade and found what cities across the country have realized: it just doesn't work. But many never thought until near the end that the Sonics were actually a flight threat. Even with a publicly funded stadium being served on a silver platter, it seemed ridiculous that Oklahoma City could be a serious alternative. After all, it's only a third of the population of Seattle, with a fraction of the Emerald City's per capita income and no history of supporting a major professional franchise. It's a textbook case for why the business of sports requires radical restructuring, because the next city to get the Sonics treatment could be your own. And trusting your own is folly.

Despite his words, Bennett had one goal and one goal only: bring the Sonics to Sooner country. In retrospect, the transparency of his master plan is breathtaking. While Bennett said all the right things about keeping the Sonics in Seattle, a team executive dinner on September 9, 2007, tells you all you need to know about the man and his motives. On that fine evening, the Sonics management, all held over from the previous ownership regime, all dyed-in-the-wool Pacific Northwesters, gathered in Oklahoma. Bennett made sure they all ate at a top restaurant, and he picked up the bill. As the Seattle execs sat down, four plates of a deep-fried appetizer were put on the table. After filling their mouths with the greasy goodness, one executive asked their waitress what this curious dish with the nutty flavor actually was. It was lamb testicles.[25] Bennett laughed at their discomfort, and the message was clear: the Sonics could suck his balls.

Bennett's arrogance was hardly well earned. He made his money the old-fashioned way: he married it. His wife is Louise Gaylord Bennett, the daughter of Oklahoma City media mogul Edward L. Gaylord. The Gaylords are the most established old-money clan in the state, giving Bennett a lifetime leg up for his every entrepreneurial aspiration. "That has certainly been a topic I have had to deal with and understand," Bennett has said of his in-law connections. "There was a time when any disparaging notion relative to that concept would [annoy me]. But I understand that perspective now. It doesn't bother me at all. I wouldn't trade it for the world. Because of a leg up, I have been able to be an entrepreneur through the years and not an employee."[26] Ah, to never have to be an employee. Now, that's nice work if you can get it.

The Gaylords are as revered in Oklahoma as the Kennedys in Massachusetts. The Oklahoma Sooners' football stadium is named the Gaylord Family Memorial Stadium. Outside the stadium, there is Gaylord Hall. The Gaylords also own the *Oklahoman,* the state's biggest daily newspaper. E. K. Gaylord Boulevard runs through the city. The tony suburb of Gillardia is called Gaylordia by residents.

The Gaylords also once owned a minority share of the Texas Rangers—later sold, as we saw, at a sweet discount to George W. Bush.

Officially, Bennett is the chairman of Oklahoma City–based Dorchester Capital Corporation, as well as the chairman emeritus of the Oklahoma Heritage Association. He considers himself a "staunch" man of the right, with a large bust of Ronald Reagan in his corporate boardroom.[27] His ownership partner, Aubrey McClendon, also gave $1 million to an organization called Americans United to Preserve Marriage, an antigay organization that pushed through an Oklahoma referendum against issuing marriage licenses to gay couples.[28] Interestingly, they took the Sonics to Oklahoma City but left behind the WNBA's Seattle Storm, a team with a sizable lesbian and gay fan base. Clearly being intimately connected to the town of "Gaylordia" hasn't made them sensitive to these issues. Bennett and McClendon also have displayed impressively deep pockets for groups such as Swift Vets and POWs for Truth, the group that called John Kerry's Purple Hearts a fraud for his combat history in Vietnam.[29]

McClendon's day job is running the Oklahoma City–based Chesapeake Energy Corporation, at its height a $23 billion company. Also on the board are former Oklahoma governors Frank Keating and Don Nickles. Governor Keating was the gent who in the 2008 election cycle said of Barack Obama, "He ought to admit, 'You know, I've got to be honest with you. I was a guy of the street. I was way to the left. I used cocaine.'"[30] If Stern wanted red state appeal, clearly he'd found it.

If the Sonics by some miracle had actually remained in liberal Seattle, Bennett and McClendon would have fit in like Glenn Beck at a mosque. Their very politics expose the kabuki theater at play. This was obvious for months before the heist would be consecrated and legal.

"When the team was bought from the previous ownership, they told us and everybody in the city that they sold it to a group that they thought would most likely keep the team in the city," former Sonics star Ray Allen, who was traded to the Celtics in 2007, commented to the *Boston Globe*. "Everybody thought that was some bullshit. How is someone from Oklahoma City going to buy a team in Seattle who doesn't have any ties [in Seattle] and has big money in Oklahoma? If things don't go right, everybody's craving for the team to move to Oklahoma City."[31]

But it was Bennett's special relationship with one of his "favorite people," David Stern, that made this a foregone conclusion. Bennett's all-powerful father-in-law became a part-owner of the San Antonio Spurs in the mid-1990s at a time when the very future of the Spurs was an open question, the San Antonio media market being roughly the size of that of a state university. The Spurs benefited from the roll of the dice, the drafting of Wake Forest's Tim Duncan, and the franchise thrived, winning four championships over the past decade.

But Bennett's dream was to see an NBA franchise in Oklahoma City. Once again, Bennett found himself bathed in the fantastic grace of Stern when in the lead-up to the 2005–2006 season, he teamed with McClendon to give the NBA's New Orleans Hornets a home in Oklahoma City after Hurricane Katrina flattened the Gulf Coast. Bennett and McClendon saw the Katrina disaster as an opportunity and treated every game like an audition for selling Oklahoma City as a major league town. They used their Oklahoma influence to make sure that all the games were well-heeled affairs, impressing Stern that big dollars could come from a smaller state. Bennett pushed the city's executives not merely to buy advertising and sponsorship deals but also to distribute thousands of tickets. "He knows exactly how much he—'window-dressed' is the term I heard—the market," said Ian Edmundson, a sports consultant who helped market the Hornets.[32]

While the Hornets were drawing 11,000 fans every game in New Orleans, Oklahoma City was averaging more than 16,000 while charging on average an extra $13 per ticket.[33] For a time it worked. Once again Bennett benefited from the hoops genius of a young rookie from Wake Forest: this time it was point guard Chris Paul. Paul's magnificent play, not to mention the novelty of the team in OKC, made the New Orleans/OKC Hornets a hot ticket. It also most certainly saved the Hornets from post-Katrina oblivion. Bennett was seen as having helped save two separate franchises. Splice in the league's push for "red state appeal" and the game was officially afoot.

In 2006, Bennett, along with McClendon, offered Starbucks founder Howard Schultz $350 million for both the Sonics and the Storm. Schultz, Seattle-born and -raised, must have been bloated on gingerbread lattes when he made the deal he later came to regret. "I regret that I accepted those assurances and am deeply sorry for the outcome," Schultz commented after the move. "Unfortunately, showing that the Bennett Group lied is not enough to turn back the clock and return the Sonics."[34]

Upon buying the team, Bennett started a charm offensive with the help of a lapdog press. A loving profile in the *Seattle Times* now reads as infamous as Herbert Hoover praising the U.S. economy in the lead-up to the Great Depression: They wrote,

> Ask anyone who knows Clay Bennett, and most say he is straightforward, a "straight shooter" as they say down here. . . . . "He's not going to say he'll do something he can't do," former Oklahoma City mayor Ron Norick told the *Oklahoman,* the paper owned by Bennett's wife's family. "And if he says he needs a new arena, that's what he needs. . . . I've never known Clay to make an idle threat. You know where you are when you're dealing with Clay."
>
> But he was sincere about not understanding the media's reaction to his claim that he wants to keep the Sonics in Seattle. Where he comes from, his word and reputation usually are good enough. He hopes that, in the end, it is valid in Seattle as well.[35]

Bennett's word wasn't his bond. Instead it quickly became bad theater, constantly mocked by columnists, fans, and players such as Seattle Storm stars Sue Bird and Lauren Jackson, who both publicly refused to move to OKC with their team.[36]

When he then insisted on a new $300 million stadium, the people said hell no. The response of NBA commissioner Stern wasn't a measured balance between the bond of a community and the needs of ownership. He treated Seattle like a dog treats a hydrant. Speaking in martial language more at home in a war room than a boardroom, Stern spoke of the need for a "scorched earth" battle for a new arena. He also said, "The presentation from Washington [State] is, 'We're going to kill you.'"[37]

Stern may have an ego the size of Shaq's waistline, but he has never been accused of stupidity. By raising the temperature on the negotiations and inflaming the local populace, he lubricated the team's move to Oklahoma City.

As Bennett found himself throughout 2007 rebuffed time and again in his quest for hundreds of millions in taxpayer cash, he retreated to his home in Oklahoma City for several weeks. He returned to Seattle to take apart a division-winning franchise, shaping the team to be as unappealing as possible. He discarded star players such as Ray Allen and Rashard Lewis and mocked a city, a fan base, and a sterling hoops tradition. He did all of this while saying publicly, "We are committed absolutely to winning championships, and as we make these decisions, we keep that goal in mind."[38] He said that even though his lawyers issued statements calling Sonics boosters agitating to keep the team a "disturbing fringe element," and also claimed that "a majority of the public has accepted the team's imminent departure. The sentiment among many is, 'Who cares?'"[39] This "disturbing fringe element" was a strong fan organization connected to former Seattle players called Save Our Sonics.

McClendon gave the game away in 2007 when he said to the *Oklahoma City Journal Record*, "We didn't buy the team to keep it in Seattle, we hoped to come here. We know it's a little more difficult financially here in Oklahoma City, but we think it's great for the community and if we could break even we'd be thrilled. They've got sixty days to make some decisions they haven't been willing to make in the past year, and if they make them in a way that satisfies Clay, then the team will stay there. If they don't meet the requirements he's laid out, the team will move and Clay has indicated they'll come to Oklahoma City.

"We started to look around and at that time the Sonics were going through some ownership challenges in Seattle. So Clay, very artfully and skillfully, put himself in the middle of those discussions and to the great amazement and surprise to everyone in Seattle, some rednecks from Oklahoma, which we've been called, made off with the team."[40] That blast of honesty caused the NBA to fine him $250,000, which he presumably found between the cushions in his couch.

After the smoke had cleared, Bennett continued to defend his efforts to try to keep the franchise in the Emerald City. "I also want to express my regret to the citizens of Seattle and the fans of the Sonics that I was unsuccessful in bringing forth a new building," he said. "We tried the best we knew how to try and did what we knew how to do and did the best job I could."[41]

But e-mails between Bennett and his ownership partners released in 2008 as part of the city's lawsuit against Bennett and the NBA appeared to show they planned to move the team to the OKC all along. In one e-mail, Bennett said, "I am a man possessed! Will do everything we can" to move the team. He said that was misinterpreted.[42]

Even sympathetic Seattle journalist Bruce Schoenfeld was incredulous. "The team captured an NBA title in 1979, reached the finals on two other occasions and, at one point in the 1990s, sold out every home game for more than three consecutive seasons. With Seattle on a roll—it's home to Microsoft, Amazon.com, Starbucks, Costco, Nordstrom—it is difficult to fathom why any team (or business, for that matter) would leave the city and its famous quality of life. . . . And why Oklahoma City? Even in its own state, Tulsa would seem to have greater national prospects, with its rolling hills, mansion-filled neighborhoods and cultural accouterments of a serious place, as opposed to flat, brown, insular Oklahoma City, where unseemly oil wells blight even the Capitol grounds."[43] Why Oklahoma City indeed? Seattle is the nation's fourteenth-largest television market. Oklahoma City is the forty-fifth. Bennett said he had done "homework on other markets," which somehow led back to Oklahoma. Schoenfeld backed this assertion, writing, "A more appropriate home for a franchise these days seems to be a smaller city on the rise, with maybe a million to a million and a half people, plenty of money, local and regional art museums and a few ambitious restaurants but not too much else for its population to do, and an excess of civic pride ready to be harnessed. A place, in other words, exactly like Oklahoma City."[44] That is what we would call an absolutely wild coincidence. "It will enhance public perception of the entire state," gushed Brad Henry, Oklahoma's governor. "We'll be on *SportsCenter* every night."[45]

The national press was less enthusiastic. As *Sports Illustrated*'s Jack McCallum, the dean of basketball writers in the United States, said to me, "If there was ever a moment when money trumped popular opinion, this was it. From a professional standpoint, who wants to see basketball in Oklahoma City when you could see it in Seattle? From a personal standpoint, who wants to see basketball in Oklahoma City when you could see it in Seattle?"[46]

Other franchise owners were brought to OKC to support the move. They were wined and dined, and this time no testicles were on the menu. The NBA owners supported the move by a 28–2 vote, with only Dallas and Portland saying no.[47] Portland was sticking up for its Pacific Northwest brethren. Dallas and their owner, Mark Cuban, didn't want the border-state competition. But the other owners, par for the course in the David Stern era, were in line like Tom DeLay himself was holding the whip.

"The voters in Oklahoma City passed $126 million in improvements to the arena," says Gavin Maloof, whose family owns the Sacramento Kings and has longed to bring the NBA to Las Vegas, where he owns multiple clubs. "That shows me they really want the team. The owner of a franchise has to be able to make money. I'm for whatever the owner wants."[48]

Meanwhile, in Seattle, there was a six-day federal trial in U.S. District Court, where the city attempted to get a pound of Bennett and McClendon's flesh on their way out the door. They settled for the paltry sum of $75 million, with only $45 million guaranteed.[49] Bennett and McClendon could now legally steal the team, and all Seattle received in return was the right to the name SuperSonics, along with the team colors. It was like losing your house and getting to keep the doorknobs.

After the trial ended, Bennett said, "It was a tough experience for all of us that were involved in it. There was just so much that happened on both sides, so much misinterpreted, miscommunicated, and misunderstood that it was difficult."[50] But Bennett and McClendon couldn't have expelled their gob of spit at the sacred hoops of Seattle without David Stern. The commish issued the following statement: "We understand that city, county, and state officials are currently discussing a plan to substantially rebuild Key Arena for the sum of $300 million. If this funding were authorized, we believe Key Arena could properly be renovated into a facility that meets NBA standards relating to revenue generation, fan amenities, team facilities, and the like."[51] This is what Stern calls a compromise. If you aren't going to put hundreds of millions of dollars into a new stadium, rebuild the old one and then we'll talk. Just make sure we get our tax dollars.

The anger toward Bennett, McClendon, and Stern's full-court press for a new stadium had the effect of pushing people away from the game itself. Dean Paton, a local political writer and sports enthusiast, said to me, "When the Sonics left town, I cheered a little cheer to myself. I was glad they were finally gone. The NBA has become something so distant from what the old SuperSonics seemed to represent that I have to say 'good riddance.' I don't know if I became more realistic or if pro basketball has just become more brazen about showing itself to be despicably crass and greedy, but over the last ten years of watching this franchise I lost all interest in the team and was left with only contempt: for the owners, for the league's 'management,' and even for a couple of the players."[52]

Another fan, Todd Klempner, wrote to me, "I am proud to live in a city which rejected what the billionaire owners had learned to expect, a resounding 'no' to publicly funding yet another multimillion-dollar sports arena. . . . Some sports pundits act like Seattle is in a major depression post-Sonics. It makes me laugh. Myself and most others that I know are thrilled that the millions we could have spent helping some rich guys from Oklahoma City who are right-wing homophobes are instead going toward transit, education, the environment, and our pockets. We miss watching professional hoops from time to time, but in the realm of what constitutes having reasoned and measured priorities, many of us progressive sports fans put sports somewhere down there way behind education, environment, equality, and the arts."[53]

The people of Seattle, drained with stadium fatigue, stood up. But the politicians, particularly former Seattle mayor Greg Nickels, did not have to stand down. The man who had tent cities cropping up called "Nickeltowns" in his honor said proudly that the settlement would cover all the rent, tax revenue, and debt on Key Arena. "I believed all along enforcing our lease would allow us time to come to a better arrangement," Nickels said. "We now have that deal."[54] Some deal. The city got its payout. Bennett and McClendon got to steal a team and call it legal. And the fans got slapped in the face. It was a sporting tragedy. It was also a lost opportunity. No one in the Washington State political class showed the courage to stand up to Stern and his cronies. They never pursued municipalization— a kind word for expropriation—and turning the team into something actually owned, instead of just subsidized, by the sporting public.

Municipalization would have meant turning the Sonics into a public utility. It would have meant following through on the efforts Maryland politicians tried to use to keep the Colts. If owners threaten to move clubs, fans need to press the state to sue for the right to buy the team. They should claim that the teams themselves are the intellectual property—the eminent domain—of their communities, and therefore the city has far more of a claim on the team than, for example, the Bennetts of Oklahoma.

Imagine if the Sonics got their new arena, but instead of the proceeds going to build another wing on Bennett Manor, the funds went to rebuilding the city's health care and educational infrastructure. Imagine seeing someone wearing a jersey of star player Kevin Durant, knowing that instead of draining the tax base of a city, it was paying for new textbooks in a school classroom.

This would have been bigger than the Sonics. This would have been about drawing a line against the subsidizing of stadiums by which public monies are delivered to private hands.

Just to see the look on Stern's face, it would have been worth pursuing.

After the smoke cleared, Stern said in a subsequent interview, "The judgment was that the prospect of continued further losses in Seattle without an adequate arena really rendered that discussion with no good answer other than the movement of the team to Oklahoma at this point."[55]

Tell that to the fans.

Sam Bernstein, another Seattle fan, said to me, "Walking or busing around Seattle, you can't help but notice the large number of people outfitted in Mariners, Seahawks, and Sonics gear. The green and yellow of the

Sonics, along with their former home at Key Arena, in the shadow of the Space Needle, are—or were—part of the heart and soul of the city. But like everything else in Seattle, our NBA team was sold off to the highest bidder, regardless of the impact it would have on the city."[56]

Some tried to say that Seattle didn't care. They are so wrong. Earlier in the 2008–2009 season, the Oklahoma City Thunder made their way to the Pacific Northwest to play Portland. Hundreds of Seattle fans made a furious pilgrimage to a city often seen as a regional enemy. They traveled to rage. "I hope they don't boo me, because I had nothing to do with it," Thunder star Kevin Durant said before game time. Sonics Superfan Carolyn Bechtel told the press, "My only disappointment is how many games [the Thunder] won this year." Bechtel said this of a team that was a woeful 13–39 at the time. "I was hopeful they would lose them all."[57]

Bennett wasn't there. Stern wasn't there. But Portland coach Nate McMillan was there to field questions. McMillan also was once known as "Mr. Sonic."

"There are no more Sonics," McMillan said. "What can you do about it?" As one writer reported, "[H]ere's what they did: They showed up by the hundreds, sporting green and gold. They wore T-shirts bearing the image of Bennett's face and an unflattering slogan. They spared Durant boos but continued to fight."[58] They will continue to fight and agitate for a team of their own. They also can at least be partly warmed by the fact that Aubrey McClendon, he of the $23 billion company, Swift Boat vets, and antigay politics, has found his fortune cratered in the recent stock market fluctuations. He has even been forced to sell his nine-thousand-bottle collection of wine.[59] McClendon could have donated it to the people of Seattle and started the healing. But this isn't about Bennett or McClendon or even Stern. It's about whether anyone has any right to do what they did and if public ownership is a logical response.

As for the Oklahoma City Thunder, they have a sharp young team that could be very good in the near future. They also signed a new center at the start of 2009, a Tulsa native named Etan Thomas. Thomas is an outspoken, proud progressive who sees himself as part of the tradition of activist athletes. I asked Etan if playing in the red state for red state owners would keep him from being as outspoken.

"Come on there, Dave, you know me better than that," he said. "I mean, Oklahoma is, unfortunately, for a while was the number-two place right behind Texas for the death penalty. And, you know, I know these statistics because I'm paying attention. And you're definitely going to be hearing about me speaking out a lot more. Nothing's going to stop."[60] The Sonics may be in Oklahoma City, but the spirit of Seattle might be there to give ol' Clay the occasional haunting.

6. Money Laundering for the Lord: Charlie Monfort and Dick DeVos Keep the Faith

You're the greatest fans in baseball! And you're the greatest fans in faith!

—COLORADO ROCKIES CEO CHARLIE MONFORT,
WARMING UP THE CROWD AT COORS FIELD
BEFORE A FAITH DAY AT THE PARK[1]

Baseball has always prided itself on being the great secular assimilator. In the early part of the twentieth century, European immigrants speaking dozens of different languages would go to the ballpark and feel unmoored from the past, and reborn as part of the grand American experiment. A similar pattern held for African-Americans and Latinos, with Jackie Robinson and Roberto Clemente both becoming powerful and enduring symbols of people fighting for their rightful seat at the American table. This history may contain a healthy measure of self-serving folklore, but it's myth that speaks to the best angels of our nature: angels that preach a secular gospel of community, acceptance, and tolerance. Today that mythical ideal has taken more than a few hits. There is a diminishing number of African-American baseball players as cities see community centers shutter and Little League teams go out of business. On the flip side, there is an exploding number of players born in Latin America as Major League Baseball invests millions in the Dominican Republic to sign raw talent on the cheap. There is also, as we now see, the rise of owners using their publicly supported sports arenas as twenty-first-century evangelical revival tents. Baseball has taken an awkward step from great assimilator to great divider.

In decades past, the baseball park wasn't used for explicit political proselytizing. Despite the fact that your local stadium was paid for by the owners themselves, games cost spare change to watch and took place in the daylight hours. Overt politics weren't part of the program. Even the national anthem wasn't part of a regular baseball game until World War II. The idea that a sports facility would be a place to press not only politics but also religion would have seemed utterly insane. But nowadays when you own the team, you set the rules. Enter Charlie Monfort and Dick DeVos. Charlie Monfort owns the Colorado Rockies while Dick DeVos leads the NBA's Orlando Magic. Both men have chosen to take the right-wing edge of the evangelical political movement and place their soapbox in the middle of their publicly funded arenas. It's known as Faith Day at the Park.

Altogether, it's a frightening, and frighteningly effective, political money-laundering scheme: our tax dollars are being funneled through a stadium and for the financial benefit of the Monfort and DeVos families, who then plow cash into think tanks, activist organizations, and efforts of the political right. When the politics then also return to the stadium, the circle is complete.

In Colorado, the money-laundering operation is in the shape of a sacred shrine called Coors Field. On this holy site, named for the holiest of beers, a team is directed not by a man but by the true Son of God. So sayeth the team's general manager and owner.

But the ballpark isn't a church, especially when, as in Coors Field's case, public financing made up more than $160 million or at least 75 percent of its $215 million cost.[2] It should also be obvious that players aren't preachers and fans aren't a flock. But a view of a typical Coors Field Faith Day demonstrates that the divides between religion, politics, and a major league baseball game are as transparent as fishing line. One Faith Day at Coors Field started with a Christian a cappella group harmonizing "The Star-Spangled Banner."[3] You can also spot the popular shirt that reads, "Jesus leads the league in saves."[4] (This shirt also is a favorite of Yankee closer Mariano Rivera, who must have at least as many miracle saves as Christ.)

There are also Christian information tables, but other than that, Faith Day during the game is a low-key operation. But as described by journalist Tom Krattenmaker, that changes dramatically once the game is over.

Out comes Monfort himself to tell the crowd of twenty thousand, "You're the greatest fans in baseball! And you're the greatest fans in faith! . . . I welcomed the Lord and Savior into my life seven years ago, and my life has never been the same."[5]

Monfort's family, it's worth noting, made their fortune in the slaughterhouse industry. Their cattle factory feedlots outside Greeley, Colorado, once produced more excrement than the cities of Denver, Boston, Atlanta, and St. Louis combined. His comfort level with bullshit is very high. He then introduces everyone onstage to the friend standing just behind him. He is a former major league pitcher who became an evangelical born again named Dave Dravecky.

Dravecky, once a starting pitcher for the San Diego Padres, lost his left arm and much of his left shoulder to cancer. Now he, along with his wife, Jan, runs an organization called Outreach of Hope. Based in Colorado Springs, that home of seemingly all things evangelical, Dravecky's nonprofit provides "gospel-based resources and inspiration to people bearing the burdens" that Dravecky suffered: cancer and amputation.[6] It also provides Christian healing for mental illness, and those who have had to "journey into the valley of panic attacks, anxiety, and depression," suffered by Jan.[7]

You would have to be made of stone not to feel the Draveckys' pain. But there is that stubborn fact that in addition to being allied with evangelical James Dobson and the ubiquitous Focus on the Family, Dravecky also was once was part of the John Birch Society.[8] The Birchers are a rabid anti-progressive organization that opposed the civil rights movement and is constantly on the watch against the encroaching "one-world Communist takeover." Monfort, like the Birchers, also seems to like a severe brand of patriotism. On July 4, 2009, small American flags were given out to fans. With the sticks bearing the brand of military contractor Lockheed Martin. On previous nights fireworks spectaculars were also, appropriately enough, sponsored by Lockheed Martin.[9]

Krattenmaker, author of the book *Onward Christian Athletes*, asks the question "But why, as the unconverted progressive inevitably asks at moments like these, is center stage of sports-world religion never occupied by a liberal?"[10] To ask the question is to answer it. This is really about religion about as much as it was when George W. Bush said that his favorite political philosopher is Christ. It's not about faith, it's about politics. This also is seen throughout Monfort's Faith Day. The day's primary sponsor is Colorado Christian University. Despite pretensions of being a liberal arts college, this is a school that once fired an instructor for including course readings that challenged notions of free enterprise.[11] (I can't imagine this book will make it to the next reading list.) But on this day, they gave out information on how to join the college Republicans and encouraged people to purchase the numerous consumer items on display. Remember, free enterprise is next to Godliness.

How did the Colorado Rockies become the "God Squad" of sports? It started in 2006 when the Rockies went public with the fact that the organization had been explicitly looking first and foremost for players with what they call "character." "Character," according to those from the Tribe of Coors, means accepting Jesus Christ as your personal savior. "We're nervous, to be honest with you," Rockies general manager Dan O'Dowd said. "It's the first time we ever talked about these issues publicly. The last thing we want to do is offend anyone because of our beliefs."[12]

Charlie Monfort said to the press that their new Christian outlook had been born of hard times. "We had to go to hell and back to know where the Holy Grail is. We went through a tough time and took a lot of arrows."[13] The team did spend quite a few years wallowing in scandal, but the fish truly did rot from the head. There was Monfort's own driving-under-the-influence charge. There were the public humiliations of signing suspect players to megacontracts, such as All-Star pitcher Denny Neagle. Neagle was eventually arrested for soliciting a prostitute and had enough wild stories whispered about him to entertain a seventy-two-hour bachelor party.[14] Some kind of change in direction was clearly needed. But instead of simply selling the team, Monfort had the team turn with him to the Holy Book.

Club president Keli McGregor, who passed away in 2010, commented at the time, "Who knows where we go from here? The ability to handle success will be a big part of the story, too. There will be distractions. There will be things that can change people. But we truly do have something going on here. And [God's] using us in a powerful way."[15]

Well, someone is using somebody, but it ain't God. Former major league first baseman–outfielder Mark Sweeney, who spent 2003 and 2004 with the Rockies, told *USA Today,* "You wonder if some people are going along with it just to keep their jobs. Look, I pray every day. I have faith. It's always been part of my life. But I don't want something forced on me. Do they really have to check to see whether I have a *Playboy* in my locker?"[16]

But General Manager O'Dowd was undeterred. "You look at things that have happened to us. . . . You look at some of the moves we made and didn't make. You look at some of the games we're winning. Those aren't just a coincidence. God has definitely had a hand in this."[17] Or maybe the management that prays together gets paid together.

Take former manager Clint Hurdle, who has since been fired for the less publicly pious Jim Tracy. Hurdle said back in 2006, "We're not going to hide it. We're not going to deny it. This is who we are."[18] One thing Hurdle isn't is employed. As Andrew Nuschler wrote on *Bleacher Report,* "Now that Clint Hurdle has failed and been shown the door, where does that fit into the narrative? . . . So did he stop being Christian? Did God stop caring about Clint Hurdle? Did It just get bored and move on? This is an all-powerful Being; surely It can handle multitasking."[19]

O'Dowd and company bend over backward to say they are "tolerant" of other views on the club, but that's contradicted by statements such as this from Monfort in 2006: "I don't want to offend anyone, but I think characterwise we're stronger than anyone in baseball. Christians, and what they've endured, are some of the strongest people in baseball. I believe God sends signs, and we're seeing those."[20] This statement sent a shock wave through Major League Baseball. The sport has players who are religious and players who aren't. There are Jewish stars such as Kevin Youkilis and Ryan Braun. The closest Monfort comes to Jewish awareness is $1 Hebrew National Hot Dog Night at Coors Field (that's an actual promotion).

In other words, whether non-Christians would be welcome on this team is an open question, at least in the minds of some players. Several college players have expressed concerns about playing for Colorado because of the clubhouse culture. As journalist Eric Weiner wrote, "Holy crap! It's enough to make me thank God I'm a Bronx-born Yankees fan . . . and a Jew. I wonder if Monfort could enlighten us as to exactly which character tests Christians have 'endured' in this country to make them stronger than people of other faiths. And exactly what does any of that have to do with winning baseball games?" [21]

Also there are as of this writing a scant number of players of color on the Rockies active roster. Is this because Monfort doesn't think these players have character? Does the organization endorse the statement of their stadium's namesake William Coors, who told a group of black businessmen in 1984 that Africans "lack the intellectual capacity to succeed, and it's taking them down the tubes"? [22] These are admittedly ugly questions. But these are questions that need to be posed when such odious policies reek through the clubhouse.

It also raises the question about what in the holy hell any of this has to do with sports. It actually has far more to do with politics.

Monfort's public piety obscures some questionable political connections. Charlie Monfort has given money not just to the Republican Party but also to right-wing zealots such as former Colorado representative Tom Tancredo (who once suggested the bombing of Mecca as a sound foreign policy alternative and lambasted the Denver Public Library system for supplying books and magazines written in Spanish) [23] and former Pennsylvania senator Rick Santorum, who has been a stalwart opponent of "the gay agenda" and its connection to bestiality—specifically, in Santorum's words, the rise of "man-dog love." [24]

The conservative messaging of his team and his political donations attempt to mask an abject hypocrisy. The millions of dollars that Monfort is now using to recraft the Rockies in his own image came from circumstances that Christ would have likely condemned. His father, Kenneth, built a massive slaughterhouse business and handed his sons, Charlie and his brother Dick, top-level positions. The Monfort empire became practically synonymous with Greeley, Colorado, the cattle butchering capital of the fast-food industry. Later, when the megafirm ConAgra bought out Monfort's company, Charlie and Dick became ConAgra execs. Now, Dick has joined Charlie and is the vice chairman of the Rockies.

The Monfort family built an empire, and they did it old-school: by union busting. After Charlie Monfort's dad hired scabs to break the union attempting to organize in the slaughterhouses, Greeley became a destination point for undocumented labor and poverty wages.[25]

According to journalist Eric Schlosser, a worker at a Monfort slaughterhouse was forced to quit or was terminated every three months. The turnover rate reached 400 percent a year.[26] Schlosser revealed that in the early 1990s, one ConAgra meat executive, Mike Coan, stated that "we're at the bottom of the literacy scale . . . in some plants maybe a third of the people cannot read or write in any language."[27] Corporate execs count on immigrant labor, especially undocumented, being too intimidated to fight back against deplorable living and working conditions. Workers today labor in underregulated conditions for $9.25 an hour.[28] Adjusted for inflation, $9.25 an hour is more than a third lower than what the Monfort family paid workers forty years ago.[29]

The Monforts' slaughterhouse legacy has been more than bad news for their workers. This tradition has infected the entire Greeley community.

As Eric Schlosser wrote in *Fast Food Nation*, "You can smell Greeley, Colorado, long before you can see it. The smell is hard to forget but not easy to describe, a combination of live animals, manure, and dead animals being rendered into dog food. The smell is worst during the summer months, blanketing Greeley day and night like an invisible fog. Many people who live there no longer notice the smell; it recedes into the background, present but not present, like the sound of traffic for New Yorkers. Others can't stop thinking about the smell, even after years; it permeates everything, gives them headaches, makes them nauseous, interferes with their sleep."[30]

It's with money earned on fast-food burgers and cheap labor that Charlie Monfort can then finance his team and his commitment to the political right refracted through his interpretation of the teachings of Jesus Christ. His publicly funded stadium then becomes an abattoir of alienation.

Krattenmaker said to me, "I have concerns about what this Christianization of the Rockies means for the community that supports the team in and around Denver—a community in which evangelical Christians are probably a minority, albeit a large and influential one. Taxpayers and ticket-buyers in a religiously diverse community have a right not to see their team—a quasi-public resource—used for the purpose of advancing a specific form of religion. Have the Colorado Rockies become a faith-based organization? This can be particularly problematic when the religion in question is one that makes exclusive claims and sometimes denigrates the validity of other belief systems."[31]

You might think that Major League Baseball commissioner Bud Selig, an observant Jew, would have something stirring to say about this issue. But Bud hasn't actually registered a pulse since the Truman administration, and has just commented meekly, "They have to do what they feel is right."[32] It's not surprising that Bud would play it soft. Bud and Major League Baseball have shown themselves to be open to the profit-making potential of Faith Days at the Park. They love it because megachurches mobilize their mighty outreach powers, fill the bus fleets, and pack the stands. The evangelical church loves it because, in the words of religious radio broadcaster Paul Ott, "God belongs in every sphere in society including the ballpark."[33] It can sound very innocent. But the closer you get, the worse it can look.

One of the Faith Days in Atlanta that occurred in 2006 gives a clear sense of what these events are and toward whom they are aimed. It starts when the team and the sponsoring religious organizations sell higher-priced tickets called "special vouchers." After the game, the stands are cleared and then only those with specially purchased vouchers can be readmitted. Those lucky chosen with the sacred disposable income were "treated to an hour and a half of Christian music and a testimonial from the ace pitcher John Smoltz."[34] Smoltz is the player who in 2004 opined on gay marriage to the Associated Press, "What's next? Marrying an animal?"[35] Good times for the whole family. On this particular Faith Day, Smoltz stomped into politics again, not merely putting out the call for Christ. He also said that Christians must choose between faith in God and faith in scientific explanations for the origins of the universe and the human race. He slams the idea that the Earth began with an "explosion" and the silly notion that "we just evolved."[36]

This is the valley in the shadow of greed. In Atlanta, one could buy a variety of bobble-head Jesuses and all the apostles you could collect. I couldn't find a big foam finger that said "God Is Number One," but there were crucifixes aplenty. The event also included a hefty helping of Christian rock led by Aaron Shust, who, according to promotional materials, is the voice behind "the hit single 'My Savior My God,' [which] reached #1 on six charts simultaneously for four straight weeks."

But Faith Days are about more than family-friendly Christian entertainment with a twist of commerce. The higher power behind Faith Days and Nights is a group called the Third Coast Sports Foundation. The Third Coast Sports website proclaims right at the top, "The mission of Third Coast Sports Foundation is summed up in 1 Corinthians 9:22: *'I have become all things to all men so that by all possible means I might save some.'*"[37]

Most of us don't go to the ballpark to be saved. Third Coast Sports president Brent High said to the press, "We've been very careful to make sure what we're not about is ambush evangelism."[38] But go to their website and it's quickly revealed who is hiding in the weeds, ready to pounce. Third Coast Sports proclaims with pride that "Focus on the Family [FOF], one of the largest evangelical organizations in the nation, has joined Third Coast Sports to sponsor 'Faith Nights' and 'Faith Days' at ballparks nationwide this summer."[39]

But the owners aren't eager to let the public in on that bit of information. In all the articles about the Faith Day in Atlanta, including the press release of the Braves themselves, there was no mention of Focus on the Family's role behind the proceedings. But there they were, using Faith Day to spread the word about a website they run called Troubled With.com, which hosts a smorgasbord of antigay pamphlets such as, "When a loved one says 'I'm gay': The paralyzing grief-stricken state of having a gay child."[40] The site also says, "Male homosexuality is a developmental problem . . . the following factors can also contribute to the homosexual orientation: . . . pornography; sexual violation . . . incest or molestation."[41]

In the aftermath, the Braves promised never to have Focus on the Family as part of the operation again. "We have asked the promoter [Third Coast Sports] to not include Focus on the Family in our other two Faith Day events," Beth Marshall, the Braves' spokesperson, said. "We do not feel it is an appropriate connection for Focus on the Family to be part of this event."[42]

Their scramble to distance themselves was understandable. According to People for the American Way, FOF is "anti-choice, anti-gay, and

against sex education curricula that are not strictly abstinence-only . . .
FOF also focuses on religion in public schools, encouraging Christian
teachers to establish prayer groups in schools."[43]

Focus on the Family's guru is the infamous and recently retired James
Dobson, a man with a laundry list of quotes that would turn the stomach
of anyone to the left of Attila the Hun. Dobson chose the second night of
Passover last year to say, "The biggest Holocaust in world history came
out of the Supreme Court" with *Roe v. Wade*.[44] Dobson often has Hitler on the brain. He also has compared embryonic stem cell research to
Nazi experiments conducted on live humans. This isn't necessarily bad,
according to Dobson, who also said, "the Nazis experimented on human
beings in horrible ways in the concentration camps, and I imagine, if you
wanted to take the time to read about it, there would have been some dis-
coveries there that benefited mankind."[45] Dobson's other pet project, the
Family Research Council (FRC), has connections to white supremacist
organizations such as the Council of Conservative Citizens (CCC).[46] In
1996, FRC president Tony Perkins paid former KKK grand wizard David
Duke $82,000 for his mailing list.[47] For what it's worth, the three major
league veterans who spoke at the three Faith Nights in Atlanta—Smoltz,
Sid Bream, and Chris Reitsma—were all white. We can only assume that
all the nonwhite players must have been militant atheists.

Dobson likes to speak of being engaged in a "civil war for values," and
Major League Baseball is his next strategic hamlet.[48]

It's easy to mock the transparent commercial trappings of Faith Days
and Nights at the Park. Major league owners are clumsily trying to maxi-
mize their manna with little concern whether Christ himself would toss
them out of the temple.

It's also easy to point out that despite PR efforts calling the Faith Days
scheme an ecumenical promotion, no synagogue, mosque, or Buddhist
temple has been invited to take part. There has been no Jewish Day in
New York City, no Muslim Day in Detroit, and certainly no atheist day,
when the park would presumably turn into an orgy of family-fun sin. And
I am still waiting for Quaker Day at the Park, when we will all just sit in
silence. It could be like an Orioles game.

As the Reverend Barry Lynn of Americans United for the Separation of Church and State said to me, "These 'Faith Days' are troubling.

Athletics has been one of the few places where Americans generally don't ask questions about religion. Who knows what, if any, religion Bruce Jenner or Willie Mays believed in. When a ballpark is turned into a Christianized venue some summer night, the non-Christians in attendance or on the field often do feel marginalized. There's no point to that in a country with two thousand different faiths and twenty million nonbelievers."[49]

Granted, many Denver fans were willing to give the God Squad some serious slack in 2007 and 2009. In 2007, the Rockies won twenty-one of their last twenty-two games to make the World Series. One fan wrote, "I think God's promise is that regardless of the outcome, He is with you. But I also know that He has power to take seemingly hopeless situations— a cancer patient being healed, a marriage restored, or an average team winning 21/22—and intervening to make something very special happen so that people might recognize something beyond just people were involved."[50] Their then star player Matt Holliday repeatedly pointed skyward during the streak. In the champagne-drenched clubhouse, where much water had clearly turned to wine, relief pitcher Jeremy Affeldt chimed in, "When you have as many people who believe in God as we do, it creates a humbleness about what we do. I don't see arrogance here, I see confidence. We're all very humbled about where this franchise has been and where it is now, and we know that what's happening now is a very special thing."[51] Monfort himself got a dose of humility when he took the field in celebration of the pennant. As Rockies fan and season ticket holder Jim Bullington recalled to me, "Do the Monforts not get that the fans in Colorado really do not care for them? One of the greatest moments ever in Colorado sports history was when the Rockies won the pennant. Of course, the topping on the cake was afterward, when they announced the Monforts on the field, a chorus of boos rained down from the stands."[52]

Humility and confidence are fine—indeed, novel—traits in pro sports. But the troubling part of operation God Squad is the assumption that Christianity by definition brings character to the table. Maybe it's because I live near Washington, D.C., a town full of politicians who invade other countries with other people's children while claiming to be guided by God. Maybe it's because I find a team using a publicly funded stadium as a platform for an event originally dubbed "Christian Family Day" exclusionary and a gross misuse of tax dollars.

Maybe it's because I think fans in Denver have the right to see baseball as an ecumenical experience. As Bullington put it, "The Monforts are nothing but religious zealots who only care about indoctrinating players into their personal vision of heaven while at the same time sacrificing the fans on the altar of mediocre ball."[53]

But for those of us who believe that freedom of religion also should mean freedom from religion at the ballpark, it doesn't matter if you call it Buddha-Jesus-Jewish-Vishnu-Islamic-Wicca Awareness Day. We just want to go to the park without feeling like we're covertly funding Focus on the Family's gay-retraining programs. Religion and sports: it's a marriage in desperate need of a divorce.

That's why it was hard not to feel a tiny taste of supernatural satisfaction upon learning before the team's 2007 World Series appearance that their website crashed following what Rockies officials called "an external, malicious attack."[54] The team's efforts to offer all its World Series tickets online was unprecedented and seen by many die-hard Rockies fans as a way to sell tickets to out-of-town corporate entities and shut out the locals waiting in line for days to buy them in person. Unless you worship at the altar of *Forbes* magazine, gouging hometown supporters doesn't seem very Christian at all. Then again, given the ticket price increases at Coors, commerce and Christ always have walked together comfortably for Monfort.

So who could be the perpetrator of this "external, malicious" attack on the Rockies' website? Was it God, punishing the team for squeezing the common fan? The Devil, trying to derail their grace-driven run? Whoever, it was hard not to smile at the biblical significance for baseball's most sanctimonious team. They could throw the money-changers out of our sporting temples, but that would leave the owners' boxes empty. And we can't have that.

But this is not where the story ends. In 2009, as mentioned, the Rockies underwent a dare-I-say miraculous transformation after firing Clint Hurdle and hiring Jim Tracy. Unlike the hyperintense "you better come to the prayer circle" Hurdle, Tracy is a mellow guy who by all accounts treats players like adults. In September 2009 he walked through the clubhouse, calm and in control, and one player who asked not to be named said to a nearby reporter, "Man, did we need that guy."

It would be very sad if the team goes into a 2010 tailspin and the manager of the year has to loudly proclaim his faith to keep his job. Such is the Monfort way. But Charlie Monfort is practically Marilyn Manson compared to Dick DeVos.

Dick DeVos: Repairing Gay People One Stadium at a Time

Forget Tony Danza, I'm the Boss. When it comes to money, I'm like Dick DeVos.

—SHAQUILLE O'NEAL'S VERSE ON THE SONG "WHAT'S UP, DOC?" BY THE FU SCHNICKENS (1993)

Shaquille O'Neal used the first recorded verse of his inauspicious hip-hop career to give props to a man richer than Croesus. Even Shaq's then $40 million contract was nothing compared to the man writing his checks, the multibillionaire Orlando Magic owner Dick DeVos. Shaq's homage recalls Chris Rock's riff about the difference between being rich and being wealthy: "Wealth is passed down from generation to generation. Rich is something you could lose with a crazy son with a drug habit. . . . Shaq is rich—the white man who signs his check is wealthy."[55]

DeVos, the Caucasian in question, certainly qualifies as wealthy. As the cofounder of Amway Corporation, he has amassed a personal fortune conservatively estimated at more than $3.5 billion.[56] Amway launched the concept of what is known as "network marketing," where salespeople attempt to lure their friends and neighbors into buying all manner of unadulterated crap. Sixty percent of what Amway reps sell is cosmetics. The rest of their merchandise is a veritable pupu platter of home care products, jewelry, electronics, dietary supplements, and even insurance.

DeVos's biggest score though didn't come through selling a truckload of moisturizer. Ground has now been broken on a $1.1 billion Orlando megaentertainment complex, the center of which would be a $480 million new arena for the Orlando Magic. DeVos and his people have publicly boasted about how much they are donating to the project. But as Neil deMause and Joanna Cagan have written,

> The actual Magic contribution toward the $480 million price tag, then, is probably somewhere around $70 million. . . . Local arena boosters, though, were just happy to see a deal struck, regardless of who was paying. *Orlando Sentinel* sports columnist Mike Bianchi was so excited that he hailed this "magical sign of the times" as having been possible "because everybody came together—[Orange County mayor Rich] Crotty and [Orlando mayor Buddy] Dyer, city and county, Disney and Universal—and realized it was time finally to get rid of the disco ball and join the 21st century." Actually, at a mere 17 years old, Orlando's current arena is about 90 years younger than the disco ball—but who's counting?[57]

Another commentator expressed the anger at this project, writing:

> This is corporate welfare in the worst sense, but the politicians don't care, they get free tickets. And what do the Magic care, the new arena will be a cash cow for them, regardless of whether anyone who makes under $100k ever walks through the doors. I say boycott them and every company that buys a suite or courtside seats in the new facility.[58]

Or as one protester put it simply, "DeVos has billions. Let him pay."[59] Employees of DeVos look at his wealth and conflate it with genius. Former Magic general manager and the team's current senior vice president Pat Williams wrote a book titled *How to Be Like Rich DeVos: Succeeding with Integrity in Business and Life.* It outlines in robustly saccharine terms the way DeVos "possesses qualities rarely found in business leaders today: leadership, wisdom, putting others first, philanthropy, patriotism, focusing on family. It is these qualities, along with his dedication to Christ, that have made him into the successful leader and beloved figure to millions that he is today."[60]

Beloved? Outside DeVos's coterie of senior executives and sycophants, the word "beloved" doesn't quite describe the emotions at play. The more people know about DeVos, the less they like. Amway has been investigated for violating campaign finance laws by seamlessly shifting from network marketing to network politicking.[61] As *Mother Jones* writers Rachel Burstein and Kerry Lauerman wrote in 1996,

> Amway relies heavily on the nearly fanatical—some say cultlike—devotion of its more than 500,000 U.S. "independent distributors." As they sell the company's soaps, vitamins, detergents, and other household products, the distributors push the Amway philosophy. "They tell you to always vote conservative no matter what. They say liberals support the homosexuals and let women get out of their place," says Karen Jones, a former distributor . . . "They say we need to get things back to the way it's supposed to be."[62]

After Bill Clinton was reelected president in 1996, one of Amway's top networkers, Dexter Yager, sent a voice-mail message—the transcript of which was leaked to *Mother Jones*[63]—to his thousands of Amway distributors, commenting, "If you analyze Bill Clinton's entire inaugural address, it is nothing but a New Age pagan ritual. If you go back and look at how it was arranged and how it was orchestrated, he talked about forcing the spring. So what they're trying to do is . . . force the emergence of deviant lifestyles, of a socialist agenda, and force that on us as American people."[64] Yager even let George W. Bush send messages through his voice-mail system during the 2000 campaign.

If the company's political practices are openly partisan, their business practices have been attacked time and again, including accusations that they are nothing but an elaborate pyramid scheme. The Internet is packed with horror stories of people being promised riches by Amway and the "beloved" DeVos but then ending up in debt. One woman tells of joining with her husband, exceeding his sales total, and being told to divorce him for the good of the company.[65] Family values here take a backseat to disposable cosmetics. Over the years, Amway has faced numerous legal challenges time and time again in the United States and has paid tens of millions of dollars to resolve them; in the 1980s, the Canadian government levied the largest customs fraud charge in their nation's history against Amway.[66]

Despite Amway's reputation, DeVos has continued to use not only his company but also his expansive fortune at the service of his politics. He could be described as the top chef of every religious-right cause on Pat Robertson's buffet table. The former head of the Republican Finance Committee, DeVos is far more than just a party man. For more than four decades, he has been the funder in chief of the Christian fundamentalist movement. The next time you wonder why the religious right has influence so disproportionate to their actual size, it is because of people such as DeVos.

Before the 1994 "Republican Revolution" elections, which made a household word out of a man named Newt, Amway, according to the *Washington Post,* made "the largest political donation in recent American history": $2.5 million.[67] In the 2004 elections, it was $4 million to groups willing to pump propaganda for Bush and company.[68] During the Bush/ Cheney years, DeVos had no cause to regret these investments as Congress passed tax cuts that saved him a fortune, and a series of work tax exemptions for people who sold Amway out of their homes. He then used these new revenue streams to further empower the nonprofit Richard and Helen DeVos Foundation. The DeVos Foundation pumps millions into groups that support radical reparative gay therapy, anti-evolution politics, and other "traditional" family values. The organizations they support include the aforementioned Focus on the Family, the Foundation for Traditional Values, the Federalist Society, the Heritage Foundation, the American Enterprise Institute, and the Media Research Center, among many others.[69]

The DeVos Foundation also supplies grants to the Free Congress Foundation (FCF), which claims that its main focus is on the "Culture War" and its hopes to "return [America] to the culture that made it great, our traditional Judeo-Christian, Western culture."[70]

DeVos also has given a small fortune to what is known as the Dominionist political movement in the United States. The Dominionists believe in fighting for a Christian theocracy in the United States. DeVos gave Dominionist leader D. James Kennedy—who died in 2007—$5 million to fund his work.[71] One Dominionist project was the "Constitution

Restoration Act," a bill that would have authorized Congress to impeach judges who don't believe in "God as the sovereign source of law, liberty, or government."

When Kennedy passed away, former president George W. Bush released a statement calling him "a man of great vision, faith, and integrity."[72] Kennedy outlined his "great vision" thusly:

> Our job is to reclaim America for Christ, whatever the cost. As the vice regents of God, we are to exercise godly dominion and influence over our neighborhoods, our schools, our government, our literature and arts, our sports arenas, our entertainment media, our news media, our scientific endeavors—in short, over every aspect and institution of human society.[73]

Their agenda makes Limbaugh look like Noam Chomsky. They want a Supreme Court that adheres to Old Testament law. They want LGBT (lesbian, gay, bisexual, transgender) people in prison and women who seek abortions to join them. For the Florida-based DeVos nonprofit, supporting this kind of work classifies as "charity."

DeVos also is a founding member of the Council for National Policy (CNP), a secret organization that makes the Masons resemble paparazzi-hungry starlets. It was formed and launched by the wealthy leaders of the John Birch Society. Dick DeVos is a two-time CNP president. According to journalist and radical right watcher Russ Bellant, DeVos was "a member of the CNP almost since its founding."[74] He also was "one of the earliest backers of behind-the-scenes efforts in the mid-'70s to stimulate the religious right and make the U.S. a 'Christian Republic.' "[75]

Another leading member of the CNP was a fellow Michigan-based billionaire named Edgar Prince. In what can only be described as a royal coupling, Edgar Prince's daughter, Betsy, married Dick's son, Dick Jr. As journalist Jeremy Scahill said to me,

> When Erik Prince's sister, Betsy, married Richard DeVos, it was like the merger of the monarchies of Old Europe. These two families basically combined to serve as a massive ATM machine for the creation of groups like Focus on the Family and the Family Research

Council and were instrumental in transforming the Republican Party into what it is today.[76]

Betsy Prince would become the head of the Michigan Republican Party, where she would pay people to protest speaking engagements of another son of Michigan who earned her hatred—filmmaker Michael Moore.

Edgar Prince's son, Erik Prince, would become first a navy SEAL and later CEO of the infamous Blackwater Corporation, a company of private mercenaries hired to help occupy Iraq, Afghanistan, and even post-Katrina New Orleans. Famous for rolling through Baghdad in black SUVs, rock music blaring, and making a hundred times the pay of a U.S. soldier, they are the outsourced army as rampaging fraternity. Since 2000, Blackwater has received $505 million in government contracts, two-thirds of which have come in no-bid contracts.[77] This isn't a vast, right-wing conspiracy; it's been an openly incestuous and highly beneficial coupling between the DeVos/Prince clan and the Republican Party.

The DeVos empire tried to take this to even greater heights when Dick's son—also named Dick, also on the governing board of the Orlando Magic—became enamored with the bright idea of becoming president. Not president of Amway, of the United States. DeVos Jr. was the Republican Party nominee for governor of Michigan in 2006. He spent more than $41 million on his campaign, running on a platform that included an opposition to the teaching of evolution; opposition to abortion in all instances, including incest and rape; and the promotion of religious charter schools as an alternative to public education. Due to his distasteful politics, DeVos Jr. was trounced by his Canadian-born opponent, Jennifer Granholm, by fourteen points.[78]

None of this should matter to sports fans if the DeVos family kept their politics out of the Orlando Magic or if they didn't rely on public funds for the team. Neither is the case.

On March 6, 2009, at Amway Arena, the DeVos family held their own Faith and Family Night. It was a carnival of Christian rock, player testimonials, and media whitewash.

This spurred the usual debate in the *South Florida Sun Sentinel* when columnist Andrea Adelson wrote that the "expression of religious beliefs has no business in sports, either before, during or after a game. . . . When I go to a game, I want to enjoy the game. I don't want to hear announcements over the loudspeaker giving me the option of staying afterward to enjoy some religious music."[79]

Paul Vigna, the sports editor at the *Patriot-News*, reported "her colleague, David Whitley, didn't agree. He wrote under the header, 'No Problem Using Religion to Sell Extra Magic Tickets,' if teams 'promoted only universally approved causes, there would be almost no promotions,' he wrote in his column. Whitley: Would the Magic have Muslim Family Night or Jewish Celebration Day? You bet if they thought either had the sales potential of Faith & Family."[80]

What an ingenious point. DeVos supports the Evangelical Christian Faith Nights because there is such a mass audience. There is *no way*, after all, a "Jewish Celebration Day" could be successful in Florida.

Adelson's column and other columns critical of DeVos, while remaining cached in search engines, are curiously not available at the *South Florida Sun-Sentinel* or *Orlando Sentinel* web archives.

Yet despite DeVos's financial largesse and accompanying self-aggrandizement, his use of the team for his own pet projects and profit has spurred protest in Orlando. To get people to protest in Orlando, you have to know you're somewhat less than "beloved."

Fans don't have to be told that there is a connection between DeVos's political pursuits and the public financing he enjoys. Outside Amway Arena, there have been demonstrations to raise awareness. One such protest opposed DeVos's contribution of $100,000 to Florida4Marriage, a group that supports Amendment 2, which would add Florida's existing ban on gay marriage to the state constitution.[81] Opponents say the measure also could deny domestic-partnership benefits for unmarried couples—gay and straight.

Proposed Amendment 2 reads, "Inasmuch as marriage is the legal union of only one man and one woman, no other legal union that is treated as marriage or the substantial equivalent thereof shall be valid or recognized."[82] The slogan of the demonstrators was straightforward enough: "The billionaire's a bonehead." "He's the biggest contributor to the amendment from Orlando," protest organizer Jennifer Foster told the *Orlando Sentinel*. "And he's getting $1 billion in taxpayers' money to build the arena. That sends a bad message."[83] Indeed. At its core, the DeVos model could be characterized as theft of public funds that turns teams and arenas into slush funds for radical right politics.

In the latest Gallup polling, only 25 percent of Americans even identify fully as Republican, let alone the Dominionist, Christian brand.[84] But because of political favors and massive contributions, our games have become an exercise in money laundering for stopping stem cell research, demonizing gays and lesbians, undermining the separation of church and state, and supporting "crusades" overseas. The idea that DeVos gets our money for his projects is abhorrent. If the City of Orlando can raise $480 million for a stadium, they should raise the same to buy him out.

7. Peter Angelos and the Shredding of the Oriole Way

There are very few people who live on after their demise. I think it's what you do now. What do they call it—instant gratification.

—PETER ANGELOS

The year of Armageddon for Major League Baseball was 1994. The players demanded a strike, the owners demanded a lockout, and the World Series was canceled for the first time in the ninety-one-year history of the contest. Two world wars and the Great Depression couldn't do it, but the battle over how to carve a rapidly expanding golden goose almost cooked the game for good. The owners were almost entirely united after a generation of getting their tails handed to them by the all-powerful Players' Association. They felt that this was one battle they were going to win. All they had to do was stick together and perhaps hire rosters of nonunion players and play, for the first time in major league history, some good, ol'-fashioned "scab ball."

But there was a big buzzing fly in the ointment: one owner who looked at the battle lines as they were lining up and sided with the players. His name was, and is, Peter Angelos, owner of the Baltimore Orioles. Angelos made it plain that in no way, shape, or form would nonunion ballplayers find their way onto Oriole Park at Camden Yards. The rest of the ownership class threatened Angelos with sanctions, including stripping him of the team because, they bleated, his actions were not in the best interests of the game. As a *Washington Post* headline blared, Angelos was "A Maverick Who Wants to Deal; He Aims to End Strike, Not Befriend Fellow Owners."[1]

"What was proposed [hiring nonunion players] was wrong so I spoke out against it," Angelos said of the replacement-player issue. "If I believe it is wrong and oppose it, I feel one has to speak out. That's an old American trait, a quality we urged upon people."[2]

At the time, Angelos had as much political and economic capital as any owner in the game. He was the overseer of spanking-new Camden Yards, a ballpark that drove baseball writers to fits of stunted poetry. He also was unique among the ranks of ownership. The man earned his money not by running a major company or inheriting the family business but by representing workers. Angelos spent decades in the courtroom fighting for unions and their members. In 1982, after patiently building a reputation among Big Labor, Peter Angelos was entrusted with the big score. He successfully led eighty-seven hundred steelworkers, shipyard laborers, and manufacturing employees from coast to coast in the groundbreaking national class action lawsuit against Fibreboard and Amchem Corp. and the ill effects of asbestos.

They won $1 billion and Angelos cleared a contingency fee of more than $330 million for his troubles. Success bred success, and Angelos then represented the State of Maryland in more class action cases against the nicotine pushers at Philip Morris and the Big Pharm company of Wyeth, makers of the dastardly diet pill Fen-Phen. It's a liberal's fantasy: to become stinking rich by actually making corporations pay for their malfeasance. It's also a working-class fantasy in that Angelos wasn't trained for this task via Harvard (or Williams College) but by working his way through Eastern College of Commerce and Law and the University of Baltimore School of Law.[3]

But just being wealthy wasn't enough for Angelos.

He wanted the whole thing. Working-class kid makes good? Check. A millionaire 330 times over? Check. Own the beloved baseball team you grew up watching? That was still on the to-do list. He said, "Money doesn't give me a feeling of power or special standing over others. It's incidental. It doesn't really mean anything other than what it permits you to do." It permitted Angelos to buy his hometown Baltimore Orioles from Eli Jacobs for $173 million in 1993, submitting the winning bid during a bankruptcy auction. The fact that Angelos was a Baltimore guy and that one of his partners was Baltimore-born filmmaker Barry Levinson made for even more local goodwill. "In Baltimore, you tend to get a small core of leaders continuing to step up," said former tennis star and Baltimore native Pam Shriver. "He is at the top of that list."[4]

As owner, he made it clear from the beginning that he would dance to his own beat. He said early on in his tenure, "Profit margins are secondary. The fans should be satisfied that they have a strong and vibrant organization pursuing a team that is absolutely and totally capable of reaching the top."[5] Profit margins are secondary? He's lucky the other owners didn't have him fitted for cement loafers.

He has even attempted to use his influence to ease the embargo conditions on Cuba. Angelos organized a series of games in 2004 between his Orioles and the Cuban national team. The Bush administration attempted to quash the entire operation. Angelos was incensed. "I think what's worse is that, once again, the U.S., this huge colossus, the strongest country in the world, is picking on this tiny, little country of 11 million. And, this time, for what? For their participation in an international baseball event? That seems to me that it makes us look like the big, bad bully that our nonadmirers say we look like."[6] In a later interview he said, "It's not financial. It's a continuation of a vendetta against one who rightly or wrongly defied our administration over the years. As far as the sport is concerned and the hierarchy of Major League Baseball, it's hard for them to act in defiance of a directive out of D.C."[7]

Angelos held the potential to truly be the anti-Steinbrenner. Like Charm City, he was rough around the edges but a fighter. "I'm just another guy from Baltimore," he was fond of saying. The early years held a terrific promise. In 1997, a stacked Orioles team made the playoffs and almost the World Series. The *Baltimore Sun* named him "Marylander of the Year" in 1998 and wrote, "Measured by professional accomplishments and contributions to his city and region, he is the Marylander of this decade."[8]

Remarkable the difference another ten years makes. Now it's no exaggeration to say that Angelos is about as popular in Baltimore as Bob Irsay. And Angelos didn't even have to move the team. No one sees him as "just another guy from Baltimore," and even fewer people from the city remember the tantalizing promise of those early days of the Angelos era.

Before Angelos, the team may have had its ups and downs, but the Oriole way was something the team and the city embraced with pride. It was the reflection of how a working-class city chose to see itself. As the poster Oriole, Cal Ripken Jr. said, the Oriole way "was about people. My dad was part of the Oriole way. I think he was there fourteen years in the minor leagues. I think seven of those years, they had the same people in place. So it was about continuity. It was about stability. . . . It was how many players you had in the big leagues that you developed."⁹ In other words, it was about doing things "the right way" and building a team worthy of the passion a city was willing to invest in it.

Baltimore's fans took the Oriole way seriously, and in return the team—before the Angelos era—took it seriously as well. They carefully managed player development and fostered the kind of atmosphere where it was not uncommon for players to stay at a "hometown discount," meaning they would actually take less money come contract time for the privilege of playing and raising their family in the area. It also wasn't uncommon to see former beloved players at the ballpark cheering on the new generation. The team would even win an occasional World Series, and the faithful would crow that the Oriole way was how their small-market team in their round-shouldered town competed with the big boys.

Today, "the Oriole way" is about as musty as Fonzie's jacket hanging in the Smithsonian. The concepts of patience, player development, and hometown connections may have been the Oriole way but it wasn't the Angelos way. As a result, the team hasn't had a winning season in a decade. Camden Yards, which used to be the toughest ticket in town, now has more empty seats than a T-Pain concert in Provo. Angelos has taken the healthiest social contract between any one team and any one city and wrecked it.

In a vast understatement, Angelos said in 2008, "There's . . . the notion that I'm an authoritarian, somebody who fires people indiscriminately— all of which is not accurate, but nevertheless there is a kernel of truth in it. So in a sports sense, [my reputation] is by and large negative."

Angelos fell into the trap of thinking that he could combine spending and browbeating to create a World Series champion. Rather than methodically putting together a team, or letting his baseball men handle baseball while he went back to the law firm, he decided that patience was for suckers and the goal would be to build a "dynasty" like the New York Yankees or die trying. As Angelos said in 1997, "We've had a Yankees dynasty. Let's have an Orioles dynasty. What's wrong with that? We've got the fan support. We've got a great local ownership group that's fully supportive of what we're trying to do. We've got the facility. It suggests something that could be very exciting."[10]

Yet instead of championships, the Orioles have suffered eleven straight losing seasons. The one area in which they have replicated the Yankees is with Angelos, bringing Steinbrenner's bombastic arrogance to Chesapeake Bay. Instead of becoming the anti-Steinbrenner, he just took his place at the head of the table.

Steinbrenner, at his worst in the 1980s, produced a sideshow of a team where young prospects and gifted management were shown the door with blasé arrogance. The Angelos tenure feels like a movie we've seen before, except this time it's John Waters behind the camera. The Orioles employed top general managers such as Doug Melvin and Pat Gillick. They didn't last. There was former Oriole second baseman and manager Davey Johnson, pushed to resign the same year, 1997, that he won Manager of the Year honors (that would be their last winning season). Then there was beloved radio broadcaster Jon Miller, who was shown the door because, according to Angelos, he "didn't bleed enough orange and black."[11] There was Hall of Fame Oriole Brooks Robinson, alienated so badly that he refused to show up for the celebration of the fiftieth anniversary of his debut.

There have been quality young players who were booted only to succeed elsewhere. There were veteran stars such as pitcher Mike Mussina willing to stay in Baltimore with a hometown discount and being told that his services weren't required. There was hiking ticket prices 22 percent in a period of declining attendance, but not until after slashing the team budget. And then there was a series of financially irresponsible and altogether impetuous signings, chief among them the inking of the volcanic Albert Belle.

Belle, a player best known perhaps for episodes of abject rage, including trying to chase Halloween trick-or-treaters with his car, was given a five-year, $65 million contract before the 1999 season despite a series of nagging injuries. Belle's career ended two years later because of "osteoarthritis" in his hip. There also was the "pitcher of the future," Sidney Ponson, whose time in the big leagues flamed out after punching a local judge on the beach in his native Aruba. Even before Ponson slugged a judge, he was an annual disappointment. His tombstone will probably read, "Here lies Sidney Ponson, future ace of the Baltimore Orioles."

Then there was Rafael Palmeiro. Other than Cal Ripken Jr., Palmeiro was perhaps the most beloved Oriole of the past twenty years. He was on an express train to the Hall of Fame, one of only four players in history to have three thousand hits and five hundred home runs. Rumor had it that his good friend George W. Bush would even induct him personally into Cooperstown. In 2005, Palmeiro was named as a steroid user by bankrupt retired All-Star and former Texas teammate José Canseco. Canseco, attempting to capitalize on steroid mania by releasing an inject-and-tell book called, appropriately enough, *Juiced*, was naming names faster than Elia Kazan on sodium pentothal. In *Juiced*, Canseco calls out every buttock that cozied up to his all-star syringe. Two of those cheeks, Canseco revealed, belonged to Palmeiro. The repercussions were immediate. Palmeiro had always presented himself as a holy Joe, a rock-ribbed Republican, and a podium thumper for the American Dream. This Friend of Bush found himself subpoenaed and forced to testify in front of Congress in March 2005. Grimacing with indignation, Palmeiro wagged his finger and said under oath, "Let me start by telling you this: I have never used steroids. Period. I don't know how to say it any more clearly than that. Never."[12]

Bush weighed in, calling Palmeiro a "friend," saying, "He's testified in public [to being clean], and I believe him. . . . Still do."[13]

The performance was convincing. So convincing Palmeiro was even named to a congressional committee in the hearing's aftermath that would work to "clean up the sport." The immediate conventional wisdom was that Canseco was the liar and Palmeiro the hero dragged through the mud. Angelos's contribution was braying that he would sue Canseco on Palmeiro's behalf for libel. The steely-eyed Palmeiro made you believe that his anger was righteous. Then the tests returned from the doctor's office and we discovered that Canseco was telling the truth and Palmeiro was one hell of a liar. His ten-day suspension was announced on August 1, 2005, right after Palmeiro secured his three thousandth hit. The problem was that Major League Baseball knew that Palmeiro had tested positive early in 2005 and alerted the club but not, of course, the public.[14]

But Selig, Angelos, and all concerned parties accepted Palmeiro's contention that the test was wrong. He must have mistakenly taken a food product of some kind that was tainted (maybe a big bowl of Steroid-ios). He was just such a good citizen such a good friend of the president, and so close to getting that precious three thousandth hit that all concerned decided they should just let him be. Angelos kept on his courtroom poker face as Palmeiro knocked that three thousandth hit. Angelos even planned an August 15 Rafael Palmeiro Appreciation Day. They did Palmeiro no favors. He looked like the one thing worse that a liar: a sanctimonious liar. The world was then informed that Palmeiro hadn't taken any kind of benign food supplement but the hard anabolic steroid stanozolol.

As Tom Boswell wrote, "In this culture, heaven help you if, after playing that once-per-lifetime, I-swear-on-a-stack-of-Bibles card, you get caught."[15]

Palmeiro reminded everyone of former Oriole Brady Anderson, who after a career of slap hitting, stolen bases, and singles and doubles, arrived at training camp in 1996 more muscled than a Vegas bouncer and set a Baltimore record, hitting fifty home runs. Even Oriole lifer Hall of Fame pitcher Jim Palmer wondered if there was anabolic evidence.[16] But Anderson was never tested and only had to endure the eye-rolling of baseball writers and skeptical fans.

Palmeiro and Anderson were just two of several Orioles on the anabolic rumor mill.

Throughout all of this, Angelos was at best benignly negligent and at worst, like many owners, was too enraptured by the box office, stadium, and cable receipts to care.

Amid this plethora of scandal, a community wanted to see the owner, the steward of their team, front and center preaching both accountability and change. Not Angelos. The "guy from Baltimore" stiffed the fans. Steinbrenner at his worst avoided the media in person and, when the going got tough, Angelos did the same. Instead he chose to issue a statement to the press that read, "I am truly saddened by today's events [the day of the positive test]. I have known Rafael Palmeiro for many years. He is a fine person, a great player and a true asset to his community. I know from personal experience that his accomplishments are due to hard work and his dedication to the game. I know that Rafael will accept the penalty under baseball's important drug policy and that he will return to be a productive member of the Orioles."[17] But Angelos never invited Palmeiro back and he left the game in disgrace. Palmeiro could take some comfort that as a friend of Bush, he has never had to answer for lying under oath to Congress.

For all of Angelos's pride in his profile, he stays away from an inquisitive, independent press. David Steele, a longtime sports columnist for the *Baltimore Sun,* said to me, "I can't remember a sports figure in my coverage area, in all the different places I've worked, whose image among fans and media was worse than Peter Angelos's. I regret, though, that in four and a half years here I have never spoken to him. I've made requests through the Orioles and dialed numbers provided by the *Sun* writers but have never reached him, and have never been in the same place he has. I just know him by reputation. Now, when writing about him, I almost have to write around him—referencing things he's proven to have done or things he's been on record to have said. And really, until the last couple of years, those things and what's resulted from them have all been uniformly bad—as the Orioles' record proves."[18]

When taken together—the firings, the scandals, the financially devastating signings, and above it all, the losing—the Oriole way becomes little more than a marketing slogan, and the delicate connection between team and community, forged over decades, becomes easily torn.

Amid this turmoil and desperate for leadership, Angelos found a new enemy: a figurative Major League Baseball team coming down I-95 to settle in Washington, D.C. For years Angelos held back the prospect of a baseball team in Washington, D.C., but not out of concern for fleeced local residents. His complaint was that the presence of D.C. baseball would "cut into his team's profits."[19]

For baseball fans not only in D.C. but in Baltimore as well, Angelos could not have seemed more tone deaf. He continued to put a terrible product on the field, annually competing for last place. The fans started to permanently stay away, and Angelos would just rail against the way baseball in D.C. was ruining his business. This is like General Motors blaming Japan for falling profits instead of their own mismanagement. It's this fundamental obtuseness that has put some remaining Oriole fans in a state of open rebellion.

Nestor Aparicio, the owner of WNST Radio in Baltimore, organized a "Take Back the Birds" protest in September 2007. Aparicio managed to get together a crew to wear all black and march to the park in unison. After taking their seats in the upper deck, and shouting "O" during the national anthem (a longtime custom), they walked out at precisely 5:08 P.M. (the "5" in honor of Brooks Robinson and the "8" for Cal Ripken Jr.).[20] Aparicio was motivated to build this kind of European- or Latin American–style fan movement out of despair at seeing empty seats and the young generation in the city with next to no interest in the team. "They're gone and they're never coming back and Peter is the only one that doesn't understand that," he said. "He thinks the ballpark is empty because they've lost for nine years. He doesn't understand how angry people are at him."[21]

Angelos responded to the anger by saying, "Whoever joins that protest has no comprehension of what it costs to run a baseball team."

Angelos even inspired a respected local songwriter, Randy Lotz, to write a tune called "Let Go of Them O's (Mr. Angelos)." As David Steele said to me, "People here genuinely hate him, which is a testament to how much they revere the Orioles, because they take it personally that they've fallen so far so fast on his watch, and that his decisions have led directly to that fall."[22]

The low point, at least until now, was the mediocre Texas Rangers beating the Orioles, 30–3, in the most lopsided loss in the 110-year history of Major League Baseball.

Amid the endless losing, the silly signings, and the fan apathy, Angelos has also damaged his own reputation as the champion of the little guy. In the last round of baseball negotiations in 2004, which skirted perilously close to yet another damaging lockout, Angelos was no maverick. He was actually one of the leaders of the hardball negotiations from ownership. He complained about the "unbelievable increase in the salary levels," as if he didn't bear some accountability for a salary structure that has created a game of haves and have-nots.[23]

It's not surprising that Angelos has flipped the script on labor in baseball. In the past, he always felt that he had the ultimate trump card for all financial woes: the continued success of Camden Yards. But as attendance dwindled because of his own mismanagement, he has joined the chorus fearful for his bottom line.

Even in these troubled times, with attendance on the wane, the number one asset for the Orioles is still their park. Camden Yards is an achingly beautiful structure that has inspired many imitators. But ideologically, Camden Yards also has served a higher function. It is usually the primary example served when proponents of public funding for stadiums state that ballparks can bring economic success and development to a neighborhood. Just get an ornate ballpark that looks like something from a newsreel when men wore ties to games, and start selling baseball nostalgia at high-end prices. Every time an owner sings from the gospel of publicly funded stadiums they say, "We can be just like Camden Yards!" We should hope not.

As sports economists Bruce Hamilton and Peter Kahn wrote in a piece called "Baltimore's Camden Yards Ballparks," "[T]here is also a widely held perception that the Baltimore experience breaks the mold, and indeed holds out the possibility that if only other cities can replicate Camden Yards magic, they too can get rich from professional sports. . . . Taking account of all of the measurable benefits of the Camden Yards investment (i.e., job creation and tax imports), we estimate that baseball at Camden Yards generates approximately $3M in annual economic benefits to the Maryland economy, at an annual cost to the taxpayers of Maryland of approximately $14M."[24]

Camden Yards is also held up as the jewel of a rebuilt waterfront. But even if we agree that the park certainly adds to the area's ambience, we also should look critically not only at the park but also at everything the surrounding service-industry development has displaced. Baltimore once was a place of union jobs at union wages. Trade unionists had power, and killer attorneys such as Angelos had their back. Today the city is a step above Detroit on the misery index. A mammoth restored factory on Chesapeake Bay is now a Barnes & Noble/Starbucks. The union jobs are now poverty-wage affairs.

This, remember, is the best-case scenario for stadium development. Recently, sports economists Dennis Coates of the University of Maryland and Brad R. Humphreys of the University of Alberta asked whether building new stadiums spurred the local economy. In their study—which spanned nearly thirty years and examined almost forty attempts to lure teams—they failed to discover a single example of a sports franchise jump-starting the local economy, including of course, the Camden Yards example. In fact, they uncovered the opposite trend: "a reduction in real per capita income over the entire metropolitan area. . . . Our conclusion, and that of nearly all academic economists studying this issue, is that professional sports generally have little, if any, positive effect on a city's economy."[25]

This is seen ever so clearly in the service jobs created not only by the gentrification that surrounds Camden Yards but the stadium jobs themselves. They are poverty-wage occupations where $7.00 an hour is the going rate.

Angelos's efforts to keep them that way, despite his union-lawsuit fortune, has further undermined his title of "Marylander of the Year." In September 2007, as the O's limped toward another lackluster finish, excitement finally came to the park because a group of Oriole Park workers said enough is enough. Organizing under the banner of the United Workers' Association (UWA), the workers fought both the resistance of the Maryland Stadium Authority (MSA) and Angelos for a living wage.[26] The UWA, a human rights group founded by homeless day laborers in Baltimore, represents 800 low-wage workers who make up the pool of the 100 to 120 people who keep Camden Yards clean. Stadium workers—the people who clean out the bathroom stalls, scrub the puke out of the club bars, sweep up the small mountains of cigarette butts, and make the Camden Yards experience as pristine and nostalgic as promised—were making poverty wages.

Because they are doing "day labor," members of the UWA who show up to work are sent home if they're not needed. The wages are so low, and the job so "flexible," that some workers live in homeless shelters. One worker was kicked out of public housing because her total pay over the course of a month couldn't match her rent.[27]

Before the Camden Yards day workers affiliated with the United Workers' Association, they were making an average of just $4.00 an hour. After an extended period of agitation, they finally got the attention of Governor Martin O'Malley and Maryland Stadium Authority officials, who agreed to a settlement that gave the Camden Yards workers $11.30 an hour, consistent with a recent Maryland "living wage" law, and higher than the $10 median hourly wage for day laborers nationally. The 2007 living wage law requires companies contracted by the state for work in the Washington-Baltimore area to pay their workers $11.30 an hour, $8.50 in rural areas.[28]

In this solidly blue state, paying stadium workers a living wage should be common sense, but it wasn't. The Maryland Stadium Authority contended that stadium workers are not eligible for the living wage because they are temporary workers. And what makes them temporary? That they don't have to work "away" games.

To get Angelos's—and Governor O'Malley's—further attention, UWA members had to wage a struggle. They held panel discussions, protests, and concerts, and even threatened a hunger strike. It's the kind of grassroots labor organizing that tends not to make the nightly news shows. But they won.

The progress made on a living wage for day laborers in a hard-edged, damaged metropolis could open a new chapter in grassroots labor organizing. The UWA was founded to try to start "a 'human rights' model of organizing led by low-wage workers themselves," Greg Rosenthal, a UWA organizer, told me. "It's all about leadership development from the ranks of the poor, a movement to end poverty led by the poor."[29] Their victory, and the citywide support that mushroomed around it, was another slap at Angelos.

As the struggle took place over years, and the Orioles continued to wither under his watch, Angelos just dug in, insisting that his management of the team—and his treatment of the stadium workers—were both above reproach. There is something tragic about the working-class kid from Baltimore who doesn't even recognize himself in the struggles of others. Those still emotionally invested in the team are saddened by the turn Angelos has made away from the city. Local Baltimore fan and sports journalist Ron Cassie described Angelos as "unfortunate."

Cassie wrote,

What's heartbreaking is that people in Baltimore and Maryland remember not only the great Oriole teams of the 60s, 70s and early 80s, but that Angelos arrived like a savior. He was a Baltimore-guy and when he bought the team nine years after the Colts left town in the middle of the night, local ownership meant everything. Baltimore's a blue-collar town and he'd made his money supporting union guys in asbestos cases. . . . He focused on blocking Washington from getting a team, rather than improving his own.

The bottom line of the Angelos legacy will be that he's responsible for allowing a beloved Baltimore and Maryland institution to wither and die. Baltimore is a city where every row house had the games on TV, and every car radio tuned in, first to Chuck Thompson, and later Jon Miller. Big and rowdy crowds used to fill Camden Yards, but this year that will happen only on Opening Day, and when the Yankees and Red Sox bring their faithful from New York and Boston. After that, it will return to be a half-filled ballpark, in a city only half interested in its own team because they know better than to get their hopes up for a winning season.[30]

Former Oriole Kevin Millar said more succinctly, "It's a beautiful stadium and a beautiful city. They've had some great tradition here over the years. But the bottom line is, we have to play better baseball and get a winning product to get our fans out to the park."[31] It will take more than a winning streak to return the fans. That would be, as the saying goes, like "giving CPR to a corpse." It would take new ownership and a sense among fans that the Oriole way is no longer a punch line, no longer a brand, but a belief that the team has returned to its community. What makes Marylanders smile is the rumor that Angelos is considering selling the team to a group led by Orioles icon Cal Ripken Jr. Angelos has publicly denied that this is on tap, but he has said that if the opportunity arises to sell, Ripken would be considered as a partner. This couldn't happen soon enough for either the workers of the UWA or the residents of Charm City.

Some fans do feel hope because of the hiring of Andy MacPhail as general manager in 2008, a baseball man with a reputation for being a patron saint of lost causes. It's seen as a start. It's also the last card that Angelos has to play other than selling the team. He will go back to the shadows and hope that a competent general manager unencumbered by his meddling can repair some of the damage. It's a savvy move by someone no one would ever accuse of being stupid. The same can't said about his boorish blood brother down I-95, Daniel Snyder.

8. Dan Snyder: When Costanza Got Hair

The general atmosphere around the team suggests Zimbabwe—
a failed state, an intractable dictator, and an impotent and
suffering populace.

—STEVE COLL[1]

I t is, along with the Cowboys of Dallas, the most prized brand name in sports. *Forbes* magazine has them at the top of their franchise value list every year, with a worth comfortably over the $1 billion mark. This platinum-plated name also is the most plainly racist in sports. The Cleveland Indians and the Atlanta Braves have nothing on these guys. Ladies and gentlemen, your Washington Redskins. Their value, so succulent to the "sports fans" at *Forbes,* has not been accrued through such proletarian concerns as wins and losses, but by the wallet-vacuuming tenacity of their owner, Daniel Snyder.

Snyder bears a striking resemblance to *Seinfeld*'s George Costanza with a top-notch rug. Like Costanza, there is a crippling insecurity that defines his tenure as owner. Walk into a Redskins game during their awful 2009 season with a homemade sign criticizing Snyder and you would find a burly member of team security ready to tear it from your hands and slam it into the trash. But unlike Costanza, his insecurity isn't accompanied by introspection. No lofty dreams of being a hand model, or napping under your desk for Snyder. His personality is more like a bulldog on crystal meth, obsessive about his own power while bleeding every possible cent out of the Redskin faithful. In return he has delivered a team built around high-priced players past their prime, producing an annual monotonous mediocrity. For years it was said that 8–8 never cost so much. In 2009 the team has sunk below mediocrity to the realm of calamity.

Like the other death-grip owners, he has convinced himself that his impressive ability to make a dollar means he knows how to run a football team. This is a team whose former players have taken to the airwaves to vent their discontent. It's also a team with a fan base on the edge of eschewing generations of support, and it's about far more than just wins and losses. There is only so much mistreatment the burgundy-and-gold faithful can take. There are the stories of Snyder's staff selling thousands of tickets to legal "ticket brokers," spiking the price of every seat. There are the homemade signs confiscated from fans, including signs that have nothing to do with Snyder or the team. It's not only the signs suggesting that Snyder use his head as a rectal thermometer that are removed. One woman had a sign that read "Hi to my husband in Afghanistan. Love you" rudely trashed.[2]

When pressured about this jackbooted practice, the team released a statement that signs obstructed views, and they were concerned about fans being poked in the eye. Then the next game they curiously distributed free signs emblazoned with the Redskins logo and the big brand name Geico. Eyes be damned.

Then there are the lawsuits. The Skins were revealed in the 2009 off-season to be suing season ticketholders such as seventy-three-year-old grandmother Pat Hill, a lifelong Redskins fan. Because of the recession, Ms. Hill couldn't make payments on her tickets, so the team brought her to court. There is no other franchise that takes this extraordinary step. Hill had been a season ticketholder since early 1962, when her young daughter danced in the halftime shows. Sitting on a sofa bedecked in the Redskins' burgundy and gold, Hill wept in a *Washington Post* photo that hit even the toughest fan right in the gut. Hill, who couldn't even afford a lawyer to contest the Redskins lawsuit, was forced to file for bankruptcy. "It really breaks my heart," she said to the *Post,* through a mess of tears. "I don't even believe in bankruptcy. We are supposed to pay our bills. I ain't trying to get out of anything." Redskins general counsel David Donovan responded by saying, "I can't guarantee everyone [who backs out of a season ticket package] gets dealt with the appropriate level of compassion, but that is our goal."[3]

It's stories like this about Snyder that caused Redskins Hall of Fame running back John Riggins to say in 2009, "This person's heart is dark."[4]

The mercenary view of the bottom line has forced more than a few lifetime Skins fans to reassess their allegiance to the team. Superfan Damian Smith said to me, "One more scandal and I am going to invest in some serious purple" (the color of the nearby Baltimore Ravens). The Ravens offer a nettlesome contrast to their Red-skinned neighbors. The Ravens are run by a general manager, Ozzie Newsome, who has proven to be a brilliant architect for the franchise. The owner, Steve Biscotti, has one directive to Newsome: "Please let me know before you make a major move so I don't hear it for the first time from my friends." Their stadium is a fans' delight, with relatively inexpensive seating and terrific sight lines all across the field of play. It's like getting a luxuriant massage. Going to the Redskins' home, FedEx Field, is like a visit to a sadistic proctologist.

Even if you disagree with every last syllable in this book, anyone who has made the pilgrimage to FedEx enduring the bumper-to-bumper drive on the infamous Washington, D.C., beltway into Prince George's County, Maryland, knows exactly what I'm talking about. It's a taxing journey that leads not to a sporting mecca but a soul-sucking structure that leaves the fan dazed and confused for the drive home. *Sports Illustrated* ranked FedEx as the twenty-eighth most "fan-friendly stadium" out of all thirty-two NFL teams, an embarrassment given Snyder's resources.[5]

For those who have never had the pleasure, FedEx Field is a 91,704-seat monstrosity. Snyder has increased the capacity of the stadium by 24,000 since he purchased the team, creating a seat structure that requires a person to be an anorexic contortionist to sit snugly. They claim a record number of sellouts, but tens of thousands of seats are empty at any given time. Daniel Snyder engineers the "sellout" mystique by dumping empty seats onto ticket brokers. (When the story became public, Snyder was said to be "livid." I was unable to get a comment whether he was livid about the practice or that they were caught.)[6]

There is an attendant dark humor to the fact that the owner of the Redskins has legitimized the professional "scalper." But even those who frequent FedEx Field are more likely to choose the warm bars inside than the seats of doom. As one fan, Jason C. from Arlington, wrote in frustration, "Before you go, take a hot shower. Then climb in the dryer and have someone set you to 'high heat' for about thirty minutes. That should shrink your body enough so you can actually sit comfortably. I was absolutely miserable, as my feet and legs were pretty much smashed against the plastic railing in front of me, and I was also rubbing shoulders (literally) with the people in the seats next to me. And there's really no room to really adjust yourself. The seats are hard plastic, and about as comfortable as sitting on concrete. That's what happens when your stadium has the highest capacity in the NFL: you don't get a bigger stadium, just tighter seating."[7]

The old Washington field, RFK Stadium, was famous for cacophonous, even deafening roars, as the die-hards shouted and stomped their feet on the awesome wooden interior. In the cavernous FedEx, the stadium is seldom loud, and empty seats dot the middle and upper decks. The prices for food are exorbitant, and the quality ranges from plain to putrid. The beer is Coors Light and costs $8.00 a pop. All the Coors Light means that you get none of that terrible beer buzz but you do get the benefits of missing a quarter waiting to take a whiz. And when you make the trip to the urinal, you are in for another surprise. The Redskins are the only team that sells you beer inside the bathrooms, which violates every health care law since the Hammurabi Code.[8]

But the food and beverages are small-time, petty extortion compared to the Orwellian parking prices. You see, for every ticket sold for an event at FedEx Field, Snyder adds a parking charge to the price. As Dave McKenna of the *Washington City Paper* wrote, "if you drove with five people . . . you will have paid $60 for a parking spot in a Godforsaken portion of Prince George's County. And if you took those same five people on the Metro with you, you will have paid $60 to not park in a Godforsaken portion of Prince George's County."[9]

We are reaching a point where taking your child to an event at FedEx Field might require a home equity loan. Snyder is a man who, tiring of fans grousing about waiting in long security lines, didn't hire more security staff or open more entrances. He instead sold fans a pass that lets them bypass those lines—for a $100 charge. After all, anyone who could afford a dangerous weapon of some sort could never have $100 lying around. Snyder, as another angry fan commented, "would charge you for the oxygen you breathe during a game if only he could regulate it." That is only slightly an exaggeration. On the fifth anniversary of the terrorist attacks of 9/11, Snyder marketed special baseball caps to "commemorate Sept. 11th" that could only be ordered through the Redskins' official website. For only $23.99, you, too, could wear what was called "a Pentagon Flag Hat," a black hat with red, white, and blue trimmings, all topped off with a patch in the shape of the Pentagon. None of the proceeds went anywhere but Snyder's pockets. No greedy 9/11 widows could make a sucker out of him. Fans also were told that at the next game against the Vikings, all the coaches would be wearing the caps so you could be just like them . . . and commemorate 9/11.

As the intrepid McKenna wrote, "Snyder's waved the flag before. Flyovers of bombers and jet fighters are common at FedEx Field. America Supports You, a Pentagon public-relations campaign to build affection for the war machine, is a big advertiser on Snyder's radio network. And [General] Peter Pace, chairman of the Joint Chiefs of Staff, took time out from overseeing this country's war successes to be in the owner's box for the Vikings game."[10]

Schmoozing Washingtonian power brokers is a proud tradition in Redskins country. President Richard M. Nixon famously had a direct line to Washington Redskins coach George Allen (whose son is the former Republican Virginia governor George "Macaca" Allen). Nixon would call in plays from the White House that Allen would immediately send into the game. They tended not to work particularly well. It pushed Redskins quarterback Billy Kilmer to say, "Nixon's really hurting us. He calls us all the time. I think I am going to ask George Allen to tell the President not to talk about the game until after we've played it."[11]

Like his predecessor, the legendary Jack Kent Cooke, Snyder gets the importance of connecting the team to the rich and politically powerful. But unlike Cooke, he has no respect for the rank and file he fleeces. He will scrounge for peanuts. Literally. It was revealed that Snyder was found to be selling peanuts in bags that read "Independence Air." The team was buying the surplus bags from the airline, which is tacky, but fine on the face of it. The problem was that Independence Air had been out of business for more than a year.[12] It's enough to make George Steinbrenner jealous. That's not the first time peanuts have exposed Snyder's avarice. Earlier, he banned the selling of peanuts still in the shell, to avoid paying people to sweep them up. (His spokesperson later said it was done out of sensitivity to people with peanut allergies. Critics were told that people who ignored the risk of a stray shell blowing into someone's mouth were being profoundly insensitive to the peanut-impaired.)[13]

This is why the stadium is so much like Snyder: a soulless, humorless, and joyless endeavor. Sportswriter Drew Magary, the author of *Men with Balls,* said it best: "The funny thing about Dan Snyder is that he's a self-made man who bought the Redskins using his own money. And yet the way he runs the team, you would swear he inherited it from someone far more noble and competent."[14]

Maybe this remarkable résumé of pettiness and greed would be tolerated if the man himself was a character of sorts. Like the notoriously colorful Charles Finley of the 1970s Oakland A's, owners can be bastards as long as they have distracting eccentricities, such as a pet mule or a young Stanley "MC Hammer" Burrell dancing in the owner's box. Even the way that Steinbrenner attempted to impose his presence on New York City gave flavor to the daily sports world. But other than playing host in the owner's box to the creepiest actor of his generation—Tom Cruise—Snyder is a man without quirks, alternating between joyless and churlish. And seeing Cruise and Katie Holmes dressed head to toe in black complete with shades was hardly an endearing moment. Snyder wasn't even trying to get a little glamour in his owner's box. He has entered into a business partnership with Cruise, underwriting his production company after Viacom severed its relationship with Cruise for excessive Scientology.

Snyder was listed as an executive producer for the Cruise film *Valkyrie,* a modest financial success. There is no truth, however, to the rumor that Cruise also appreciates Snyder's company because he makes Cruise look tall.

Delicately pointing out Dan Snyder's modest stature is more than a cheap shot. Snyder has become a caricature of the very concept of a Napoleonic complex. His height is somewhere between that of Danny DeVito and Michael J. Fox, but Snyder accompanies his small stature with a seething stink eye at all who can look down on his head. He is the guy who never got picked for the team who ends up buying the team but still hates you. He is the boss who makes coaches thirty years his senior, and even other owners, call him "Mr. Snyder." He is the owner who hangs in the locker room after games, as the cameras have witnessed, ferociously slapping muscled asses that hit him at eye level, yelling, "When we play physical, we win!"[15] But even the winning and the ass-slapping don't inspire the man to smile, only to set his scowl a little deeper into his face.

It wasn't always this way. When Snyder burst into the league with a spectacular $800 million purchase of the team before he turned thirty-six, reporters loved the angle of the superfan/boy genius who grew up middle-class, got rich, and bought the team.

Paul Attner, a football writer for the *Sporting News,* penned in 2000, "Like him or not, embrace his style or not, Snyder is going to be in your face, pushing the norm, scratching for revenues, defying you to slap him down and shut him up. He's quickly become the guy everyone else in the league loves to hate—and beat. If you are looking for the NFL's future, stop your search. . . . For the kid who was the outsider, it is sweet revenge."[16]

In a moment of machismo, after his purchase was approved by the owners' club, Snyder proudly warned an assembly of employees that he was a "prick."[17] The room laughed. He didn't. The problem with being a prick is that it just gets less amusing with time.

Stories began to accumulate of petty firings of longtime employees and dressing down subordinates in volcanic fashion for calling him "Dan" instead of "Mr. Snyder" or for looking directly in his eyes. Even other owners were aghast to see this young man publicly dress down a hotel employee at the league meetings for not putting him in a proper suite.[18]

His firing of several dozen Redskins employees, some with more than twenty years of service, led ESPN's Chris Berman to do the previously unthinkable. Berman, normally a Barnumesque broadcaster/carnival barker who rarely lifts an eyebrow in criticism of anybody (except for profanity-laced tirades aimed at production assistants when he thinks the cameras are off), slammed Snyder for his lack of respect for his employees and coaches. Berman said on the air that Snyder needed to get some "class," which is sort of like being called ugly by a toad, but the point was well taken.

Despite the signs of Snyder being an insufferable "prick," Attner wrote back in 2000 that even though the man may have an edge, "He just might be as smart as he thinks."[19] When it came to making the kind of megamoney that allowed him to fulfill his fan-boy dream of sports ownership, he was absolutely as smart as any of us could hope to be. Snyder got his start when he exploited the highly profitable link between college students and spring break. He dropped out of the University of Maryland at age twenty to lease jets to fly students to the inebriated orgy of their dreams. He is fond of telling people that he made his first $1 million at this venture working from his parents' bedroom. As the *Chicago Business Weekly* wrote, "Money [from a very young age] mesmerized Dan Snyder and school was 'unimpressive!' "[20]

Snyder then, as his hagiographers always insist, went out with a feral tenacity and just "refused to fail." "What made me decide I wanted to invest in him and be a partner when he was just 22 or so was that he was a 'PSD'—Poor, Smart and Desperate to be rich," recalls Redskins minority owner Fred Drasner, a publishing magnate who helped arrange financing for Snyder's first huge business success.[21]

"He was the ultimate PSD who wanted nothing more in life than to succeed. That kept you with him even in the tough times. He would go 24 hours a day, fly to three cities a day. He could not allow himself to lose. He wanted OUT."[22] To call Snyder "poor" says more about Drasner than Snyder. Danny grew up in the Maryland suburbs. His father, Gerry, was a freelance writer who wrote for the now defunct United Press International and *National Geographic*.

But for all the fawning praise of the man with more than $1 billion in assets, Snyder made his money in a fashion familiar to the journey of Dallas Mavericks owner Mark Cuban and many others in the bloated 1990s: He started a business—in this case, a company outsourcing direct marketing and mailing campaigns for *Fortune* 500 companies—and got it traded on the New York Stock Exchange when he was thirty-two. He then sold it for a wildly inflated $2.3 billion to a French firm and bought himself a sports franchise.[23]

After pocketing his stock market cash, Snyder went from being a megafan with his own Redskins belt buckle to the guy living the dream. Since his purchase, Snyder has gone about vacuuming the pockets of the Redskin faithful down to the lint. One reason for this strategy is that in these more challenging economic times, his business acumen, like that of so many of the so-called geniuses of the 1990s, is showing its limitations. In 2005 he invested $50 million into the famed amusement park Six Flags. Six Flags' stock price went from $12 a share to $1.91 and it filed for Chapter 11 bankruptcy in 2009. His best business move may have been cutting down 130 fully mature trees in front of his $10 million Potomac, Maryland, riverfront property. It earned him the anger of environmentalists and a fine of a whopping $100 from the federal government.[24] But it added as much as $1 million to the value of his home. These off-field actions certainly rankle the average fan, but no one would really care if only he could field a decent team. And no one doubts that Snyder desperately wants a white-knuckled grip on the Super Bowl Lombardi Trophy. But his method for building a team makes football experts simply shake their heads. Most championship teams build their rosters in a painstaking manner, through the draft. Snyder in his early years attempted a radically different philosophy of trading draft picks and spending lavishly on a group of fading Pro Bowlers. It was a daring strategy, but by every measure, the plan failed. And yet instead of climbing out of the hole, Snyder chose to keep digging.

Along with the stupefying signings, Snyder has chosen to meddle in every aspect of the team, as if a lifetime of making money transfers magically into football expertise. Drew Magary made it plain: "It's not as if Dan Snyder hasn't been criticized for his stubbornness and his lack of football acumen before. He has. Repeatedly. And that's the problem. Snyder has owned the team for a decade now. In that time, he has displayed a lack of self-awareness that borders on the sociopathic. And after ten years, it's fair to assume now that he will NEVER change. He will never listen to reason. He will never acknowledge failure. He will never accept that the hundreds of thousands of voices telling him he's fucking it all up may have a point."[25]

Just as Steinbrenner was compared to Mussolini, Snyder has been called "the D.C. dictator." Magary wrote directly to Snyder, "You are a tiny little sociopath who should be wearing giant old person sunglasses and running one of the Koreas."

He may have the light, feathery touch of Kim Jong Il with his employees and the fans, but when it comes to sportswriters, Snyder is even worse.

The local press believes that Snyder has made it his business to punish journalists who criticize the team, limiting their access and undercutting the ability of local papers to expand their coverage. Snyder makes clear with each and every one of these moves that he just can't stand to be criticized. Steinbrenner believed that all publicity is good publicity. Snyder's maxim fits more with the old adage that "a free press is fine as long as you can buy one." After purchasing the club, Snyder's next acquisition was the *Redskins Journal,* a northern Virginia–based independent fanzine that followed the team with a trenchant eye. Once again, the man bought out a fanzine.

In 2006, Snyder did Ted Turner proud by buying the D.C. Metro-area flagship sports radio station Sports Talk 980 and turning it into ESPN 980, "Your Home for the Washington Redskins." Sports Talk 980 was always essential listening for those who loved the Redskins but wanted to hear a more analytical discussion of the team and its direction. The team's executive vice president in charge of football operations, Vinny Cerrato, seen as Snyder's Waylon Smithers of *The Simpsons,* had for years been the station's all-purpose punch line for what ailed the Skins. After Snyder's buy, Cerrato was given his own show on the station.

Two long-standing hosts on the network, Andy Pollin and Steve Czaban, to their great credit, vented their displeasure with Cerrato. "As a Redskins fan for forty years, forty-two years," said Pollin, "I am angry about this because I like to see my team, the team I have rooted for, the Washington Redskins, WIN GAMES. And management of the Redskins and ownership is telling us that positive spin on what they are doing is more important than spending time helping the team to win."

Czaban responded, tongue planted firmly in cheek, "Where will he find the time to [run the team] AND do a radio show?"[26] Yes. How would Vinny find the time to run the team and argue with Jimmie from Silver Spring?

If the Sports Talk 980 purchase seemed like classic overreach, for Snyder it merely whetted his appetite. He has since purchased three more Washington-area radio stations, including a liberal talk-radio affiliate, which he turned into a financial news station. Then there was television. Snyder's entertainment wing participated in producing five weekly television shows and two additional weekly radio shows about the team. This placed, directly or indirectly, every television station's news department, with one exception, on the payroll of the franchise they were being asked to critically cover. But Snyder wasn't done. He then became the first owner to buy an already existing fan internet site: ExtremeSkins.com.

In a move that would make a generalissimo blush, Snyder then proceeded to relaunch the site with a personal message to all the local media outlets that dare raise an eyebrow of criticism in his direction. He posted, "I would encourage the local media to follow the example of the national outlets like *USA Today* which refuses to use unidentified sources. Most obviously have personal agendas."[27] I don't know if "follow the example of *USA Today*" should be the guiding principle of a free press. When a "fan" (perhaps Cerrato in an adjacent room) asked what has been the most difficult challenge as an owner, Snyder answered, "The inaccuracies in the media. The portrayal of people and the use of the coaches, the players and the owners to sell their newspapers."[28] Jack Shafer of *Slate* magazine wrote that Snyder sounded like "a crazed press baron from the yellow journalism era."[29]

It doesn't stop with Snyder. Skins chief spokesperson Karl Swanson has long been rumored to be a "lurker" at the site, posting under the name "Andyman" and blasting the press, particularly the *Washington Post,* at every turn. Swanson denies this furiously, but for a lurker, Andyman seems to have a curious amount of knowledge about what is actually happening behind the scenes at FedEx Field. Other posters on ExtremeSkins .com are actually paid by the franchise to stroke Snyder on the boards and attack the beat reporters trying to cover the team.[30] Snyder rewards the paid lurkers with both money and a place in the team press box, where they whoop and holler while the newspaper reporters cringe, curl their toes, and fill out law school applications.

It's either an ambitious effort to turn sports journalism into a version of the direct mail/corporate marketing where he made his fortune, or the chief Redskin has more Costanza in him than he lets on. Maybe instead of imperious, the undersized college dropout might just be profoundly insecure. *Washington Post* sports columnist Mike Wise said to me, "For all his impulsive ways as a sports owner, Dan Snyder is undeniably a tycoon—a man who clearly understood the art of making a deal to obtain the wealth and stature he has. But it must eat at him down deep in his gut that all the money in the world cannot buy him the one thing he really covets: the adoration of his fan base. He's at once the man who has everything and nothing."[31]

Wise has a firm place on the Snyder enemies list. This isn't just because he has been a critic of the direction of the team. It's also because he has been a constant voice against the team name. This Snyder cannot stand.

Snyder's effort to protect the $1 billion brand also has meant brooking no discussion, dissent, or even dialogue on whether, in the twenty-first century, the Redskins' moniker might be past its time. Here is D.C., Chocolate City, in a town presided over by the Obama First Family, and we have a football team name that is a racial slur.

The name Redskins is a constant canker sore in D.C. for people on both sides of the issue. There is a whole network of radio stations, and even several newspapers, that have a policy wherein they only refer to the Redskins as "the Washington football team" or "the burgundy and gold."[32] When the Redskins played the Seattle Seahawks in the 2007 playoffs, the *Seattle Times* only mentioned the team name on first reference. Otherwise writers would have been violating the paper's antidiscrimination policy. Snyder insists that there is nothing wrong with the name. It would therefore be marvelous theater to see Snyder enter a South Dakota Black Hills bar or a Salt River, Arizona, public park and wave the Redskin flag. They would be lucky to leave with a punch in the mouth—and for good reason. In the old days, trappers would kill a Native American, slice some bloody skin off the top of his head, and then they'd have a "redskin" to go with the deerskin, bearskin, and other nonhuman skins.

It's not just activists or football-hating liberals who have spoken out against the name. Former Skins Pro Bowler offensive lineman Tre Johnson said to the *Sporting News,* "It's an ethnically insensitive moniker that offends an entire race of displaced people. That should be reason enough to change it."[33]

"Redskins," the defenders will say, is more than just a name. After years of wins, losses, and a trunkful of Super Bowl glory, it is the closest thing to a common culture there is in the city. Entire row houses in Northeast D.C. have been painted burgundy and gold. This team is the sun around which all other local sports must gravitate. "It's just a name," they say. "This is about preserving tradition."

The sensitive new-age line from Karl Swanson is that the name was "derived from the Native American tradition for warriors to daub their bodies with red clay before battle."[34] Their media guide—on page 272, no less—reads that "the term redskin . . . was inspired not by their natural complexion but by their fondness for vermillion makeup."[35]

This is their argument: that the name must stay because it was actually born of a deep cultural respect for "redskin warriors."

Since Swanson and company brought it up, it's worth examining the roots of this particular Washington football "tradition." The great Redskin patriarch who brought the team to D.C. in 1937 was a man named George Preston Marshall. Marshall, in the words of the late sportswriting legend Shirley Povich, "was widely considered one of pro football's greatest innovators and its leading bigot."[36] Marshall, as the story goes, wanted to pay tribute to his coach who was supposedly of Native American ancestry, William "Lone Star" Dietz. But it seems that Dietz was in fact a white man "who began taking on an Indian identity as a teenager and ultimately seized the past of a vanished Lakota tribesman and made it his own."[37]

Marshall's Skins were the last NFL team to integrate, finally taking the plunge in 1962 and only when the Kennedy administration's interior secretary, Stewart Udall, issued an ultimatum: sign an African-American player or be denied use of their new government-financed fifty-four-thousand-seat stadium. Marshall responded by making Ernie Davis, Syracuse's All-American running back, his number one draft choice. One problem: Davis's response was a forthright "I won't play for that SOB." Davis was traded to Cleveland, which in return sent African-American All-Pro Bobby Mitchell.[38]

Marshall's racism was more than just the bad ideas knocking around his brain. It was the material foundation upon which the Redskin empire was built. He had brought his football team to Washington with a plan to make them "the South's team." He signed TV contracts with stations in southern cities, and he drafted players mostly from southern colleges. The team, once again to quote Povich, "became the Confederates of the NFL."[39] In fact, in the original version of the ever-present fight song "Hail to the Redskins," the line "Fight for Old D.C." was "Fight for Old Dixie."

In the face of this history, it is hard to imagine Marshall as a student of the cultural intricacies of vermillion makeup. Far more likely, he was merely marketing a minstrel show in shoulder pads, preying on bigotry for big bucks.

But Snyder won't hear any criticism of his precious brand, even though several of his players have expressed their own discomfort.

Former player Chad Morton described his feelings to Mike Wise upon seeing antinickname protesters outside a team banquet in Virginia. "I use to look at them and think, 'Why don't you guys do something else with your time?' Now I look at them and think they're right. I mean, if you look at that logo and you really think about the name, it is racist."[40]

Snyder's spokesman Karl Swanson sneered at the suggestion: "I know a guy who wants to paint the Redskins logo on the bottom of his swimming pool," Swanson said in response.[41] I know a guy who bought a Confederate flag bikini for his teenage daughter. It doesn't make it right.

The power that comes with this $1 billion brand means that Snyder can buy loyalty if not affection. Sonny Jurgensen, the Hall of Fame Redskins quarterback legend who has become something of a talisman to Snyder, said in 2000, the year after Snyder's purchase of the team, "This franchise was treading water, wandering aimlessly. There's nothing wrong with him being involved."[42] But treading water is exactly what the team did in Snyder's first decade in charge: 7–9, 8–8, 8–8, 7–9, 5–11, 6–10, 10–6, 5–11, 9–7, and 8–8. For all of Snyder's spending, the team has been basically an extended flat line, until tanking to 4–12 in 2009. Snyder undermined his second-year head coach Jim Zorn by bringing in a sixty-seven-year-old retired coordinator named Sherm Lewis to call the plays. When Lewis was hired, he was working as a bingo caller in a retirement community. Zorn spent the rest of the season standing on the sidelines, looking for something to do. Meanwhile, Snyder's $100 million off-season pickup, bulbous defensive tackle Albert Haynesworth, was a wheezing mess, functioning only on every other play. (When Steve Czaban was asked if Haynesworth was out of shape he said, "Well, round is a shape.") Nothing was spent on the offensive line, which led their quarterback, Jason Campbell, to practice the time-honored art of "chuck and duck."

The suffocating public pressure finally had its effect. By January 2010, the utterly inept executive vice president for football operations Vinny Cerrato and head coach Jim Zorn were both gone. Like Angelos, Snyder is bringing in a real GM, Bruce Allen (the brother of "Macaca" Allen), and Super Bowl–winning head coach Mike Shanahan. As Sally Jenkins wrote in the *Washington Post*, "If what Snyder has in mind is a management team that will act coherently—starting with a proven, competent personnel man who will have the back of the head coach, who can build a staff that operates in concert, and who cultivates chemistry instead of finger-pointing and second-guessing—it will be a welcome experiment. It's something they haven't really tried before."[43]

There is no question what would happen if the team was reclaimed by its rightful owners: the people of Washington, D.C. First, we would return the team to the district. No more treks on the beltway to the Maryland suburbs. Then we would let the coaches coach, and stop signing people on the wrong side of thirty to disastrous contracts. The $1 billion in value could act as a support beam for a city fallen on tough times. Would the name change? That might take some time. But at least there could be an honest discussion. Maybe we would just take the advice of D.C. sports radio and *Pardon the Interruption* host Tony Kornheiser and keep the name but just put a red-skin potato on the side of the helmet. Or perhaps we would call ourselves the Washington Freedom. Not because D.C. is an emblem of freedom and democracy, but because we would be liberated from an owner who controls the press, gouges our wallets, and exploits people's grand affections, all in the service of profit and ego. But lest this be seen as uniformly negative, we must say this about Snyder: we thankfully have no idea what he looks like shirtless. We can't say the same about Donald Sterling.

9. Donald Sterling: Slumlord Billionaire

Please don't forget the children, they need our help.

—DONALD STERLING

I t takes a certain flair for racism—a panache for prejudice—to find yourself facing two different discrimination lawsuits simultaneously. Meet Donald Sterling, the owner of the most regularly rancid franchise since the Cleveland Spiders: the Los Angeles Clippers. Since Sterling's purchase of the club in 1981, his team has by far the worst record in all of the National Basketball Association. The Clippers have made the playoffs only four times in Sterling's twenty-eight years as owner, never advancing past the second round. It's been said that the NBA should rename its annual players draft the Donald Sterling Draft Lottery. The writers at ESPN.com named him the nation's worst owner because of his blithe disregard for fielding a winning team as long as he could turn a buck.[1] It stands to reason that in 2000 *Sports Illustrated* named the Clippers "the worst franchise in professional sports."[2]

But Sterling transcends the stereotypical Scrooge-like miser. He is so much more colorful than just a man snoozing in his luxury box on a large pile of cash.

Sterling is like a side character in a James Ellroy L.A.-noir novel. He is ruthless and toothsome, a man who unabashedly reinvented himself in Los Angeles's healing sunshine. Former L.A. mayor Tom Bradley once said of the City of Angels, "People cut themselves off from their ties of the old life when they come to Los Angeles. They are looking for a place where they can be free, where they can do things they couldn't do anywhere else."[3]

Bradley could easily have been talking about Donald Sterling, real name Donald Tokowitz. After moving to L.A. from Chicago as a child, he came of age in the rough-and-tumble neighborhood of Boyle Heights. Donnie Tokowitz was the only son of an immigrant produce peddler. As a young boy, he worked boxing groceries and showed a skill for saving money. "As a kid, Donald never had enough of anything," said a friend. "With him, acquiring great wealth is a crusade. He's psychologically pre-disposed to hoarding."[4] His mother was not impressed with his ability to hustle a dollar and insisted that he go to college and become a lawyer, and if you think this story sounds like a Jewish Horatio Alger story, you're not alone. (Full disclosure: I'm Jewish and very bad with money, which might make me a touch alienated from this story.)

Young Donnie Tokowitz worked his way through the Southwestern School of Law, graduating at age twenty-three. To help pay his way through, he worked nights selling furniture. It was there that he changed his name to Sterling. "I asked him why," a coworker told *Los Angeles Magazine*. "He said, 'You have to name yourself after something that's really good, that people have confidence in. People want to know that you're the best.' "[5]

After success as a real estate attorney, he started buying property throughout Los Angeles, and kept buying and flipping real estate until he earned enough to buy the then San Diego Clippers for $13 million, $10 million of that on layaway. By ownership standards, he was practically proletarian.

Before fleeing to Los Angeles, he crippled any prospects of professional basketball in San Diego by being the most personally repellent owner in the game. In San Diego, he preened like a peacock. "It's the start of a new era!" he promised in an open letter to fans. "I'm in San Diego to stay and committed to making the city proud of the Clippers. I'll build the Clippers through the draft, free agency, trades, spending whatever it takes to make a winner."[6]

They were gone within five years.

As *Sports Illustrated* wrote in 1982, "Sterling is a good example of the kind of ownership problems the league has had in recent years. . . .

He started his crusade with a campaign to boost ticket sales that, oddly enough, featured Sterling's grinning face on billboards throughout San Diego County." After they won their opening game of the 1981 season, Sterling skipped around the court, shirt open, handing out hugs and high-fives to players and the coaching staff. This behavior would be charming if that same first season he wasn't accused of stiffing players on their paychecks.[7]

It also didn't help that his "special assistant general manager" was a woman named Patricia Simmons, an ex-model who had what one San Diego newspaper described gently as "no known basketball background."[8] When Clippers coach Paul Silas was in China on a Players' Association exhibition tour that summer, Simmons moved into his office. Upon Silas's return, he found his belongings stacked and boxed in the hallway.

This kind of bizarre behavior is why in 1984, team president Alan Rothenberg predicted about Sterling, "You're going to call him the Howard Hughes of the NBA."[9] But Hughes was a recluse. Sterling wants everyone to see him, no matter how long his hair and fingernails.

The San Diego Clippers averaged fewer than forty-five hundred fans per game for three consecutive seasons. Sterling could have stuck it out, but instead he packed up and, urged on by his friend Los Angeles Lakers owner Jerry Buss, moved the team to L.A. in 1984. Sterling undertook the move without first receiving approval from the league, which fined him $25 million for the play. Sterling countersued for $100 million but withdrew when the new commissioner, David Stern, dropped the fine to $6 million.

While Sterling has cobbled together a terrible team, he is seen as a visionary at the art of turning his franchise into a cash cow, dumping contracts, pocketing the team's share of the league's television revenue, and collecting his share of the luxury tax charged to teams that spend beyond the salary cap, something Sterling has never done.

The cheapness of Sterling is the stuff of legend. During his first season as owner, he asked Coach Silas if the former power forward could double as the team trainer and take up the duties of taping players before games.[10] During the 1998–1999 NBA owners' lockout, when almost half the season was canceled, Sterling chose simply not to hire a coach for six months. (The Clippers finished the lockout season with a "sterling" 9–41 mark.) Not one of Sterling's nine lottery picks before 1998 re-signed with the team.

"Being a Clipper can be real tough," said retired point guard Pooh Richardson, who played for the Clippers from 1994 to 1999. "It's almost a given that you won't win and that the team won't hold on to its best players."[11]

"At some level Sterling must be content being the losingest NBA owner ever," said superagent David Falk. "All the criticism he has gotten hasn't changed the way he runs the team one degree."[12]

Sterling says he hates to lose. He said plaintively to a reporter, "Basketball is the only aspect of my life in which I haven't been a winner. I want to win badly, I really do. It hasn't happened yet, but it will. Don't you think it will? . . . It must. It simply must."[13]

But if Sterling really wants to win, he just loves being an owner even more. He's never come close to winning a championship and compensates by holding NBA lottery parties at his Beverly Hills estate. As *Sports Illustrated* reported, "Sterling has often prepped for his parties by placing newspaper ads for 'hostesses' interested in meeting 'celebrities and sports stars.' "[14]

Prospective hostesses per custom are interviewed in the owner's office suite. One former Clippers coach recalled dropping in on Sterling during a cattle call. "The whole floor reeked of perfume," he said. "There were about fifty women all dolled up and waiting outside Donald's office, and another fifty waiting outside the building."[15] Those chosen get to mingle with D-list celebrities, such as his friend of twenty-five years Leon Isaac Kennedy, the star of *Penitentiary I, II,* and *III.* (Full disclosure: I love *Penitentiary II,* which featured the film debut of Mr. T.)

Sterling has even been penurious enough to share an arena with the Los Angeles Lakers. It certainly makes business sense. Since leaving the L.A. Sports Arena and sharing the Staples Center, Sterling has finally opened up his wallet for players such as Elton Brand and Baron Davis (both signings, disasters). But the comparison between the two clubs is rather consistently unkind.

The Lakers, as of this writing, have been to thirty-five NBA finals and won fifteen championships. The Clippers have the most sixty-loss seasons in NBA history. It's the prince and the pauper sharing space at Staples. As comedian Nick Bakay wrote, "the Lakers' luxury box is prawns, caviar and opera glasses while the Clippers stock Zantac, barf bags, some good books, and cyanide."[16]

Sterling dismissed the comparison, saying, "Let's say you take your child to see Shirley Temple onstage. And let's say you tell yourself, 'Wouldn't it be nice if that was my child up there?' And you think, 'My child will never be Shirley Temple, but I love her all the same.' So you send her for dancing and singing lessons and hope that one day she'll have all the qualities you admire in Shirley Temple. But she'll never be Shirley Temple."[17] It's lines like this that have led him to be described as having "the furtive, feral charm of an old-time movie mogul."[18]

He likes to present himself as a self-made Gatsbian figure. He even has "white parties" at his Beverly Hills home where guests all wear white "like in the book."[19] He's a Gatsbian who appears to have never read *The Great Gatsby*. Jay Gatsby was running from his past, hiding his rough background behind the artifice of taste and wealth. Sterling presents himself as the tony developer of high-end properties in the Hollywood Hills, but plays it much closer to the street.

You might be tempted to think that playing for Sterling would at least be interesting. The man is a character, not a suit. But in addition to being cheap he also is verbally abusive. Sterling stormed into the team's locker room in February 2009 and unleashed what was described as a "profanity-laced tirade," calling young forward Al Thornton "the most selfish basketball player I've ever seen." When Thornton looked beseechingly to his coach, Mike Dunleavy, Sterling told Dunleavy to "shut up."[20]

This is why Clipperland has always been a place where any player with potential is either not re-signed or desperately tries to leave before his potential is squandered. In 1981 they picked Tom Chambers with the number eight pick, and then in 1982 they nabbed Terry Cummings number two overall (he won Rookie of the Year honors). The two appeared in six combined All-Star Games and 228 combined playoff games . . . none with the Clippers. Both got the hell out of Dodge by the summer of '84.

Would that hoops incompetence were the full extent of Sterling's sins. But it's his business practices that create grounds for his removal. Sterling is a slumlord billionaire, a man who made his fortune by building low-income housing, and then, according to a U.S. Department of Justice lawsuit, developed his own quota system to decide who gets the privilege of renting his properties. In November 2009, Sterling settled the suit with the Justice Department for $2.73 million, the largest amount ever obtained by the government in a discrimination case involving apartment rentals.[21] Reading the content of the suit makes you want to scrub with steel wool. Sterling just said no to renting to non-Koreans in Koreatown and just said hell no to African-Americans looking for property in plush Beverly Hills.[22] Sterling, who has a Blagojevichian flair for the language, says he did not like to rent to "Hispanics" because "Hispanics smoke, drink and just hang around the building." He also stated "Black tenants smell and attract vermin."[23]

The slumlord billionaire has a healthy legal paper trail that creates a collage of someone very good at extorting rents from the very poor. In 1986, the spiking of rents in his Beverly Hills properties—the "slums of Beverly Hills"—led to a full-scale tenants' march on City Hall.

In 2001, Sterling was sued successfully by the City of Santa Monica on charges that he harassed and threatened to evict eight tenants living in three rent-controlled buildings. Their unholy offense that drew his ire was having potted plants on balconies.[24] Talk about hands-on. How many billionaires drive around their low-income housing properties to look for violations? That's Donnie Tokowitz in action.

Two years later, Sterling evicted a tenant for allegedly tearing down notices in the building's elevator.

In 2004, Sterling led a brigade of other landlords to smash Santa Monica's ultrastrict tenant harassment ordinance.[25] The ordinance stated that issuing repeated eviction threats to tenants was a form of harassment. Sterling and his crew believed that they should be allowed to harass to their heart's content. There are only so many potted plants a man can stand.

And in 2005, Sterling settled a housing-discrimination lawsuit filed by the Housing Rights Center, which represented more than a dozen of his tenants. He paid nearly $5 million in legal fees to the plaintiffs along with a reportedly massive, albeit confidential, sum. Not all the plaintiffs, though, lived to see their windfall. According to court filings, on July 12, 2002, "Kandynce Jones was under threat of eviction by [Sterling] even though she had never missed a rent payment. Ms. Jones, who is a senior citizen and a person with a disability, suffered a stroke caused by the stress [of Sterling's] housing practices. On July 21, 2003, Ms. Jones passed away as a result of that stroke."[26]

Peter Keating wrote in ESPN the Magazine that Jones had repeatedly walked to the apartment manager's office to plead for assistance, according to sworn testimony given by her daughter Ebony Jones, "Kandynce Jones' refrigerator dripped, her dishwasher was broken, and her apartment was always cold. Now it had flooded. [Sumner] Davenport [one of Sterling's four top property managers] reported what she saw to Sterling, and according to her testimony, he asked: 'Is she one of those black people that stink?' When Davenport told Sterling that Jones wanted to be reimbursed for the water damage and compensated for her ruined property, he replied: 'I am not going to do that. Just evict the bitch.'"[27]

Amid this scandal, the NAACP presented Sterling with a lifetime achievement award, raising the question if either party was about to be Punk'd. "I really have a special feeling for this organization," Sterling said at the award gala. The billionaire gives $10,000 to $15,000 a year to the L.A. chapter.

As sports columnist Bomani Jones wrote, "Though Sterling has no problem paying black people millions of dollars to play basketball, the feds allege that he refused to rent apartments in Beverly Hills and Koreatown to black people and people with children. . . . You gotta love racism, the only force in the world powerful enough to interfere with money-making. Sterling may have been a joke, but nothing about this is funny. In fact, it's frightening and disturbing that classic racism like this might still be in play."[28]

Our good friend NBA commissioner David Stern, always so PR conscious when it comes to where players mingle, how players dress, and who they consort with after hours, has turned a blind eye to this disturbing pattern. Now these chickens have returned to Stern's back porch to roost.

In addition to the housing discrimination settlement, there is a second racism lawsuit buzzing around Sterling's helmet of hair. This other suit has come from inside his own NBA offices: his longtime general manager Elgin Baylor. Baylor, an NBA legend with the Los Angeles Lakers, has spent more than two decades making a series of personnel decisions that have ranged from depressing to enraging. Baylor was called without irony by a television commentator a "veteran of the lottery process," watching the Ping-Pong balls bounce around to see who gets the number one pick. The Clippers' draft picks under Baylor's tenure—and their entire roster— have largely been a dyspeptic horror show. According to Baylor, one reason for their continued ineptitude was Sterling, in telling Baylor to limit his picks to "poor black boys from the South and a white head coach."[29]

A Clipper draft pick who could actually play was Kansas star Danny Manning. Manning didn't last in L.A. This might be because Sterling, according to Baylor, would grumble that he didn't like being in a position where "I'm offering a lot of money for a poor black kid." The lawsuit claims the team has "egregious salary disparities" based on race. Baylor claims he was told to "induce African-American players to join the Clippers, despite the Clippers' reputation of being unwilling to fairly treat and compensate African-American players." It also stated that Sterling made clear to Baylor that hiring an African-American head coach was not his preference. This is why Baylor's lawyers accuse Sterling of having a "vision of a Southern plantation–type structure."[30]

This news is hardly the public relations boost that David Stern relishes. And it's not the first time Sterling has humiliated the league. Donnie had to testify in open court in 2004 that he regularly paid a Beverly Hills hooker for sex, describing her as a "$500-a-trick freak" with whom he coupled "all over my building, in my bathroom, upstairs, in the corner, in the elevator."[31] Stern, as one commentator noted, "normally has to explain away the behavior of 20-something athletes, not married 70-year-old club owners worth nearly a billion."[32]

I guess a billion buys a lot of Viagra. Sterling went on to give the woman in question credit for "sucking me all night long" and said that the "best sex was better than words could express."[33] The very married Sterling had a blunt appraisal of this "exciting" relationship: "It was purely sex for money, money for sex, sex for money, money for sex."[34] (I will now tear out my eyes with a shrimp fork.)

In an even greater leap toward the absurd, the lawsuit was not initiated by the vice squad or any controlling legal authority. It was spurned by Sterling himself against his "$500-a-trick freak" because he just couldn't bear the thought that she was occupying a home she claimed he gifted to her. He wanted her evicted and went to court to do it. He also seems to have wanted to proclaim to the world that at seventy, Donnie Tokowitz could still throw down in the sack. If Sterling wants to be a geriatric Charlie Sheen, that's his business. But in a sport that so aggressively polices the character of its players, it seems the height of hypocrisy that Sterling skates.

If evicting his tenants and frequenting hookers are Sterling's work and leisure activities, his charitable practices are a further descent into the bizarre.

Although his hobby is unjust evictions, Sterling's pet project is helping the homeless. It's like Dick Cheney becoming the spokesman for the electric car.

Sterling's homeless "activism" consisted of him buying an $8 million warehouse with big plans to turn it into the $50 million Donald Sterling Homeless Center. We know of Sterling's plans not from any press conference with homeless rights activists or a ribbon-cutting ceremony or even efforts to secure permits from the city. We are aware of his unparalleled generosity because Sterling bought a series of full-page ads in the front section of the Los Angeles Times to tell us how generous he is.

The ads do more than trumpet Sterling. They seem designed by him as well, or by a man who would unbutton his shirt to the waist in public. Each ad contains Donald Sterling's massive head, complete with a smile showing a mouth of capped teeth, hair by Blago, and skin stretched tighter than a Sunset Boulevard miniskirt. Underneath Sterling's head it reads, "Please don't forget the children, they need our help."

Sterling has taken out full-page ads before, oftentimes ones that proclaim him the recent recipient of some "humanitarian of the year" honor. But the shelter ads were worse because they raised the hopes of an entire community in L.A. starved for funds and relief.

As Patrick Range McDonald wrote in the LA Weekly, "The advertisements promise a 'state-of-the-art $50 million' building on Sixth and Wall streets, whose stated 'objective' is to 'educate, rehabilitate, provide medical care and a courtroom for existing homeless.' . . . These days, though, Sterling's vow to help the homeless is looking more like a troubling, ego-inflating gimmick dreamed up by a very rich man with a peculiar public-relations sense. . . . From homeless-services operators to local politicians, no one has received specifics for the proposed Sterling Homeless Center. They aren't the least bit convinced that the project exists.' "[35]

Tom Gilmore, who served for six years on the Los Angeles Homeless Services Authority, said, "I'm generally a very optimistic person but this thing smells like shit. The *L.A. Times* ads aren't cheap. He could've stopped buying the ads and spent that money on homeless people." Gilmore, who's been working downtown since 1992, adds, "I've never seen [Sterling] down here in my life."[36]

The Reverend Alice Callaghan, who works with the four thousand people on L.A.'s skid row at any given time, was even more blunt: "It's the lowest of the low if he's using the homeless to make himself look good," she said. "Or it's the dumbest of the dumb. No one builds those kinds of shelters down here anymore. He's a businessman. He can make anything happen. So if it's not happening, there's a reason for it."[37]

When we consider the terrible budget deficits and constant crisis the State of California finds itself mired in—and when we couple that with the colorful train wreck that is Donald Sterling—perhaps the Clippers should become the first of the teams to go the way of the public utility. Then they might actually get some fans.

10. The Wal-Mart Way: David Glass and the Kansas City Royals

I see Wal-Mart as a big speeding truck just waiting to hit something.

—DAVID GLASS

What can you say about a 2009 Kansas City Royals team that can have a Cy Young Award–winning pitcher in the dazzling Zach Greinke and still finish in last place with ninety-seven losses? What can you say about a team that's had only one winning season since 2000 and has averaged almost a hundred losses every year? What can you say about a team that has still managed to double in value over the past decade? What can you say about a team that won the 1985 World Series, yet now seems to be permanently locked in last place? You can look at the owner's box and say simply, "Karma."

The death-grip owner in question is a national unknown named David Dayne Glass. Glass might not have the glossy profile of the other death-grip owners, but there is no one in any other owner's box that's had a greater day-to-day impact on all of our lives, whether you're a sports fan or not. Glass may not be the meddling, headline-grabbing type of owner such as Daniel Snyder or the family Steinbrenner. He will never undo his shirt to the navel like Donald Sterling. But it is only with a touch of hyperbole that Royals fan Louis Dimas calls his work "viral in its destructive powers,"[1] for David Dayne Glass earned his fortune as the

CEO of Wal-Mart. Running Wal-Mart from 1976 to 2000 taught Glass some fundamental lessons on how to squeeze every last dollar out of your business. The "Wal-Mart way" means cutting labor costs, driving out local businesses, and bilking taxpayers. When you apply that business model to a major league team, you get a disaster. You also provide ample justification for the citizens of Kansas City to force the Royals out of his hands.

Now this once-proud team is a whisper, a rumor, of a franchise. But it doesn't have to be this way. My first baseball memories are of a hearty appreciation for the Kansas City Royals. I grew up an unreconstructed New York Mets fan, which means that anything that came in Yankee pinstripes made me break out into hives. In the 1980 American League Championship Series, the Royals knocked the vaunted Yankees off their perch when American League MVP George Brett faced down a Goose Gossage 100 mph fastball in the decisive third game and crushed it into the Yankee Stadium upper deck. Brett's shot sent the Yankees home and the Royals into the World Series. KC's team faltered that October against the Phillies, but they eventually climbed the mountain in 1985, winning the World Series over the St. Louis Cardinals. They didn't have a team so much as a movie cast. There was Brett, the gap-toothed, pine-tar-lovin' Hall of Fame third baseman. There was Dan Quisenberry, the All-Star relief pitcher closing games with a submarine delivery that rendered him unhittable. There was second baseman Frank White, the player with the same name as Christopher Walken's cold-blooded drug lord in *King of New York* (that counted for a lot in the 1980s). There was Willie Wilson, with his record 705 at-bats in 1980. There was Bret Saberhagen, the 1985 Cy Young Award winner. There was the terrifically named Buddy Biancalana at shortstop. And we didn't even get to Amos Otis and Willie Aikens.

In 2009, with the exception of Greinke, there isn't a Royal who would be recognized outside the city limits. The team regularly holds bobblehead nights in commemoration of former players who haven't played in decades. In 2005, the satirical newspaper the *Onion* blared the headline "Dying Boy Brought in to Cheer Up Kansas City Royals." The article then "quoted" first baseman Mike Sweeney saying, "I can't even explain how uplifting it is to see somebody who soon won't have to put up with the pain and misery anymore. Even though we have to endure the same terrible fate again come April, Danny, unlike the Royals organization, will be in a far better place."[2]

Glass has a ready answer for why the Royals are so bad. He lays ultimate responsibility upon the "rich team, poor team" financial dynamic in Major League Baseball. This past season, when the losses started to stack up, Glass said, "When you're as thin as we are—it hurts. We just don't have the depth that the big-market teams do."[3] It's undoubtedly true that the Yankees, Mets, Cubs, and Red Sox can spend in ways that other teams simply can't. In the past fourteen years, the Yankees have made it to the World Series seven times. They've also had the highest payroll in baseball for nine straight years. As mentioned, they won the 2009 World Series after spending $423.5 million during the 2008 off-season on free-agent pitchers CC Sabathia and A. J. Burnett, and first baseman Mark Teixeira. The final four teams in the 2009 playoffs all had payrolls of more than $100 million.[4]

But the "small market" excuse just doesn't hold water. While small-market teams are at a financial disadvantage, baseball has more competitive parity than any other major sport. The Kansas City payroll in 2009 was $70 million and ranked twenty-first in player salaries, the highest it has ever been under Glass's reign. This is actually higher than that of small-market contenders such as the Minnesota Twins, the Texas Rangers, and the Tampa Bay Rays (formerly Devil Rays but ownership—in a controversial move—renounced Satan). The Rays made the World Series in 2008 with a $43.8 million payroll. Yet the small-market blues is always the Glass excuse.

While there may be a financial imbalance in Major League Baseball, competitive imbalance is a myth, with seven different teams having won the World Series in the past nine years. But the Royals have been unable to buy or play their way out of futility. Instead Glass has been accused by fans, media, and anyone with a working brain of pocketing checks from the "luxury tax" imposed on the big-market clubs, while doing next to nothing to improve his own franchise. Every time the Yankees engage in one of their "only the Yankees" spending sprees, Glass gets richer. He is the welfare queen of Major League Baseball.

The evidence abounds. In 1999, the Royals had three future all-stars in Jermaine Dye, Johnny Damon, and Carlos Beltran. Most small-market teams will invest in one or two of their top prospects and cut someone loose. Glass chose to invest in none of them. After a serious push by their dwindling fan base, they finally started spending money two seasons ago. But they spent it poorly, which, as the other death-grip franchises can tell you, is the easiest way to go from a lousy season to historically awful.

As *Kansas City Star* columnist Jason Whitlock wrote for ESPN, "a franchise that thrived in the '70s and '80s powered by owner Ewing Kauffman's passion for the club and the city was reduced to accepting the efforts of a half-assed owner who started every year with a half-baked plan to win half the club's games in hopes that half the stadium would be filled."[5]

This is the "Wal-Mart way," and that's not merely a rhetorical flourish. You can't understand the rot at the heart of the Kansas City Royals without grasping what was wrong with the David Glass era at Wal-Mart.

Taking over directly from Sam Walton himself, Glass led Wal-Mart for more than thirty years, resigning from the board in April 2009. The period of Glass's tenure also saw a profound shift in wealth across the United States as the poor became poorer and the rich wealthy beyond the dreams of J. P. Morgan. Wages dipped, unions were busted, and personal debt exploded. Amid the financial chaos, like a life raft for consumers, was Wal-Mart. Glass sold discounted products to workers living on low wages and drowning in debt. In the process, under Glass's leadership, Wal-Mart moved into other industries. It became your pharmacy, your toy store, and your grocery store. Mom-and-pop shops went the way of the Betamax, alongside the very concept of a living wage. Wal-Mart also set up relations with Chinese and other Asian sweatshop factories that paid pennies, imported the products, and sold them at rock-bottom prices. This process achieved its own name in the American lexicon: Wal-Martization.[6]

In 1992, *Dateline NBC* interviewed Glass about these ostensibly legal but morally untethered business practices. *Dateline* broadcast damning scenes of Bangladeshi children slaving away at Wal-Mart products. When asked to defend this practice, Glass said simply, "You and I might, perhaps, define children differently."[7] He then pointed out that since the Asians he knows are very short (that would be news to Yao Ming), the children could have just been vertically challenged grown-ups. The *Dateline* reporter then confronted Glass with a horrific picture of a factory that had burned to the ground with the children workers locked inside (locking in is a standard sweatshop practice to keep children workers from pocketing the plastic, shiny goods they're assembling with their small hands). Glass looked at the picture and said, "Yeah . . . there are tragic things that happen all over the world."[8] He then stomped out of the interview, which kept him from having to answer why signs in Wal-Mart that said "Made in America" were hanging over goods made by Bangladeshi children.

As recently as January 2004, the *New York Times* exposed an internal Wal-Mart investigation demonstrating "extensive violations of [US] child-labor laws and state regulations requiring time for breaks and meals."[9]

But while the new Wal-Mart way has been often imitated, it's never been duplicated. Glass articulated Wal-Mart's goals thusly: "First we dominate North America, then South America, then Europe and Asia."[10] This was furthered with the opening in Mexico of their new chain of stores, "Walmex."

Under Glass's leadership, Wal-Mart became the largest employer in the United States, taking in more revenue than any other publicly traded corporation. This revenue comes in off the skin of their employees, called "associates" in Wal-Mart-speak. On average, a Wal-Mart employee makes $10.84 per hour, for an annual income of $19,165.[11] That's $2,000 below the federal poverty line for a family of four. As the group Wal-Mart Watch put it, "They call them 'associates' and treat them like interns."[12] (Fittingly for Wal-Mart-world, the CEO who replaced Glass, Lee Scott, makes $30 million a year.)

You might think this would make Wal-Mart an industry pariah. But the company has received more than $1.5 billion in direct subsidies from the federal government per year. Through it all, just as the earnest face of Mao is always watching his Chinese laborers, the cult of Sam Walton is forever, even in death, mindful of his charges. Walton, the Wal-Mart founder, died in 1982, the richest man in the United States. Despite the sacrilege, execs are known to say, "In Sam we trust."

Lee Sustar, a tech writer, told me the following tale about the cult of Sam. "I went to [Wal-Mart headquarters in Bentonville, Arkansas] in '98 for a tech writing job about Wal-Mart's data networks. The offices were spartan and ugly—metal desks rammed together in an old warehouse. Everywhere, though, there were giant posters of Sam Walton with quotations—just like that Genius of the Carpathians, the Great Conductor, Nicolae Andruță Ceaușescu. Here's a typical Sam Walton quote: 'Appreciate everything your associates do for the business. Nothing else can quite substitute for a few well-chosen, well-timed, sincere words of praise. They're absolutely free and worth a fortune.' Compliments to workers, yes—it cost nothing. A living wage, that's another story. Walton and Ceaușescu had identical views about the threat posed by independent unions, of course."[13]

This process of exploiting workers both at home and abroad, all under the watchful eye of the Cult of Sam, was a very profitable method of operation for Glass at Wal-Mart. But it's a hellish way to run a baseball team.

As chairman of the Royals' board in 1994 following the death of beloved owner Ewing Kauffman, Glass was a strong proponent of the lockout that canceled the 1994 World Series. He led the owners' charge to oppose any settlement with the Players' Association and stood ready to destroy the game in order to save it. Glass advocated fielding replacement players and playing a year of scab ball. This wasn't an idle threat. He even had a planeful of replacement players ready to travel for the opening of the season when he received word that the lockout was over.[14] Unions just weren't the Wal-Mart way. As Judge Sonia Sotomayor put it in her gruff decision that put the game back on the field, the owners had been acting in bad faith, with no effort to reach a settlement and seeing the destruction of the Players' Association as the only appropriate outcome. They had, in Sotomayor's words, "placed the entire concept of collective bargaining on trial."[15]

Glass responded to losing the labor battle like a machete-wielding adolescent throwing a tantrum. He couldn't shut the game down like it was a Wal-Mart store trying to unionize. But he could take a very promising 1994 club and smash it to smithereens. Glass cut the team's payroll from $40.5 million to $27.6 million in 1995. Then, by 1996, he cut it to $18.5 million.[16] Gone was a team that was 64–51 at the time of the strike. Traded were 1994 Cy Young Award winner David Cone and the very skilled Brian McRae. Unsigned were free agents such as Tom "Flash" Gordon. And fired was the manager: Brian's father and Royals legend Hal McRae.

Glass had no competitive passion for what the 1994 Royals could have been. The general manager of that team, Herk Robinson, told the

Kansas City Star, "Who knows [what would have happened] if there'd been an owner who felt the emotion of what we were doing? Maybe then it's, 'Hey, let's bring everybody back.'"

"I was happy to go," said Brian McRae, "because I didn't think the organization was going to be worth a damn."[17]

For six years, from 1994 to 2000, Glass, as chairman of the board, cried to the press that he would sell the team, but there was no one who would do the charitable work of running a small-market club such as the Royals. The real charity began when Chairman Glass bought the team in 1999 over a competing bid by businessman Miles Prentice, even though Prentice's offer was reportedly 25 percent higher.

Then Glass made his first move as owner: making his son Daniel team president. Daniel's previous job experience was working at Wal-Mart. Clearly Glass's lack of sentiment for the McRae family didn't extend to his own brood. Family hookups are the Wal-Mart way for executives, not for workers.

The Wal-Mart way also was seen in the profits Glass pulled despite pleading poverty and small-market despair. *Forbes* magazine put Glass's annual profits from the Royals at more than $20 million.[18] That's also the Wal-Mart way, cutting corners to profit off a lousy product.

The taxpayer-financed renovations on the Royals' Kauffman Stadium mean that the franchise is now worth nearly double the $96 million that Glass paid for it in 2000. In 2006, by a 53 to 47 percent margin, both the Royals and the Kansas City Chiefs won a public referendum worth $425 million in stadium renovation subsidies. The slender margin of victory was courtesy of a ferocious PR campaign involving George Brett, Negro Leagues legend Buck O'Neill, and Chiefs Hall of Famer Marcus Allen. But the clincher was Glass arguing that without more sports bars and luxury boxes in Kauffman Stadium, the team would move.[19] Your money or your team. Taxes went up, and so did the Royals' profits. The team, however, stayed down.

This is also the Wal-Mart way. In addition to the more than $1.5 billion in federal government subsidies per year, the store chain also depends heavily on the U.S. taxpayer to pick up the slack for health care and child care costs for their underinsured/poverty-wage workers.

Also per the Wal-Mart way, the lower you were on the Royals' food chain, the worse you were treated. As Sam Mellinger of the *Kansas City Star* reported, "Minor-league teams struggled to get new uniforms or screens for batting practice. One year, the Royals ran out of money to sign draft picks after the sixth round. Other years, anybody taken after the fourth or fifth round was offered no more than $1,000."[20]

Glass also is not shy about his right-wing politics. He donates thousands of dollars to the Republican Party, including hard-right-wing pols such as Kansas senator Sam Brownback, a Republican flat taxer who opposes not only abortion but also contraception. It's hard to imagine that this kind of political support is what fans had in mind when they stuffed Glass's pockets with public subsidies. But alas, this also is the Wal-Mart way. In 1996, Wal-Mart execs gave 98 percent of contributions to Republicans. Since then, in either a dramatic political shift or a savvy display of public relations, executives gave only 52 percent to Republicans. But in 2008, the accusations flew that Wal-Mart managers were pressuring employees to vote for McCain.[21] They also have been accused of pushing their working-class customers and "associates" to support Republican candidates. The *Wall Street Journal* reported that Wal-Mart executives held mandatory meetings with store managers and department supervisors and warned that a Barack Obama win would mean more union rights, and more union rights would mean some sort of Armageddon.[22]

Glass has never hosted Sarah Palin Bobblehead Night, or anything of the sort, but he has overseen Faith Nights at the Park. It is an exercise in vertical management when Faith Night comes to town. General manager Dayton Moore is a member of the Fellowship of Christian Athletes. The new manager, Trey Hillman, says, "I knew there was a plan and a purpose, and for that plan and that purpose, I needed Christ. I made God a promise a long time ago, and that promise was, 'Give me an opportunity with a platform in professional baseball and I will never be hesitant, I will not be shy about professing my faith.' That's my job as a Christian."[23] But neither God, nor Christ, nor managers and general managers touched by the heavens can change a thing as long as ownership is by Wal-Mart. The Wal-Mart way works in retail, but it has wrecked a proud baseball franchise.

11. James Dolan: Serpent in Eden

All decisions at the Garden I make on my own.

—JAMES M. DOLAN

The dream is to have an owner who leads a winning team with grace and class. The Rooney family, who command the Pittsburgh Steelers, are the prototype. If you can't have the Rooneys, most fans would want a winning team even if the boss spits on the floor and only occasionally wears pants. Most would love to have a home team like the Lakers led by Dr. Jerry Buss winning with a kind of shabby Runyonesque sneer. After that there is the often imitated, rarely duplicated Steinbrenner model: win but feeling somewhat queasy about who is pulling the strings. Then we would have the lovable losers: the owner who genuinely cares about his or her community. The late Abe Pollin, who owned the Washington Wizards, presided over decades of futility, but people perceived him to be a person of dignity.

At the bottom of the food chain we have people such as James Dolan. Dolan is by all accounts a rager, a screamer, a narcissist, and someone who has helped create a work environment about as agreeable to women as a *Girls Gone Wild* video shoot.

"Jim actually doesn't care whether you love him or hate him, as long as you *know* him," says one former Madison Square Garden executive. "Why else does he sit in the very front row? Why else does he come in late? He wants everyone to know: *I am in charge.*"[1] What he is actually in charge of is another question.

·　　·　　·

In an ordered, sensible universe, the NBA team out of New York City would be America's Team. Basketball is the city game, and without New York, basketball might still be a game played with peach baskets. It was the city—through the Irish, Jews, and African-Americans—that took a game designed by Dr. James Naismith to give idle college students something to do over the winter and gave it a soul. The New York Knicks should be representing that soul at the professional level. Instead, they need an exorcist.

The team plays at Madison Square Garden, our hoops Eden, also known as "the World's Most Famous Arena." Like the Yankees and the Mets, they have financial resources that other teams in the NBA could only envy. But the Knicks are a nightmare. They have had eight straight seasons losing at least fifty games. They haven't been relevant in a dozen years. They have spent money like a coked-up 1980s stockbroker. They have been less a basketball team than a reality program, with a series of off-court incidents that put a proud franchise to shame. And for all of that, and then some, we can thank the man in charge, who in his own words makes every decision, James Dolan. But don't take my word for it. Commissioner David Stern, who would sooner shave his head with a cheese grater than criticize a resident of the owner's box, actually said of the Knicks, "they're not a model of intelligent management."[2]

James Dolan has taken that sacred strand that connects the team and the city and flossed his teeth with it. Count me among those who, even though it hurt like hell, have simply said, "Enough." The first Knick squad that captured me whole was in 1984, when number 30, the most underrated player of his generation, Bernard King, scored fifty points in consecutive games. Those King teams didn't win championships, but at least they had a sense of planned order. There was the steady point guard Rory Sparrow, the defensive stopper in Darrell Walker, and Bill Cartwright in the middle. They all revolved around the fierce will of King, a man whose turnaround release was so quick it looked like he was setting a volleyball. The team took the Celtics to seven games in the '84 playoffs, and the question of whether Bernard or Larry Bird was the better player was debated for two glorious weeks.

Ten years later, the Knicks made the finals. This was a bruising blue-collar team coached by Pat Riley. In an alternative universe, Riley led the showtime Lakers in the 1980s. Now he helmed a team that would proudly win 74–65. Winning ugly was a way of life. They were led by Patrick Ewing and Charles Oakley, two guys who couldn't hurdle a magazine. Their most dynamic player was John Starks, a shooting guard with a disturbing tendency to head-butt opponents. This was a team of survivors. In 1994, they survived both Reggie Miller's dazzling twenty-five-point fourth quarter, when he taunted Spike Lee, and the Jordan-less Bulls. They might have survived the Rockets in the finals, if the mercurial Starks hadn't gone 2 for 18 in game seven. This team was about as fun as watching an apple turn brown, but they had an identity. Now their identity is defined by feckless ownership.

Dolan came to run the Knicks because of the power of genetics. Dolan's father is the one and only Charles Dolan, the founder of Cablevision. Cablevision owns Madison Square Garden, and the teams that call it home, the New York Rangers and Knicks, therefore James Dolan had himself a job.

It's not just that the fifty-four-year-old Dolan is unqualified. James Dolan's early years were marked by drugs, alcohol abuse, and mug shots. He has said that his midthirties were "a festival. It was not a festival of love, it was a festival of self-abuse. Like any other alcoholic and chemically dependent person, every binge, every event, is a little more than the one before. To be honest, there are stories that I've heard that may be true, but I don't remember them."[3]

If he were poor, he'd probably be sitting in a prison cell serving a mandatory minimum.

But he's a Dolan, so he gets to run the Knicks. Operating the team seems like his father's version of boot camp for the wayward son: a way to teach him responsibility and the value of a dollar. If only he'd been given a paper route. Instead the team is run by a man named by *Sports Illustrated* as the worst owner in the NBA (and in a league with Donald Sterling, that takes some serious effort).[4] As S. L. Price of *Sports Illustrated* wrote, "The tales of Jim's drug-and-drink-addled past, his volcanic temper, his shifting moods, were already legendary, fueling the image of a spoiled boy who had been handed the keys to perhaps the most prized property in all of U.S. sports."[5] Dolan's demons, as he himself has said, stem from living in the specter of his übersuccessful father. The *Hollywood Reporter* wrote of

Cablevision that it is now "the North Korea of the cable business. No one understands what they are doing, but everybody is concerned."

Like a certain ex-president with youthful substance abuse issues and a desire to be bigger than Daddy, Dolan has turned Madison Square Garden into his own personal Baghdad. The owner's box may be his Green Zone, but the product is bombed out and depleted.

Becoming a Knick used to be a dream destination for free agents. But the last decade has seen some of the more dynamic players in the NBA sapped of their strength once they don the orange and royal blue. At one point under Dolan, they were starting two nearly identical shoot-first six-foot point guards, Stephon Marbury and Steve Francis. At another, they were starting two nearly identical tubby low-post big men allergic to salad, Zach Randolph and Eddy Curry. There was no sense to it. It got so bad in 2006 that Dolan had to formally deny he was mentally ill. "I believe in the plan, I believe in the strategy, I believe in the guys who are executing it. Maybe some people think I'm brain dead because of that and the record. But you know what? Time will tell."[6] But time has already told.

The Knicks at present are trying to dig their way out of this sporting hell with the help of the best coach and the best general manager money could buy: Mike D'Antoni and Donnie Walsh. Day by day that brave duo have attempted to pry the team from Dolan's financial and emotional death grip. They have been trying to remove an insane $410 million in contracts off the books and dump a current roster whose destiny is in the basketball witness protection program eating egg noodles with Henry Hill. For two dreadful years the plan has been to cut the flotsam and sign a marque free agent such as LeBron James or Dwyane Wade in the 2010 off-season. If D'Antoni and Walsh feel at times like they are shoveling sand in the ocean, the emotion is shared.

The list of James Dolan's offenses is longer than his father's shadow. They constitute a steaming bouillabaisse of incompetence and abuse, making Knick fans across the city glassy-eyed with stunned frustration.

There was the unceremonious firing in 2004 of Hall of Fame announcer Marv Albert, who Dolan believed was too critical of the Knicks for his tastes. Albert had been announcing Knick games since 1967, his voice spanning the eras from Willis Reed to Patrick Ewing. And he was gone.

There was Dolan's revolving door of coaches. He signed head coach Larry Brown to a five-year, $50 million deal in 2006 and then dropped the Hall of Famer after one season. Brown settled with Dolan for $18 million, which meant that the well-traveled coach made $28 million for one year of work. As former NBA player Steve Kerr said, "The only winner in this mess is Larry Brown's accountant."

Then there were head coaches Don Chaney (2001–2003) and Lenny Wilkens (2003–2005), both of whom are being paid years after termination. And, of course, there was the operatic drama of Dolan's codependent relationship with Isiah Thomas. Thomas, a former Detroit Piston point guard, was out of basketball, looking for any scrap of work and seemingly unhirable. The Hall of Famer had been tagged as the failed commissioner of the Continental Basketball Association, the failed general manager of the Toronto Raptors, and the failed head coach of the underachieving Indiana Pacers. Dolan looked at this résumé and inexplicably made Thomas the president of the most valuable basketball team in the world.

With Isiah in charge, there were a series of moves that were as baffling as they were enraging. These critiques aren't made in hindsight. In real time, writers, fans, even sports-radio hosts knew these moves were destined to fail. It didn't take Red Auerbach to know in 2004 that signing out-of-shape, three-hundred-pound center Vin Baker, whose previous contract, with the Celtics, was terminated for "violating the terms of his alcohol treatment program," wouldn't work. Thomas said, "I think we are catching him at a good and unique time in his life."[7] Perhaps Baker was in a better mental state. But he still averaged only 1.4 points per game in twenty-four games and was gone. Thomas (always with Dolan's approval) also signed rotund center Jerome James to a five-year $30 million free-agent contract after a season when he averaged 4.9 points and 3 rebounds a game. Any time you can give $30 million to a perpetually out-of-shape player nicknamed "Big Snacks," you just have to do it. Chris Mannix of *Sports Illustrated* wrote that the Knicks signing James "was a mistake before he ever took the court at Madison Square Garden. The day the Knicks announced his signing, they were universally panned by executives, experts, journalists—really anyone with a voice box."[8] He arrived at his first training camp in 2006 out of shape, and in his first season he averaged only 3.1 points and 2.1 rebounds in 9 minutes per game. In 2007–2008, James played two games and made $5.8 million.

Then, in 2005, the Thomas/Dolan team traded for the woefully out-of-shape and underachieving center Eddy Curry. When asked by a reporter in 2003 what Curry needed to do to become a better rebounder, his Chicago Bulls coach, Scott Skiles, simply replied, "jump."[9]

But Curry had potential that the Bulls were willing to gamble on until the team doctor discovered that his "genetic makeup leaves him susceptible to cardiomyopathy, a heart condition that, combined with arrhythmia, could prove fatal."[10] Anytime you can sign an underachieving player with heart troubles to a long-term contract, you have to do it. Then there was Zach Randolph. In 2007 they traded for Randolph, a player with a six-year, $84 million contract and a career as a malcontent. Randolph's high school coach once said, "I just don't want the day to come where I pick up that paper and it says [Zach] shot someone, or that he was shot. Every day that goes by that I don't see that, I feel good."[11] This experiment also failed, but the year after leaving New York, Randolph became an All-Star in Memphis.

In 2007 they also traded for a broken Steve Francis. In this deal, they gave up a sharp young player named Trevor Ariza. It cost $15 million. Then there was the drama of Stephon Marbury. Marbury, the wildly explosive and widely criticized point guard with a Q rating commensurate with a dog-fighting stockbroker, was ground to dust during his tenure in New York. In 2007, after learning that Dolan and Thomas wanted him out of the starting lineup, Marbury and Thomas actually came to blows on the team plane, and then Marbury said to the press, "Isiah has to start me. I've got so much shit on Isiah and he knows it. He thinks he can fuck me. But I'll fuck him first. You have no idea what I know."[12] In a proud Knick moment, it was the first public blackmailing of a coach in history. After Thomas was fired, D'Antoni and Walsh decided it was best to pay Marbury $20 million not to play.

The painful part of these stories is not just the signings. It's that the Knicks can afford this idiotic spending in part because they have the highest ticket prices in the NBA, forcing out the fans who bring the noise.

Going to a game in recent years has meant seeing more people texting on their various tech gadgets than watching the damn game.

Dolan's team management was noxious by any measure, but it's the embarrassment to the Knicks' name that should be grounds for expulsion. As mentioned in the Sterling saga, Commissioner Stern speaks often about accountability for off-court behavior for players while owners get a pass. This certainly proved true for Dolan, even when there was the little matter of sexual harassment.

Former Knicks vice president Anucha Browne Sanders walked out of a New York City courtroom in 2007 with $11.6 million in damages, winning a sexual harassment trial that made you want to delouse. The jury determined that Isiah Thomas and James Dolan created a workplace so toxic that Sanders simply couldn't do her job. Dolan then took the heroic step of firing Sanders for having the temerity to complain.[13]

You might expect Thomas and Dolan to show a measure of contrition after such a public flaying. But in the aftermath of the verdict Thomas said, "I want to say it as loud as I possibly can: I am innocent."[14]

Thomas wasn't nearly so eloquent in his trial testimony when he said to much fanfare, "A white male calling a black female a bitch is highly offensive. That would have violated my code of conduct." But as for a black male calling a black female a bitch, Thomas said it would bother him "not as much. I'm sorry to say, I do make a distinction."[15]

Dolan wasn't much better. In videotaped testimony, after much hedging, Dolan finally acknowledged that it was inappropriate for anyone to call a woman a "black bitch." Then he said with a shrug, "It is also not appropriate to murder anyone. I don't know that that happened, either."[16]

The drama caused many to make the entire case an issue about gender relations in the black community. Harvard sociologist Orlando Patterson wrote an op-ed in the *New York Times* that linked the Thomas/Sanders lawsuit to something symptomatic of a "social calamity" between black men and women defined by the "central role of unstable relations among the sexes and within poor families."[17]

But the Thomas/Sanders lawsuit is not an issue of social pathology. It's also certainly not an issue of poverty. It's men such as James Dolan and Isiah Thomas in positions of power creating an atmosphere for women that should be deemed entirely unacceptable. It's millionaires and billion-aires behaving badly. It also mirrored stories of Dolan's tenure as the head of his father's company, Cablevision.

"It was a boys' club, a boys' network, and the boys could do whatever they wanted to do," said Richard Saavedra, who worked at Cablevision for thirteen years between 1989 and 2002.

From the beginning, Dolan and Thomas attempted to paint Sanders as an incompetent, and her lawsuit as a craven grab for money. This didn't quite explain why they had promoted her to vice president and awarded her hefty bonuses on top of her $260,000 salary.

It didn't explain why Sanders, the highest-ranking African-American woman in the world of sports, would risk her position and promise of fu-ture millions on a lawsuit that will most likely result in her never finding hire in the league again.

It also didn't explain why Sanders, at age forty-four, would walk away from a job that on the surface, at least, was an absolute dream. At Northwestern University, Anucha Browne, as she was then known, was a basketball superstar. A three-time All Big Ten selection and two-time conference player of the year, she still holds the conference records in points and rebounds.

She was charting new ground for all women in the upper manage-ment strata of sports. Now those days are done. But Sanders may have done more good by raising awareness that sports is no longer a club for aging frat boys.

We need to be as brave as Sanders and challenge Dolan's authority. There is no reason why the world's worst owner should hold sway in the world's most famous arena. If there are Oedipal issues to be worked out, let that be done on a psychiatrist's couch. And let's make the Garden once again a place of honor and greatness, as it was before the serpent slithered in through the back door.

12. The NHL: Skating on Slush?

The National Hockey League may have some of the worst owners in sports. Granted, as of this writing the sport has to be feeling somewhat healthy. For the first time since the disastrous 2004–2005 lockout, the troubled league has increased both its attendance and its ratings.

"We're particularly pleased this year because the world around us is a lot different than it's been in a long time," said NHL deputy commissioner Bill Daly. "Most businesses would have reasons to be concerned about a downturn, and so far we haven't seen it."[1] Of course, when you're starting at zero, and literally there were games that garnered ratings of 0.0, the space for improvement is relative, but the NHL has genuine reason to cheer.

Ten of its thirty teams in the 2008–2009 season played at or near 100 percent capacity, including all six Canadian clubs, the Minnesota Wild, the Pittsburgh Penguins, the New York Rangers, and the Chicago Blackhawks. An outdoor January game between the Blackhawks and the Detroit Red Wings played at Wrigley Field in Chicago drew more than 4.4 million viewers, making it the most-viewed NHL regular-season game in thirty-four years.

A crop of young stars such as Alexander Ovetchkin and Sidney Crosby and the rise of high-def television, which allows people to actually follow the puck at home, have been godsends to the sport.

But the health can be illusory. As Richard Garner, former host of the Canadian sports talk show *Drive This,* said to me, "It's impossible to argue with revenue growth and franchise value increases. . . . But the moral of the recent economic story is that as quickly as things can grow, they can collapse even faster, especially if built on a faulty foundation. . . . And if you think that type of talk is alarmist or premature, ask the record industry how they're doing."[2]

While some markets have seen a recent rise in television ratings, other cities have seen hockey telecasts rank just above a test pattern. The Florida Panthers, for example, averaged a league-low 0.15 local rating.

The NHL also has fallen off the map in much of the United States, not with a bang but a whimper. The Phoenix Coyotes, despite being led by legend Wayne Gretzky, filed for bankruptcy, and the franchise is now a sporting "ward of the state" owned by the NHL. The league's difficulties should stand as a five-alarm warning to ownership groups in every major sport. If you abuse the fan base long enough, if you market your product with an eye on short-term gain instead of figuring out how to make your team a permanent part of the community, people will simply find something else to do. It's a shame, because hockey still is a great live sport. The hard-core fan base that comes to games is passionate in a way the bored yuppies at most NBA contests couldn't hope to match.

When I was growing up, we would have fierce school yard debates about the New York Rangers versus the Islanders, and whether the Islanders' "drive for five" consecutive championships was "barely alive." Today, the Islanders play in front of a nearly empty arena. In 2010, I don't know where kids would get in a playground scuffle over the NHL outside of Manitoba or maybe Detroit. While it's common currency to say that the league is in a healthy place, it's worth remembering that when the season was canceled in 2004 due to a lockout of the players, there were no peals of outrage. Unlike baseball's full-scale cancellation in 1994, no one claimed that the end of civilization was nigh. The opposite of love, in sports, if not life, is not hate but indifference. Hockey's cancellation met with a jarring reverberation of indifference. There was no outcry in the streets. There was no Million Hockey Fan March. Seventy-seven percent of *Canadians* said in a poll that if a lockout had to happen, then so be it.[3] Nationally televised NHL games were garnering a miserable 0.2 rating, just below anything on CNBC. "It's not a good sign when your replacement programming is outperforming the NHL," said one ESPN executive.[4] In short, the sport was a corpse. The National Hockey League owners took a terrifically exciting sport with reservoirs of support in the northern United States and Canada and turned it into something unrecognizable. The NHL's journey was starting to resemble De Niro's Jake La-Motta in *Raging Bull*. At the beginning he's rough around the edges, but also magnetic, lean, and lethal. By the end, he's a bulbous, repellent, gassy clown—a human car wreck. This—in all its ugliness—was the NHL.

As Travis Sedore, a fan, said to me, "For the record, the hockey played today in 2009 is great. The game should be changed in no way. It's the league itself that has, in a sense, lost its way. The league has been living in the shadow of the NBA, MLB, NFL, and I think the reason for that is the way the NHL has been managed. I don't like to use absolute statements, but I feel that the NHL has tried to copy the other leagues, both in the number of teams and emphasis on the United States market. I feel that the NHL should have traveled its own path instead of expanding to an excessive amount of teams."[5]

Their road to Armageddon began when ownership hired a slick NBA marketing whiz named Gary Bettman to be their commissioner. Bettman boasted that he had never set foot in an NHL arena, but knew how to "grow" the sport. Unfortunately he also knew zero about hockey, probably thinking Guy Lafleur was a Montreal-based escort service. Bettman took one look at this blue-collar league built on the backs of hardscrabble French Canadians, toothless grins, and rabid fans, and recoiled. He examined its base in northern deindustrializing cities and shook his head at the absence of short-term revenue streams. He saw the future of ice hockey and, unfathomably, saw Dixie. Bettman expanded the league to thirty teams, putting the sport in places such as Nashville, Atlanta, Raleigh, and, of course, Phoenix. NHL owners sat back and collected hundreds of millions of dollars in expansion fees, giving out fat contracts along the way, with no thought to the long-term consequences.

Predictably, these new revenue streams were barely wading pools. The big national TV contract Bettman promised never came, and the NHL was left with unknowable new teams with names such as the Hurricanes, Coyotes, and Predators playing in half-empty arenas. Today, while the Canadian teams, as mentioned, operate at or near full capacity, Bettman and the owners never realized that now defunct hockey towns such as Winnipeg and Quebec were part of the league's appeal. The NHL was selling a culture as much as a sport. Of the five places with the lowest attendance, four of them are the Columbus Blue Jackets, Atlanta Thrashers, Nashville Predators, and Phoenix Coyotes.[6] All are part of the southern strategy. There is too much product, too many periods, too much hockey. When I asked hockey *fans* what they would change about the league, the most common answer was a call for a shorter season and less teams.

As sportswriter Dan Wetzel put it, "There is no denying that under [Bettman's] stewardship the NHL has been run into the grave. The league has been mismanaged, misplaced, overexpanded and overpriced, all because Bettman turned his back on the core fans—believing there was a pot of television and corporate [fool's] gold at the end of the small market rainbow."[7]

The money wasn't there. Attendance, which accounted for 80 percent of revenues, was down. The new territory was showing as much chance of success as an ice rink in hell. None of this was helped by a defense-oriented style of play that limited scoring to historic lows. Bettman, who didn't know a hockey puck from a sausage patty, was clueless on how to tweak the rules to present a more exciting, offensive-minded product. As *Sports Illustrated* pointed out, the top-scoring team in 2003–2004 would have ranked twenty-first in 1985–1986.

Instead of taking a hard but necessary look at their product, the owners chose to take their crisis out of the players' hides. Even though in 2004 the union offered an unheard-of 24 percent pay cut across the board to save the season, this was not enough.[8] The owners decided to risk the league on what is called a "hard cap." A "hard cap" is when owners decry the evil—for the first time in their lives—of the free market and demand external restraints on their ability to spend. This is a hypocrisy players had every right to stand against. Why should there be a cap on what owners can pay them? This would be unacceptable to the owners and their ilk in every other walk of life. We don't see a hard cap on executive Wall Street bonuses or the price of a computer or a gallon of milk. When it comes to our spending, we get credit cards, interest rates, and the right to bankruptcy court. They, like owners in every sport, want formal limitations on what players can earn. It was a transparent effort to collectively bargain their way out of a crisis of their own making.

NHL union chief Bob Goodenow caved on the hard cap in the end, to the anger of many players, but it still wasn't enough to save the season. Bettman snubbed him, more concerned with making sure the season stayed canceled than saving it with an eleventh-hour deal. Why not? After all, several owners said that the sport was bleeding so much cash, they actually lose less money with the game shuttered than if they were paying salaries. Caring nothing for the tradition of the game, owners from the Deep South to Buffalo made clear that they would sooner rent out their arenas for Toby Keith concerts and monster truck shows than nurture the sport back to health.

The poor state of the NHL was further revealed during the labor stoppage when a coven of Boston businessmen offered to buy the entire league, down to the last Zamboni, for $3 billion. In the language of the megarich, their $3 billion offer is the equivalent of saying that the league is worth little more than a carton of fried rice and a pack of Kools.

But the great humiliation was not so much the offer. It's the fact that NHL commissioner Gary Bettman felt like he had to take it seriously. "We felt we should hear them out," said a Bettman spokesperson. This was a definitive statement that the NHL, once one of the Big Four North American sports along with the NFL, the NBA, and Major League Baseball, was on a tier with indoor soccer and box lacrosse. Bettman's NHL limps not only behind the aforementioned Big Three but also NASCAR, men's and women's college basketball, college football, and the Westminster Dog Show. A terrier with a silicone snout had more star power than anyone in Bettman's locked-out, shut-down, sclerotic NHL. Even the now canceled Arena Football League was more popular.

In the past three seasons, young players Alexander Ovetchkin and Sidney Crosby have been trying gamely to turn it around. We will see if individual stars can overcome leaguewide incompetence.

As sports economist Andrew Zimbalist said, "What [the $3 billion offer] does say is that there are people out there that see much more potential and value in hockey if the league is run properly. They think the asset value of the franchises has been so depreciated by mismanagement and the lockout that there's an opportunity to get a bargain."[9]

To make matters worse, Bettman publicly threatened permanent replacement players as well.[10] Yes, the one thing that could have saved the NHL, in Bettman's mind, was scab hockey.

The scab suggestion signified that Bettman had been in the Sunbelt too long. Using scab players would in fact have violated Canadian labor law, where unionists are protected against job loss while on strike or locked out. This would have made games in places such as Montreal, Toronto, and Vancouver the site of picket line combat and a potential legal nightmare. Also, while U.S. workers have no such labor protection, the key cradles of U.S. hockey—union towns such as Detroit, Chicago, Philly, and Pittsburgh—don't take kindly to picket line crossers.

As Al Strachan of the *Toronto Sun* wrote about the prospect of scab hockey, "It's a desperate step, a virtual legal minefield, but [Bettman] has no choice now. He promised too many owners a hard cap [mandatory spending limits on players to make up for budget problems rooted in overexpansion], and he is backed into a corner. If the owners think replacement players will restore credibility to their sport, they have been misled. It will only make the NHL more of a travesty than it is already."[11]

The game may have emerged with a better foundation without scabs, but all the problems remain: a bloated league with too many teams that thinks marketing Sarah Palin is the road back to relevance. If Ovetchkin and Crosby can save the league, they deserve to be named Sportsmen of the Century. The greater lesson to draw from the NHL, though, is one that the NBA, Major League Baseball, and even the NFL should take to heart: sports leagues don't necessarily end with a bang. They can die slowly with little more than a whimper. Like an accordion wheezing out its last note, pro sports as we know it will limp to a close unless ownership asserts leadership in the interest of the games over profits. If that means fewer games, or if that means fan ownership of failing clubs, then that should be on the table. Otherwise, the Phoenix Coyotes won't be the only team that sees bankruptcy court as a suitable option.

13. The Unholy Gall
of the Paulsons

*We're talking hundreds of billions. This needs to be big enough to
make a real difference and get at the heart of the problem.*

—FORMER TREASURY SECRETARY HENRY PAULSON

I n the United States, politicians drill into our heads that these are
tough economic times, and tough times mean we have to do more
with less. But as any teacher, nurse, or Gus from *The Wire* can tell
you, you don't do more with less. You do less with less. But thanks to
Henry Paulson, we know that while there were no funds for evicted families, crumbling schools, or hospitals, there is cash aplenty for bailing out
his compadres on Wall Street. The swan song of the Bush presidency was
Paulson's securing $700 billion in tax money to save investment houses
on Wall Street.

It's socialism on crack, a world where we collectivize debt and priva-
tize profit—call it the Paulson doctrine. While the bank bailouts have extended into the reign of Paulson's Goldman Sachs brethren Tim Geithner
and Larry Summers and the Obama administration, it was King Henry
who showed us that as long as there are toxic assets to buy, there will be
tax money to spend. It's an economic model that shocked many Americans already in debt and trying to figure out what makes an asset "toxic."
But in sports, we have seen these bizarre economics play out for a generation. It is, as we discussed earlier, stadium politics on a national scale:
you take public money and through a magical alchemy taught in Harvard
Business School and the Goldman Sachs boardroom, transform it into

private profit. Paulson may have learned the way of the athletic industrial complex not at Goldman Sachs, but at his family dinner table.

Like father, like son. Meet Merritt Paulson, the Harvard M.B.A. off-spring of Henry Paulson. Merritt is in fact his actual given name. I suppose if Henry had named his son "Legacy" it would have been too blunt.

The thirty-six-year-old Merritt owns the Portland (Oregon) Beavers, a minor league baseball team, and the Portland Timbers, a United Soccer League First Division squad. At the same moment his father was demanding $700 billion of our money to bail out banks, Merritt was agitating for his own little piece of the action. He embarked on a public campaign for $85 million in public funds from the City of Portland to build a new sports complex for the Beavers and an upgrade on the Timbers' stadium ($85 million is called, among Portlanders, "the Liars Club estimate").

Merritt is not the sole owner of the Beavers and the Timbers; he has only an 80 percent stake. The man with the other 20 percent stake is—wait for it—his father, Hammerin' Hank. If you can keep the bile out of your mouth for a moment, you have to give the Paulson family credit for unholy gall. You can almost imagine the scene: the Paulsons sitting around the dinner table, munching on bald eagle pâté, and wondering, "What's $85 million more?" The Paulsons' proposal has them paying rent for the facilities but coughing up not one solitary dime for construction.[1] And as the Lerners of Washington, D.C., showed us, rent for these folks is a fungible entity.

We haven't seen a family of rustlers like this since Frank and Jesse James. Keep in mind that Hank Paulson is worth $700 million on his own (he just loves that 700 number). So forget the obscenity of any sports owner having the temerity to ask for public funds for a sports stadium at a time when families are seeing their homes foreclosed across the country while we are bailing out banks across the nation. Forget the lunacy of making the case that you need $85 million from a city that, despite its lush rose gardens and microbreweries, has 16 percent of all its children living below the poverty line. Forget that Portland General Electric (PGE), the local utility company whose sponsorship blares from the side of PGE Park where the Timbers play, is paying its former CEO Peggy Fowler a whopping $11 million parting package as she rides off into the corporate sunset. Forget all humanitarian and economic considerations. Ponder that the Paulsons could easily pick up the tab themselves in partnership with PGE, whose net income in 2007 was a cool $145 million.[2] Surely PGE could help cover the stadium renovations for the Timbers and at the same time finally live up to the stadium naming rights they're currently getting on the cheap (about $1 million a year). But that's just not how they do business. These aren't masters of industry. They're grifters.

Merritt Paulson has laid the groundwork for this budget grab by trying to present himself, in the best liberal Portland tradition, as a community-minded idealist with a belief in local responsibility. (This is a city where even the airport can only have stores that are local businesses—although one of those "local" businesses is a Beavertown, Oregon, cobbler known as Nike.)

In an interview with a popular sports business site called Biz of Baseball, Merritt said, "I think sports is such a unique vehicle in terms of being able to shine light on areas of the community that could use the help. It's something that everybody relates to. I think that players getting out and making appearances and using the media attention that follows them to really focus on areas that could use a lot of public support—that's terrific, and it's not all about money."[3]

He also, as the glowing puff piece made clear, gave $10,000 to the local Little League. This is a very modest investment if you have $85 million in public funds as an ultimate goal.

Of course, Merritt makes the case that such a public expenditure would be economic steroids for the community. But that's not holding water, not even with die-hard local fans. As Jules Boykoff, a professor at Pacific University, former pro soccer player, and a Portland Timbers fanatic who brings his six-year-old daughter to the games, wrote in the *Oregonian*,

> More jobs? Economic development? Sounds great! The only problem is that it's not true.... This plea comes from someone who loves soccer: I played college ball at the University of Portland, professionally for the Portland Pride, and was fortunate enough to play on the U.S. Olympic team in international competition. And I would love for Major League Soccer to come to Portland. But it's unfair to have working people and their families pay for the venture when

the already cloudy economic future is anything but a sure bet. If Merritt Paulson's affection for Portland is real—and I'm willing to give him the benefit of the doubt that it is—it's time for him to step up and put his money where his mouth is. Should he do so . . . my daughter and I will be the first in line to buy season tickets.[4]

I think there are many others like Boykoff who will happily support their local sports teams but don't want to feel like suckers in the bargain. Economic times are rough. Working people across the country are being forced to step up to save the financial system. It's time for Merritt Paulson to do the same.

The fact that there is no logical reason to support Paulson hasn't stopped support from the press. Columnist Anna Griffin is tragically typical in how the media will pretzel itself to defend the indefensible: "We shouldn't use urban-renewal money to improve PGE Park. We shouldn't be adding to the city's debt when essential services face cuts. Guys rich enough to buy professional sports teams should pay for their own pretty new ballparks," she writes.[5]

"Yet at the end of the day, as much as it pains me to admit this, Portland leaders should say yes. Not because soccer is the world's biggest sport. Not even because city commissioner Randy Leonard, apparently our de facto mayor these scandalous days, wants it. Put plainly: This town needs more people like Merritt Paulson. A reality check for those of us who don't care a whit about soccer: Major League Baseball and the National Football League aren't coming to Portland, at least not until a few *Fortune* 500 companies relocate this way. In other words, not in this lifetime. Instead, the city's economy—the financial engine for the entire state—will rest on the shoulders of small-business owners in sustainable industries who are willing and financially able to take risks. People like Paulson."

It's enough to make you want to hammer nails with your forehead. The great risk takers at work here are the taxpayers of Portland. And as for the argument that Portland is too small for an NFL team, we should look at Green Bay and what it takes to actually bind a team to a community. It means elevating more than sports. Adam Sanchez, a worker at Portland's famous Powell's Bookstore, showed more courage than the city leaders ready to hand the money over without complaint. He wrote in the *Orego-*

nian, "If the Paulsons want new stadiums for the sports teams they own, they should pay for them themselves, just like the bankers should be paying for this crisis. But if they insist on begging for money from Portland taxpayers, we should get voting shares in return. Portlanders should have a say on where the profit generated from those stadiums will go. Because if we did, we could use the money to keep our schools open and to create public works projects that would create jobs instead of lining the pockets of the Paulson family with more of our money. Portlanders voted for change in November, but the Paulsons want more of the same."[6]

14. For a Few Steroids More

Angry Cleveland Indians Fans Demand Team Take Steroids.
—ANDY BOROWITZ, *THE HUFFINGTON POST*

When you press fans about what disgusts them about sports, they invariably speak about steroids and performance-enhancing drugs. The frustration ranges from the understandable to the irrational. Players are cheaters. Sports has become pro wrestling. We are just rooting for the team with the better biochemist. And Barry Bonds might be at least a distant cousin to Satan.

But wherever one may fall on the question of performance enhancers, there continues to be an unasked question: where do the owners fit into the anabolic agonistes? As we wring our hands in anguish, there is no investigation or even discussion in the mainstream press of their accountability. I was on ESPN as a proud yipping head debating "who is at fault?" for the steroid soap opera that annually threatens to smother Major League Baseball. Fans were then asked to vote online for whom to blame. The choices were "players," "the union," or "the commissioner."

This is like telling the story of *Star Wars* and leaving out Darth Vader. Nowhere is the question asked, What did owners know and when did they know it?

In February 2005 MLB commissioner Bud Selig said about steroids, "I [had] never heard about it."[1] The problem with that argument is that it strains credulity to the breaking point. As sportswriter D. K. Wilson wrote, "General managers know if a player reported to spring training at 185 one season and 215 the next and whether that newly added 30 pounds was fat or muscle, or a combination of both. As does the team owner."[2]

The issue of performance-enhancing drugs had been discussed at Major League Baseball's winter ownership meetings dating back to 1988.[3] Selig at the time owned the Milwaukee Brewers. Assuming he was awake at these meetings, Selig would have heard the warnings of former Cleveland Indians trainer Brent Starr. "Here's the thing that really bothers me," Starr said in 2007. "They sit there, meaning the commissioner's office, Bud Selig and that group, and the Players' Association, Don Fehr and that group . . . they sit there and say, 'Well, now that we know that this happened we're going to do something about it.'

"I have notes from the Winter Meetings where the owners' group and the Players' Association sat in meetings with the team physicians and team trainers. I was there. And team physicians stood up and said, 'Look, we need to do something about this. We've got a problem here if we don't do something about it.' That was in 1988."[4]

Sportswriter Stew Winkel was even more pointed about the selective amnesia on display. "I would compare that to a parent who walks into the kitchen, sees paint all over the refrigerator, sees a child covered in paint, but believes it when the child says, 'It wasn't me.' . . . Selig's failure to act for years, until forced to, means one of three things—either he is too stupid to notice what was going on in the sport he was trying to run, he knew and just didn't care, or he knew, cared, but decided not to act because more home runs and more strikeouts meant more money. All are unacceptable."[5]

At best we are talking about a case of benign neglect and at worst, malignant intent. As one player said to me, "The problem with steroids is that punishment is an individual issue but distribution is a team issue."[6]

Not to sugarcoat the issue, but Major League Baseball's steroid policy is hypocritical, idiotic, and altogether morally bankrupt. It's also rooted not in Selig's dumbfounding ignorance or even in a backroom conspiracy, but in the owners' greed. The juicing of the game began in earnest in 1994, when a players' strike mutated into an owners' lockout that led to the cancellation of the World Series. The game's popularity had sunk to historic lows. Then the muscles started growing and the bucks along with it. Owners milked the new powerball to the hilt and used cartoons of freakishly muscled players as part of ad campaigns. They also embraced the puckishly sexist slogan coined by Nike, "Chicks Dig the Long Ball." Increased offense and media buzz meant increased revenue. In 1995, with the sport on life support, MLB sold their broadcast rights for $565 million, which represented a major loss. By 2001 they sold the playoff rights alone for $2 billion.[7]

Balls were flying over the fence at a record, ungodly pace. It was far more pervasive than the heavily promoted Mark McGwire/Sammy Sosa home run chase in 1998, when both players broke Roger Maris's thirty-seven-year record of sixty-one home runs. Consider that between 1876 and 1994, a player had hit fifty or more home runs eighteen times. From 1995 to 2002 it was done another eighteen times. Slap hitters were hitting twenty homers. Twenty-home-run guys were up to thirty. The idea that owners and GMs "dug the long ball" while leaving the very conditioning of players to themselves simply strains belief.

But that's why you get former Senate majority leader and Boston Red Sox board member George Mitchell to issue the Major League Baseball–sanctioned "Mitchell Report" on steroids. Sanctioned by Commissioner Bud Selig's office, the Mitchell Report was seen by some as an unprecedented act in sports: a $20 million internal investigation aimed at rooting "performance-enhancing drugs and human growth hormones" out of the game. Mitchell's much-lauded report, while criticizing both baseball owners and the union for being "slow to act," was a sanctimonious fraud, absolving those at the top and pinning blame on a motley crew of retired players, trainers, and clubhouse attendants. It was truly the old saw of the magical fishing net that captures minnows but lets the whales swim free.

The Mitchell Report certainly contained a great deal of sexy sizzle. First and foremost, it named names, including former MVPs Mo Vaughn and Miguel Tejada as well as All-Stars like Eric Gagne and Lenny Dykstra. It also names a man being called the Moby Dick to Mitchell's Ahab: seven-time Cy Young Award winner Roger Clemens. For some time, people in the game whispered about Clemens being on the juice. And the few times he was asked, Clemens denied all charges, as a compliant media lapped it up.

As Dan Wetzel wrote, "Year after year he peddled the same garbage, Roger Clemens was so dominant for so long because he simply outworked everyone. It played to the nation's Puritan roots, made Clemens out to be this everyman maximizing his skills through singular focus, dedication and a commitment to eating his spinach. It's all gone now, the legend of Rocket Roger dead on arrival of the Mitchell Report; one of the greatest pitchers of all time, his seven Cy Youngs and 354 career victories lost to history under a pile of lies and syringes."[8]

The Mitchell Report confirmed not only suspicions about Clemens, but also the existence of an outrageous media bias and double standard. While seven-time MVP Barry Bonds was raked over the conjecture coals for years, Clemens got a pass. Two players, both dominant into their forties, one black and one white, with two entirely different ways of being treated. It doesn't take Al Sharpton to do the cultural calculus. And yet, flaying Clemens shouldn't excuse the gross whitewash at work.

There were three fundamental problems with the Mitchell Report:

1. Mitchell himself. George Mitchell, the former Senate majority leader best known for helping negotiate the peace deal in Northern Ireland, has a massive conflict of interest when it comes to baseball. The man is on the boards of both the Boston Red Sox and the Walt Disney Company. The Disney Company owns ESPN, baseball's number one broadcast partner. Joe Morgan has spoken out about how in the 1990s, ESPN execs encouraged him not to state his suspicions about steroid use on the air. As Morgan said, "I would be broadcasting a game and there would be players hitting balls in a way that they had no business hitting them."[9]

   As for Red Sox Nation, the two most prominent players from the Red Sox championship team of 2004 have since tested positive: David Ortiz and Manny Ramirez. But magically, neither was mentioned in the report.

2. No testimony from players. The only active player to speak to Mitchell was then New York Yankee Jason Giambi, and he spoke under threat of suspension. Mitchell says he invited the accused, those named as dirty, to come clear their names, but no one took him up on this generous offer. If you were an MLB player, why would you come forward to legitimize a process in which you wouldn't even have the opportunity to face your accuser? This is a process where Mitchell was judge, jury, and executioner. The Mitchell Report ruined reputations, and the essential "truth" of the report is still based on hearsay.

3. Same old story. Mitchell paid lip service in his press conference to "slow-acting" owners—calling it "a collective failure." At one point, Mitchell said—without explanation—that baseball execs were slow due to "economic motives." Yet the overarching narrative is that the owners and general managers were merely ignorant or obtuse, with a complete absence of malice. The real fault lay with players and independent-acting clubhouse attendants, such as Mets clubhouse worker Kirk Radomski, who says he secured the juice for players and named names. Radomski was described by former Mets GM Steve Phillips on ESPN as "the guy who would pick up the towels or pick up a player's girlfriend from the airport." Yes, Kirk Radomski, a regular Pablo Escobar.

Mitchell went on to say that players have actively and on their own made great efforts to foil the owners' poorly organized efforts to clean up the game. This is the same kind of political cover that the mainstream press gave the Bush administration on Iraq. Errors made are just well-meaning people with good intentions who had to make difficult choices. Those who suffered from these choices are blamed for their backwardness. When Baghdad was looted and destroyed, Iraqis were pilloried for their greed. Rumsfeld, Bush, and Cheney were critiqued for being "overly optimistic" and "trusting them too much."

This is poppycock, whether we're talking about the Bush cabal or Major League Baseball owners. This is the way people in power stay in power during times of crisis: take some heat, blame the underlings, cry some tears, and call it a day. Now baseball has a setup akin to water torture, thanks to the Players' Association. Once arguably the most powerful union in the United States, the MLBPA has in its possession the infamous list of the 104 players who tested positive in 2003. That year a deal between the owners and the union was supposed to be based on anonymity and trust. If more than 5 percent of the players tested dirty, more testing, with suspensions, would ensue. The union promised its members that it would destroy the list. Instead it inexplicably held on to all the names long enough for the government to seize it as part of the Bay Area Lab Company (BALCO) investigations into steroid distribution. This has made the union look terrible. As one fan, Dorsey White, wrote me, "The recent divulging of a list of over one hundred names that was to have been destroyed months or years ago, illustrates the evil that is the players association. . . . All of the owners of major league teams said yes to the billions of dollars generated by these players who engaged in this activity . . . yet, when the day of reckoning came to pass, the white hankie of innocence was waved and the blame was selectively laid on the players to take the heat for the league . . . the sanctimonious sacrifice to cleanse the mantle of Major League Baseball."[10]

The big kahuna implicated in the list leak was the man known as A-Rod, Alex Rodriguez. The three-time MVP and owner of the largest contract in team sports history, $275 million over the next nine years, was on the magic list. The flamethrowers at the *New York Post* summed up the mood of the moment with one blaring headline: "A-FRAUD." ESPN senior writer Jayson Stark was no less overwrought; his headline proclaimed, "A-ROD HAS DESTROYED GAME'S HISTORY."[11] When it comes to steroids, no one, as A-Rod's alleged paramour Madonna might say, is like a virgin. Before we gather the torches and pitchforks, let us round up some of the real villains. For instance, there's MLB commissioner Bud Selig, who touted A-Rod as the man who would replace the "unclean" Barry Bonds as the all-time leader in home runs.

New York City mayor Michael Bloomberg and the Steinbrenner family certainly have anabolic egg on their faces. They were depending on A-Rod to be the cherry atop the sundae of the new $1 billion Yankee Stadium. Finally, there are the owners at large, who have yet to face any kind of congressional subcommittee, grand jury, or operatic media melodrama for their role in cheapening the sport. Stark, in his piece blaming A-Rod for shredding the very fabric of baseball history, writes, "In baseball, we love our numbers. And we love our heroes. And that brings us to Alex Rodriguez, a man who has committed a crime he doesn't even understand: a crime against the once-proud history of his sport."[12] But Stark ignores two key points. The first is that every hallowed statistic in baseball is deeply flawed. The only time I have ever agreed with Bud Selig was when he once said, "There is no such thing as an era in baseball without taint."

Every record set before 1947 was achieved under the shadow of segregation. And baseball's major leagues didn't fully integrate until 1959.

The period of segregation was always known as the "gentleman's agreement." There was never any formal rule, never any paper trail. It was just done. The "steroid era" has a similar echo. If we are upset about the way numbers and hallowed records have become cheapened over the past fifteen years, ownership is the problem—and it extends far beyond steroids.

Owners actually had a multifaceted strategy to make baseball more like beer-league softball—and it was about as subtle as a tabloid's back page. As baseball writer Bob Klapisch said, "Somewhere someone decided that baseball needed more runs. It was made at a very fundamental level. And little by little, step by step, this became the new reality. There has been too much to write it off as coincidence."[13]

The reasons for the home-run boom extend far beyond the steroid dealer. The boom reverberates in every urban budget, every underfunded school, and every library that closes early. It's in the rash of cozy, publicly funded ballparks. The shorter fences at these parks are engineered to yield more home runs. They are supposed to be fan-friendly—that is, unless your child happens to go to a public school whose budgets paid for the tab.

Then there are the balls and bats. Countless baseball insiders believe that the ball is now wound tighter than it was twenty years ago. As for the bats, as recently as fifteen years ago, players used untreated ash bats. Now the bats are maple and lacquered for a cleaner crack of the bat.

Then there is the strike zone. The area where a pitched ball can be called a strike has shrunk, in the words of former Atlanta general manager John Schuerholz, to "the size of a postage stamp."[14] The owners consciously engineered this trend toward the microscopic strike zone. When umpires refused to agree to a uniform strike zone, Major League Baseball crushed their union and installed a machine to monitor their abilities. Hall of Fame pitcher Jim Palmer has said that the loss of the high strike "has changed the game more than any pill."[15]

But an equally big reason why home-run numbers are up is that the game finally shed its nineteenth-century view of strength conditioning. The training standard until the 1990s was that if Joe "Ducky" Medwick didn't do it in the 1930s, then it shouldn't be done. For example, it has been the conventional wisdom for most of baseball's history that weight lifting would destroy your swing. Many teams even fined or suspended players if they were caught pumping iron. Weight lifting is now as much a part of every team's regimen as shagging fly balls.

Yes, Alex Rodriguez was torn to pieces by columnists, fans, and the sports radio blabbocracy. Yet as soon as he started hitting homers in the 2009 playoffs, it became a memory. That's what owners count upon: our own short-term memory. But other than the revelations that A-Rod has a portrait of himself as a centaur over his bed—sorry, just threw up—he hardly deserves our scorn. Reserve that for the owners, political leaders, and Bud the commissioner—who robbed our cities blind and distracted us with dingers so we wouldn't notice.

15. "What's a Scouser?" Tom Hicks Goes European

We work real hard not to get an attitude of arrogance or haughtiness, which you see in this business all the time.

—TOM HICKS SR.

P retend for a moment that you are Tom Hicks Jr. Your father, Tom Hicks, is a billionaire, worth, according to *Forbes* magazine, a cool $1.3 billion. He is that twenty-first-century master of the universe, the Texas billionaire.

He's also the owner of the Texas Rangers, the National Hockey League's Dallas Stars, and half owner of the English football (soccer) club Liverpool FC. Granted, your dad hasn't always had the Midas touch. He did head the committee to get former New York mayor Rudolph Giuliani elected president (the most money spent for the fewest primary delegates in American political history). He also gave former Texas Ranger shortstop Alex Rodriguez $252 million over ten years to lead the Rangers to last place, only to sell his contract to the Yankees at a mammoth loss. But other than those minor league snafus, to be a Hicks is to lead a charmed life. Your dad has actually made you a "director" of the Liverpool club, and now you are making your first visit to see this strange land of Liverpudlians (or, as they are known, "Scousers," a name derived from a local stew).

You may be a director of this treasured club with a fiercely loyal fan base, but in the end, you are a tourist from Texas who happens to share a name with the franchise boss.

You proudly strut among the Scousers, in the working-class town that gave us the Beatles, and think not without some justification that you are the man in charge. You may know that the team is nicknamed the "Reds." You may not know that the team is seen throughout the league as openly "socialistic" because the fans really do believe that they have first claim over the club, no matter whose name in on the title.

You walk into the famed, cacophonous fan hangout known as Sandon Pub located near your team's Anfield Stadium, but not before snapping some photographs of the pub's exterior and some locals. And besides, there is nothing Europeans like more than posing for candid photos taken by Americans. You then enter the pub feeling fine, excited, as you say later, to engage in some "direct talk with some of the supporters."[1]

You feel especially confident that you will be greeted with flowers and sweets because Liverpool had just beaten Middlesbrough, 3–2. In Texas, winning ranks just behind breathing and slightly ahead of chewing. Surely that will translate across the pond. You have arrived a conquering hero. You make a big show of entering the pub amid a phalanx of bodyguards, who won't be an obstacle to that "direct talk" you crave. You are Joaquin Phoenix in *Gladiator*. You rule the roost by grace of bloodlines. It's your team. You hope the gratitude coming your way isn't too sloppy.

Then the unexpected occurs. *Liverpool Echo* reporter Tony Barrett was right there in Sandon and witnessed what happened next: "As his bodyguards got closer one fan swilled Hicks junior with a pint of lager— and given the price of a pint in the Sandon after the match that's quite a protest. Another spat in his direction."[2]

Yes, the son of the owner of the beloved Liverpool FC had beer poured on his head and was spat upon—and after a Premier League victory, no less. Spit and beer. Not exactly candy and sweets. Hicks Jr. later said, "I did have several constructive conversations in my short visit and look forward to following up with them next time I am in Liverpool."[3] He will probably need an umbrella and a raincoat for the follow-up, for there was no bonhomie in the suds and saliva. This wasn't a Liverpudlian male bonding ritual. It happened because Junior forgot, in the words of one Liverpool FC–loving blogger, "that his father is the most hated man in Liverpool."[4]

It happened because of who his namesake is, and what he represents to the die-hard fans of Liverpool. It happened because of the exporting of American-style ownership into the field of European football. In U.S. sports, the owner is the man on the throne, looking out from the owner's box like a modern Caesar. U.S. fans are far more likely to complain about players than an owner. They are more likely to be angered by an athlete's salary than the price of tickets, or the profit margins on an $8 hot dog. U.S. owners expect to be treated like they are life's great winners and they are allowing fans to join their party. It's an approach that has not served Tom Hicks Jr. well, and the response by the Reds to his clumsy management has allowed the fans of Liverpool to chart a map for fans to follow the world over, but especially in the United States. It's a story of fans organizing and asserting their moral and historic will over the so-called ownership.

It started on February 6, 2007. It was almost exactly a year to the day after Liverpool's greatest triumph, beating archrival Manchester United 1–0 in the Football Association Challenge Cup, the oldest soccer tournament in the world. Liverpool's win over their hated rival was their first in eighty-five years of Cup play. Life was good. With Hicks Sr. buying the club along with his friend George N. Gillett Jr., some fans thought it would get even better. American—even Texan—ownership wasn't seen as an automatic negative.

Hicks and Gillett bought Liverpool FC for $432 million, borrowing the money against assets of the club, making Liverpool the third English Premier League team to be bought by U.S. businessmen. And yet there was little uproar upon the immediate takeover, certainly nothing to suggest that the progeny would find himself bathed in beer.

As British journalist Dave Renton said to me, "At first thought this is striking: the most 'socialist' football team in Britain was bought by people with no history of supporting it, no connection to the sport, and no proclaimed motive other than capital accumulation—and there was no protest."[5]

This is especially stunning because just a scant eighteen months earlier, there was a fan revolt that received international attention when the Florida-based Glazer family, owners of the NFL's Tampa Bay Buccaneers, bought Manchester United.

But in some ways, according to locals, the Man U purchase made it far easier for Hicks to be initially accepted. It was now a given that such a previously unheard-of phenomenon—a wealthy Yank buying a precious FC—was in fact possible. Also, the provincial rivalry against Man U meant that many Scousers didn't want to "copy" their hated rivals with their own knee-jerk protest movement. There was the cold truth that Liverpool was in financial straits. European fans are perpetually conscious, if not obsessive, about the financial health of their clubs. But the most important difference was that the Glazer family borrowed money immediately against Manchester United to buy the team, putting the club in serious debt. Hicks and Gillett promised they wouldn't do this, even though they did end up financing the purchase in just this manner.[6]

It can't be overstated how harmful this was to their standing in the community. Following the money management of a franchise is to Britain what fantasy sports and statistical obsession are in the United States. It was thought by the Red amateur accountants that a Texas billionaire could supply the filthy lucre to put Liverpool over the top, or at the very least help it stay in the game.

Shaun Harkin, a Liverpool FC fan and former professional player in the Irish leagues told me, "We initially had almost a TINA approach to the sale. We thought, 'There is No Alternative.' All of the other top clubs were being bought by billionaires and this was seen as the sad price of success, of getting back to the pre-1990 winning ways and restoring dignity to the team and city. Silence, however, doesn't equal agreement."[7]

It helped that upon buying the club, Hicks and Gillett Jr. tried—like Clay Bennett in Seattle—to say all the right things. They promised to break ground for a new stadium within sixty days. They issued a buffed-to-a-shine statement that hit on all the right notes: "Liverpool is a fantastic club with a remarkable history and a passionate fan base. We fully acknowledge and appreciate the unique heritage and rich history of Liverpool and intend to respect this heritage in the future. The Hicks family and the Gillett family are extremely excited about continuing the club's legacy and tradition."[8]

And yet there is little to suggest that Hicks or Gillett knew anything whatsoever about the history of Liverpool FC, a history so sprawling and intense you would need Tolstoy to do it justice.

Dr. Grant Farred wrote a book called *Long Distance Love* about how he became a Liverpool obsessive from his hometown in Capetown, South Africa. After speaking the solemn catechism that Liverpool FC is "truly God's gift to football," he said to me, "The club has been massively successful, and part of its success is founded on a very intimate and close relationship and proprietary relationship between the Scousers and the club. So the fans have a deep, deep interest. When they say Liverpool FC is my team, my club, they're not just saying that in a kind of explanatory way. But there is a very real bond between the club and the city, the people who live there."[9]

It's this bond that makes fans in Liverpool feel a sense of ownership over the progress of their team. When fans tell stories about the five championships and nineteen league titles, they speak in the first person plural. They are a "we." Their revered late coach Bill Shankly would say of the fans, "They can suck the ball right into the goal by sheer will power."[10]

But Hicks and Gillett were like tourists walking around Vegas, fanning themselves with $50 bills: the clueless and the vulgar. Gillett admitted as much in 2009 to a Canadian radio station when he said, "It was really amazing . . . it's just shocking how popular Liverpool [FC] is. So it surprised me."[11]

Some token research, or even an undercover trip to Sandon's without a team of bodyguards, perhaps could have cushioned the North American owners (Gillett is Canadian) to the shock.

The team dates back to 1892. They were, from their inception, an outsider squad, fielding a crew of Scotsmen who were able to win against their English opponents. They were even called the team of the "Macs," since many of their players had, in the Scottish tradition, the prefix "Mac" connected to their names.[12] They were William Wallace on the pitch, the redheaded stepchildren, calloused and even somewhat dangerous, and they wore it proudly.

The stadium, like most British soccer stadiums, was in the heart of the working-class section of the city, among the council houses, an organic part of the neighborhood.

Back then, the crowds cheering on their Reds were as orderly as ushers at Sunday Mass. It's hard to believe now, but to look at old footage is to see working-class crowds dressed to the nines for game day. The flags, the cheers, the songs, and the booze that make up the modern soccer audience were not part of the action.

That changed in the early 1960s, and, according to historians of the game, the first team to make that great leap into fanaticism was Liverpool. Some of this was linked to the conditions—the very soil of Liverpool—that gave the world the Beatles: an alienated feeling of frustration at gray, industrial life and the desire for a primal scream of relief. It also was linked to the arrival of the most storied name in the history of Liverpool FC, manager Bill Shankly.

Shankly arrived in 1959 and started Liverpool on a streak of success that continued almost without interruption until 1990. In this period Liverpool FC established itself as the most successful football club in the country's history. As Shankly was fond of saying, "Football is not a matter of life and death. It's much more important than that."[13]

Journalist Dave Renton spoke to me about how Shankly transformed the character of the Liverpool fan base. "Liverpool fans have all sorts of ideas to explain what sets us apart. It starts in the 1960s when Shankly built more than a team: he built a social organization. Through the 1960s and 1970s, the largest single employer in Liverpool was the docks followed by the car industry. The people watching football were very largely dockers and their children. Many were also recent immigrants from southern Ireland. In this same period, along with Glasgow, Newcastle, and London, Liverpool was the city that saw the most strikes. Between 1967 and 1969, there were seven times as many strikes in Liverpool than in Britain as a whole. As well as the building of Shankly's football club, this is also this period in which Liverpool earned its cultural association with industrial militancy."[14]

Shankly joyfully channeled that militancy into fandom for his team. He once said, "The socialism I believe in is everyone working for each other, everyone having a share of the rewards. It's the way I see football. It's the way I see life."[15] He also said of soccer: "Train the right way, work hard for each other. It's a form of socialism without the politics."[16]

In the 1965 FA Cup Final at Wembley Stadium, a policeman's horse trampled a Liverpool fan's scarf. Shankly pushed the horse and the policeman aside and said, "You don't ever show that kind of disrespect to a Liverpool scarf. That's somebody's life, son."[17]

The team and the labor movement were the dual pillars of pride that sustained Liverpool through hard times. But the 1980s would deal both the industrial base of the city and the team terrible, near mortal, blows.

Heysel and Hillsborough

Located in Brussels, Heysel Stadium was a decrepit wreck of a structure. By 1985 it was simply an accident waiting to happen. Enter the Reds.

Liverpool FC was facing off against the Italian team Juventus for the European Cup championship. A group of Liverpool fans, with neo-Nazi skinheads infiltrating their ranks, charged through a thin police line to brawl with the Juventus supporters. It was an ugly melee, with families caught in the middle. It also was not that uncommon in the U.K. soccer world. Prime Minister Margaret Thatcher had even set up a "war cabinet" to combat soccer hooliganism. But to brawl in crumbling Heysel Stadium was to invite tragedy. A wall collapsed and thirty-nine people were killed, thirty-eight of them Juventus fans.[18]

The disaster, called "the day football died," was put at the feet of Liverpool and the "thug culture" that pervaded the fan clubs across the country. There was no patience for examining whether the aging stadium itself was unsafe. It was easier, and cheaper, to blame the thugs. The UEFA (Union of European Football Associations) made the unprecedented move of banning all English teams from European competition until 1990.

The unspeakable Heysel tragedy and cheap scapegoating that followed were not even the worst calamities to befall Liverpool FC in the 1980s. It could get worse. And it did.

In 1989 the Heysel tragedy was exceeded by what is known as the Hillsborough disaster. Hillsborough is the home of another storied British club, this one residing in the industrial town of Sheffield. On April 15, 1989, hundreds of Liverpool fans were crushed against Hillsborough's perimeter fencing. Ninety-six people were killed, with 766 more injured. The photos of fans trying to avoid suffocation against the steel guardrails would haunt the hardest of hearts. It was the deadliest stadium disaster in the history of the sport.[19] A report after the fact put the blame on police and stadium security for not organizing the flow of people more effectively. In the aftermath, England quietly changed the layout of their stadiums to be "all-seaters," no more free standing room, to avoid a repeat of the stampede tragedy. That didn't stop columnists from going on a rampage about the "savagery" of fans who were likened to "animals."[20] Rupert Murdoch's *Sun* newspapers led this charge, with an infamous and immediate declaration that alcohol was the primary reason for the deaths. An informal boycott of all things Murdoch exists in Liverpool to this day. The British political class, both Tory and Labour, have since chosen to ignore the pleas for justice and closure from the families of the ninety-six dead. They have done so at their peril.

At the twentieth anniversary of the Hillsborough disaster, in 2009, thirty thousand Scousers gathered in silent tribute as the names of the dead were read. But the crowd turned raucous when Prime Minister Gordon Brown's minister of sport, Andy Burnham, rose to speak. He quickly discovered that no one wanted a politician on the premises.

As soon as Burnham expressed that he was there to bring a message from the prime minister, he was drowned out by boos. Burnham had the microphone, but thirty thousand people were chanting, "Justice for the ninety-six."[21]

When he paid tribute to the Hillsborough families, they chanted, "Hypocrite!" When he reasserted "Today I represent the PM and the government," the response was, "Fuck off Gordon Brown!"[22]

What amplifies the tragedies of Heysel and Hillsborough for fans is that they took place as Liverpool's economy was getting crushed under the weight of Tory prime minister Margaret Thatcher's draconian cuts to social services and and her equally severe attacks on the trade unions. It was tragedy on top of misery. Early under Thatcher's reign, in 1981, there were riots in the Liverpool community of Toxteth, but it was a rage against the dying light of a once-thriving industrial town. Many of Thatcher's cuts were beaten back, but most were not. These two aspects of Liverpool identity—soccer and industrial struggle—entered the 1990s on life support, with only intermittent prospects of revival.

If there was one moment in the 1990s that brought the worlds together with a sense of the old joy, it was due to a player named Robbie Fowler. Fowler, a Liverpudlian, had fulfilled the Scouser dream of becoming a star player for his hometown team. He never forgot those roots. In March 1997, while a Liverpool dockers' strike raged outside the arena, Fowler raised his soccer shirt on the pitch to show he was wearing a solidarity T-shirt underneath. He was joined by teammate Steve McManaman. The fans loved it, and the league fined him the equivalent of $2,000.[23]

Fowler's moment of courage and confidence helped signal a new moment—if not for the city, then the team. A dynamic new manager, Rafa Benitez, helped bring Liverpool FC back to its feet and earned the fierce gratitude of Reds the world over.

The point of relaying this incredible odyssey of tragedy and resilience is to make clear that Tom Hicks bought a team with more scar tissue than a battalion of boxers. Liverpool is an emotional ecosystem with a delicate balance of history, tragedy, and resilience that has sustained an entire city. It's them against the world. What Hicks did not understand is that he was the world. The billionaire was in over his head.

The problems for Hicks started soon after he bought the club. In the United Kingdom, fans actually expected his word to be his bond. Hicks promised to break ground for a new stadium within sixty days, but the ground remained firm. When pressed for comment, Hicks stonewalled the press and the fans. That kind of American arrogance was about as welcome as Euro Disney.

In November 2007, Hicks and Gillett engaged in a very public spat with the beloved Benitez. In a press conference, when asked about his relationship with the owners, Benitez simply answered, "As always, I am focused on coaching and training my team." He then gave this precise answer twenty-five consecutive times.[24]

Benitez undertook this act of performance art because Hicks and Gillett were treating him like the hired help. It was later revealed that when he pressed Hicks and Gillett about his personnel, he was told by Hicks to "shut up and coach."[25]

The Texas Ranger then took this tense situation, and rather than defuse it, brought out the blowtorch. It was "leaked" to the press—in classic Steinbrennerian fashion—that he had held two meetings with German soccer legend Jurgen Klinsmann, whom Hicks had met while on a skiing vacation. There were rumors that Rafa would be out on his ear. When the media pressed Hicks on his German flirtation, he said merely, "He's an impressive man."[26]

For fans this was like someone driving on the wrong side of the road. In response, *EPL [English Premier League] Talk*, the most widely read Premier League blog in the world, posted an article titled, "Why Hicks & Gillett Are Giving Americans a Bad Name."[27]

The blogging Scouser wrote, "This decision by Hicks to blurt out the [meetings with Klinsmann] to the *Liverpool Echo* newspaper, the paper that many Liverpudlians read, was inane. . . . Unfortunately, it's another dagger that Brits can use to pierce Americans with. They can use it as the perfect example of how 'Americans' don't understand football."[28]

Hicks, coming from the United States, where baseball managers are as expendable as a soiled Kleenex, seemed baffled by what he unleashed. In November 2007, as fans feared that Rafa was not long for Liverpool, thousands took to the streets before a win over FC Porto to raise their voices in protest. They chanted Rafa's name, held banners, and even produced placards with their coach bearing an unmistakable likeness to Che Guevara. They also produced an immense framed picture of their coach, proclaiming him as the "Rafatollah." Others proclaimed that they were leading a "Rafalution."[29]

As all this drama played out, that new promised stadium was still a figment of ownership imagination. Hicks finally had to comment on the broken promise, saying that the global credit crunch "no one could have anticipated" was causing him to cease all projects in Texas and Liverpool.[30] But the financial problems of a billionaire didn't exactly pluck Scouser heartstrings.

Liverpool Supporters Club secretary Les Lawson responded, "When Hicks took over . . . he said a spade would go into the ground at Stanley Park within sixty days; eighteen months on we are still waiting. . . . If the Americans can't finance the club and what it needs to get back to the top they should make way for someone who can."[31]

If British soccer fans have difficulty abiding mendacity and arrogance, incompetence might be an even greater sin. As Hicks started to feel a torrent of criticism, his partner and "great friend" George Gillett said on a radio station back in Canada, "We get as many as two thousand e-mails a week. Ninety-five percent of them have been directed at some of the comments made by my partner. The thing that angers fans the most is the prospect I might sell even one share of my stock to my partner." He spoke of the death threats received by him and his family and pointed his finger not at those issuing the threats but at Hicks himself.

"Frankly, I don't think it's fair for me to put my family in that kind of danger," Gillett said. "So, instead of thinking about selling, I might think about buying [out Hicks]. . . . This partnership has been unworkable for some time."³²

Gillett even attempted to sell 98 percent of his interest last year, but Hicks blocked the transfer. This has led fans to see Hicks as the primary culprit, a profiteering pirate with little or no interest in the fans,

As one longtime fan said to me, "I don't think that Hicks got that Liverpool has never been about making money. Liverpool's a modest club in a poor city, peopled by working-class folk. You have to act with a certain kind of modesty, and most important, humor, and you also have to be able to muster the same amount, if not a greater amount, of passion. And Hicks has never, at any moment, given himself over to that team. This is the thing about Texans, right? It's a place big on everything except self-deprecation. I mean have you heard Texans laugh at themselves? If you wear cowboy boots and a pair of Levi's or Wranglers that are three sizes too small and crotch-hugging, how can you not laugh at yourself?"³³

Connected to this cultural alienation, fans also were feeling priced out of the game. Peter Hooten, who does the public relations for Save Our Scousers, said, "The first game I went to in 1983 cost me seventy-five pence. A game I went to this season cost thirty-five pounds."

It's not the feverish community passion that Hicks and Gillett want. It's the thirty-five-pound ticket multiplied by the forty-five thousand who attend every game.

This is an absolute mess. But unlike fans of the Pittsburgh Pirates or Kansas City Royals, where locals are choosing to turn the channel (an effective albeit passive response to chronic mismanagement), the fans are now striking back. There is an organization called Share Liverpool FC that is attempting to recruit a hundred thousand shareholders to purchase the team outright from Hicks and Gillett. The two bosses deny that they are selling but have, according to the *Times* of London, contacted a broker at Merrill Lynch to facilitate the process.³⁴ In an open letter to Hicks and Gillett, Share Liverpool cites the Green Bay Packers as their working example of community ownership. They take Shankly's dictum of "everyone having a share of the rewards" very seriously. They write,

> We understand you have decided to relinquish your ownership of
> Liverpool FC and are actively looking for a buyer. Along with the

vast majority of Liverpool fans, we agree with your decision to with-draw. We would like to buy the club on behalf of the fans, and invite you to sit down with us to agree to a deal. We are confident that if you're willing to sell to us for a fair price, we would have sufficient backing [either from the fans alone, or with a suitable partner]. We want the club we love run solely in the best interests of a successful team, the fans and the community. We believe we represent a real opportunity for both of you to bring to an end a troubled period of ownership; an "exit strategy" which would lead to admiration and respect from many.

Doing the honourable thing and selling the club to the fans would return it to the values that made it the most successful foot-ball club in England and one of the best supported in the world.[35]

The people of Share Liverpool aren't alone in organizing to make Hicks's British sojourn a difficult one. In January 2008, 350 Liverpool fans crammed into that same Sandon pub where Hicks Jr. would find himself doused, and announced the formation of the country's first Football Sup-porters Union. In their founding statement, they wrote,

"If we stand together and speak with one voice, regardless of language or accent, we can make a genuine difference to our football club, the city of Liverpool and indeed the wider footballing world."[36] The new union was spearheaded by a fan group called the "Sons of Shankly." They have since held a series of spirited demonstrations that, for the U.S. sports fan, needs to be YouTubed to be believed.

In September 2008, four thousand supporters marched in the streets of Liverpool. They called for a national boycott of the Royal Bank of Scot-land if it extended Hicks and Gillett any more credit. What is particularly fascinating is that all of this has made its way back to Tom Hicks's home ground in Dallas, where in 2008, the Texas Rangers wrapped up yet an-other dispirited season. The Dallas Observer wrote acidly, "Thousands of Liverpool FC fans took to the streets on Saturday night to protest Tom Hicks' ownership of their beloved, beleaguered team—four thousand folks, by some counts, or the same number of people expected to turn out total for Texas Rangers home games between now and the season's blessed end."[37]

The buzz was so intense, George Gillett himself had to meet and do a personal sit-down with the wild-eyed Sons of Shankly. But the SOS didn't budge. In their comments later about the meeting, they said, "We also reminded him that we, as a union, wanted both himself and Tom Hicks to sell up and leave."

The *Dallas Observer* chimed in again, "Alas, looks like they're stuck with Hicks. Aren't we all."[38]

Hicks is a terrific example of making an owner fear the fans, instead of fans fearing the next move of the owner. He thought he was getting a piece of one of the most valuable sports "brands" in the world. Instead he finds himself confronted with "Reds" under every bed. As Grant Farred said to me, "[Being a Liverpool FC fan is] the ultimate act of love, which is to say to make yourself vulnerable in the face of possible defeat. It's to take on the history of tragedy and triumph. And unless you can do that, unless you can effectively give yourself entirely to this club, you will never know what it means to be a Liverpool fan. They may be the owner of Liverpool Football Club, but they will never own Liverpool Football Club. It belongs to a history, to a people, who understand pain, tragedy, triumph, and the small joys in life, as well as its many devastations. Unless you can do that, unless you can sink yourself into that history, and commit yourself to it fully, vulnerably, you have no right to call yourself the owner of Liverpool Football Club."[39]

There are protests, there are efforts to collectivize the team, and there is a culture that seethes with impatience from the promises of ownership. Liverpool is in many respects showing us the way. Fandom doesn't have to be a slouching, passive exercise and club supporters the world over don't need to just meekly consume whatever thin gruel the owners serve.

Outro: Looking Toward Green Bay

I just love it that the team is not owned by some rich guy.

—GREEN BAY RESIDENT DEBBIE KENYON[1]

T here still may exist those owners who see community first and profit margins second, but on the whole, today's generation of team CEOs have irrevocably damaged the world of professional sports. I have friends who can name the entire starting lineup and bench of the 1991 Pittsburgh Pirates but couldn't tell you one player on their 2010 roster.

Teams have been hemorrhaging money even in advance of today's recession realities, and more fans, and most perilously, the children of fans, are voting with their feet. If we want to reclaim sports in all its wicked glory, we need to make demands about how we expect our teams to be run. We need a fans bill of rights that lays out a few basic bare minimum expectations from ownership.

- We should have the right to withhold tax money for a stadium unless a public advocate is added to a team's board of directors.
- We should have the right to demand not salary caps but salary floors in every league so owners are bound to put a competitive product on the field.
- We should have the right to take our families to a game without worrying about having to tap into little Janey's college fund.
- We should have the right to publicly question owners about how they

are running the team. That includes opposing their use of the team as a platform for their political pet projects. No more Keyser Sozes in the ownership box!

- We should have the right to see the death of the blackout rule in football so we can see our local football team every week, no matter the attendance at the games.
- And most important, there is simply no place on Earth that an American beer should either cost $8 or be served to us in a public restroom.

If owners can't fulfill these basic tasks, then states should have the option of buying them out and turning both team and stadium into public enterprises. Governments enforce "eminent domain" laws when they need to get us out of our homes to clear space for stadiums. We should have the right to impose "eminent domain" on them. Fans should be organized to buy shares of a club and keep it rooted and affordable in the city it calls home, regardless of the vicissitudes of the economy.

This may sound like a far-fetched fantasyland, where fan ownership and inexpensive beer exist just to the left of Lollipop Fields. But this is the reality in the small city of Green Bay, Wisconsin, a place that delivers good beer, better cheese, clean public restrooms, and cleaner business practices.

In Green Bay, a city of about 100,000 people also known as Titletown, there is an ownership structure for their beloved Packers that needs to be at the heart of a debate from sports radio to city council meetings across the country. It is the only publicly owned, not-for-profit, major professional team in the United States. The Pack have operated under this structure since August 18, 1923.

The Packers were named for both Green Bay's cheese packers and its manufacturing workers. Now fans wear large Styrofoam cheeses on their heads as a memory of those days past. (They also wear large Styrofoam cheeses on their heads because, as a fan told me, "It's frickin' Wisconsin. It's what we do.")

The team was skating perilously close to bankruptcy in the 1920s until the community stepped in and reorganized the franchise into a nonprofit entity, selling shares in the team to the community at large. Volunteers from local charities today work home-game concessions with 60 percent of concessions, 60 percent of every last foam cheese head, going to charity.[2]

A total of 4,750,934 shares are owned by 112,015 stockholders, not a single one of whom receives any dividend on the initial investment. Those who own stock in the Packers get nothing more for their money than a piece of paper suitable for framing. These stockholders reside throughout all fifty states, plus Guam and the U.S. Virgin Islands. More than sixty thousand of the new shares sold during the 1997–1998 offering were purchased by residents of the state of Wisconsin. An unpaid board of directors and a seven-member executive committee govern the corporation. To protect against any single person making a power grab and taking control of the team, the articles of incorporation prohibit any person from owning more than two hundred thousand shares. As Pat Vance, a Packers fan who lives in Dubuque, Iowa, commented on this altogether unique ownership structure to *Mother Jones* magazine, "Every dollar they make on football they put back into the community and into football. No one is skimming money off the top."[3]

Another Wisconsin native, Jesse Zarley, voiced a similar vote of confidence to me: "The important thing is that they can never move. Because it's publicly owned, the Packers can't ever pack their bags and leave the State of Wisconsin. That's the beauty of it. An owner can't extort concessions from local communities. There's no greedy owner demanding new stadiums with public funds who can move if he's turned down."[4]

It is a story as remarkable as it is underdiscussed. In an era defined by free agency and an oft-abused salary cap, one of the dominant modern teams in football has not only survived but also thrived. The team has sold out its 72,928 seats well into the foreseeable future, with 50,000 people still on the waiting list. Season tickets have been fought over by children in court when a parent dies, and divorces have led to pitched battle over who gets the seats.

The nonprofit team is financially solvent, competitive, and deeply connected to the community. It has created something beautiful: a throwback that is also forward-looking. It deserves to be replicated. So, of course, the NFL has it written into the rulebook that no way, nohow, can any community replicate the Green Bay model.

The late NFL commissioner Pete Rozelle, in 1960, wrote into the league's constitution that no one could ever again "nonprofitize" their team. According to Article V, Section 4:

(a) New members must pledge that their organization is primarily for the purpose of operating a football team.

(b) Charitable organizations and/or corporations not organized for profit and not now a member of the league may not hold membership in the National Football League.

(c) All stockholders in a corporation or persons owning any interest in a franchise in the National Football League must be approved by a ten-twelfths (10/12) vote and any transfer of stock or of any interest in a franchise must also be approved by a ten-twelfths (10/12) vote of the membership.

(d) If any stockholder or holder of an interest in a league franchise violates this provision, said stockholder or the holder of the interest involved must sell or dispose of his stock or his interest in a National Football League club within thirty (30) days. The price and terms of such sale or disposition shall be fixed by two arbitrators, one of whom shall be chosen by the league member and the other by the stockholder or the holder of the interest involved. If said arbitrators fail to reach agreement on the price or terms then the two arbitrators shall select a third arbitrator and the decision of the majority of said arbitrators shall be binding on both parties. (This provision shall not take effect until January 28, 1960.)

In other words, beneath the legalese, Green Bay must simply never, ever happen again. Even if you buy a team and as an act of goodwill try on your deathbed to bequeath your $1 billion franchise to your hometown, you will find yourself wheeled into court on a gurney.

Interestingly, the league declared this constitutional decree at the same time it adopted sports' first revenue-sharing plan, distributing all sales of tickets, gear, and all revenue from merchandise, television, and gate receipts equally among teams. This collectivizing of the wealth, which made small-market teams viable, is why the team in Green Bay is able to compete. But imagine if Rust Belt cities such as Gary, Indiana;

Akron, Ohio; or Decatur, Illinois (original home of the Chicago Bears, when they were the Decatur Staleys), were permitted to practice community ownership. Pro football franchises could have turned the Rust Belt into a cordon of Titletowns. But there is no money in keeping teams as a public service in a community, even if it does work.

David Meggyesy, the recently retired NFL Players' Association western regional director, said to me, "As we understand it, *the players are the game,* and in the same way, NFL football and its thirty-two teams belong to the communities that support them. The Green Bay Packers are a shining example of how successful a community-owned team can be."[5]

Major League Baseball also has banned community ownership, even though it is not in the bylaws. As the *American Prospect* reported, "In the 1980s when Joan Kroc, widow of McDonald's founder Ray Kroc, offered to donate the Padres to San Diego along with $100 million to cover operating expenses, the owners nixed the idea. Bud Selig, baseball's current acting commissioner—who as owner of the Milwaukee Brewers coerced Wisconsinites into building him a new stadium—has vowed to kill any community ownership proposal because it would be an 'awkward' arrangement for the league."[6]

It is always awkward when profit, held as sacred, becomes inconvenient. In the NFL's case, community ownership would work for the same reason that revenue sharing works. It gives teams a chance to compete on a more level field. Otherwise you get Major League Baseball and the permanent financial inequality that allows the Yankees to be an empire unto itself.

From the perspective of NFL commissioner Roger Goodell and the thirty-one owners, the move to keep the ban on nonprofit ownership makes logical sense beyond the obvious point that nonprofits aren't great for profits. If a team isn't publicly traded, its books remain closed and protected by antitrust laws. Teams can continue to cry poverty and demand subsidies. It also would take the power away from owners to move clubs and break hearts.

If the Sonics were publicly owned, David Stern and Clay Bennett wouldn't have been able to break the lease at the Key Arena and smuggle the team to Oklahoma.

If the Washington Redskins were publicly owned, the team wouldn't be sacrificing its financial health by signing wintry free agents or serving us bathroom beer. If the Philadelphia Flyers were publicly owned, Sarah Palin wouldn't have a captive audience. If the Baltimore Orioles were publicly owned, the fans could have a say in restoring the Oriole way. If the L.A. Clippers were publicly owned, Donald Sterling could devote his attention full-time to evictions and hookers.

As one of the fans I spoke with, Yuseph from Montreal, said to me, "Why can't they be public? I live in Montreal, and I always joke around with my buddies that the province should take over the Habs [the NHL's Montreal Canadiens]. I mean, it would be a cash cow just like Hydro-Quebec or the liquor board."[7] Perhaps Yuseph doesn't see the downside to this. You don't get a rich guy to kick around in the papers. You do get a team not just connected but also bonded to the community.

The people who own shares of the Packers don't make a dime, no matter how successful the team is. Even executive committee members buy their own tickets to games. The Packers have been sold out at home for an astounding eighteen years. These aren't fake sellouts, as in Redskins land, but real, live fans trying to will their team to victory.

Brad Knapp, a Green Bay resident, said, "This is not some corporate team. They are not going to pick up and leave." He then commented on a recent bond issue passed to make improvements to Lambeau Field. "You know all that money they raised? It wasn't for a new stadium. It was to improve the old stadium. That building is going to stay right here, and so are the Packers."[8]

Another resident, Carole Tising, said, "This team is owned by the people, and that will never happen again."[9] Tising's point was echoed in a discussion I had with a member of the Packers' board of directors, Rick Chernick, who expressed doubts that other communities could do what the Packers do. They are an exception, he believed, not an example. "I'm just not sure in today's day and age a team could follow the Packer way," he said. "The cost of ownership is a ton today, thus being almost an impossible task without deep pockets. Green Bay is truly a special, special situation that started many years ago. It is owned by the community and shareholders around the country. It's a pretty neat deal we have but truly a worry if the salary and other costs continue to accelerate. The Packers belong to the people, and that's a wonderful thing!"[10]

Chernick makes a good point. But there is a strong counterargument as well. It may be exorbitantly expensive to run a team, but team owners don't run their squads as a civic service. There is money in being an owner. The television contracts alone run in the billions. The new 2006–2011 contracts for the National Football League are valued at approximately $3 billion annually, $800 million more than the previous broadcast agreements. In addition, the NFL has recently signed a contract with News Corp's DirecTV for about $700 million per year through the 2010 season. It seems that while Green Bay is a "special situation," it doesn't need to be.

Even if we take Chernick's point to heart, one thing is absolutely certain: if we want our teams to endure as living, breathing parts of our cities, then we need to make more demands on ownership. As consumer advocate Ralph Nader said to me, "In any tax-supported sports facility, the fans should become shareholders because they're taxpayers. The stadium and ballpark should be called 'Taxpayer Stadium,' not some sold-off brand name, or some bank, or computer company. More important than that, there should be organized fans' groups that can sit at the table. Anything that intersects public policy with the sports teams, the fans have got to have representatives at the table."[11] We all have an interest, players and fans, in making sure that sports owners are forced to be more accountable to the public. As All-Pro NFL player Adalius Thomas said, "If you want to cry about money, then open your books up to an independent audit to really show how much money you're making. If you really want to cry about money, open your books up [and] put what you really make in the paper like you have put our salary in the paper every year so the fans can say, 'They're making this much money. Why aren't they doing this?' "[12]

Robert McChesney, author of *The Death and Life of American Journalism* and a student of the political economy of sports, said to me,

When one evaluates the evidence, it seems obvious that local or community ownership of some kind is the most rational way for a professional sports team (and league) to be organized. The University of North Carolina cannot shake down people around the nation to get a better deal and move to wherever it can get the best deal, like, say, South Florida. Why should a sports team built upon the support and love of generations in a community be permitted to do so to enhance the profits of some greedy and egotistical hot-head who may have only recently inherited or purchased the team? Profits and sports are an unholy marriage. The Dodgers should have never left Brooklyn, the Colts Baltimore, the Sonics Seattle, and on and on. Sports teams and leagues should be nonprofit entities, likely a monopoly, a public utility of sorts. That way the massive public investments in infrastructure always benefit the community. It also means that the hearts of millions of sports fans who dearly love their local teams cannot be broken by callous owners who play franchise hopscotch, and season tickets need not necessarily cost a mint. And it rids our nation of this most worthless and parasitic class of varmints—sports team owners. Let these guys go on reality TV shows with the likes of Donald Trump [a former sports team owner himself] to get their rocks off. Maybe they could mud-wrestle each other or have a cookie-baking contest or see who can gain the most weight in three days. Just leave our treasured sports teams alone. If some existing sports team owner is really good at the job—and there are a few who fit that description—he or she can possibly earn a position with the new community-owned team. Otherwise, take a hike.[13]

Take a hike is right. Whether you love sports or not, this question of reclaiming the games is far bigger than just the sports page. It's a question of fighting for the future. We all have a stake in breaking the passive pose of the fan. We all have a stake in demanding that our local owners live up to the dreams their teams inspire. There's a time to cheer and a time to seethe. We all have a stake in knowing the difference.

Acknowledgments

There is no way I write this book without the ideas and input of Colin Robinson, formerly of Scribner and currently at O/R Press. Colin looked at an outline/collage of half-baked ideas and helped me find a book.

There's also no book without the work of the fantastic Anna deVries and Brant Rumble at Scribner. Anna is the Mariano Rivera of *Bad Sports*: the closer. Many thanks to William Drennan as well.

But I don't even get the chance to put pen to page without the people from Haymarket Books and the New Press. Thanks to Julie Fain, Anthony Arnove, and Sarah Macaraeg at Haymarket. And thank you to Ellen Adler, Diane Wachtel, Anne Sullivan, and Marc Favreau at the New Press.

Much appreciation to Andy Shallal, Don Allen, and Pam Pinnock at Busboys and Poets and Mike G at Politics and Prose in Washington, D.C.

There also are several books that helped immeasurably with this project, particularly *Onward Christian Soldiers* by Tom Krattenmaker, *Field of Schemes* by Neil deMause and Joanna Cagan, and *Steinbrenner* by the late, great Dick Schaap. The writing, sports and otherwise, of D. K. Wilson, Patrick Range McDonald, Jules Boykoff, and Frank Lidz also proved invaluable to the final product.

These are the people who keep me happily employed: Susan Price, Lang Whitaker, and Ben Osbourne at *SLAM*, Matt Rothschild at *The Progressive*, Katrina vanden Heuvel, Peter Rothberg, Emily Douglas, and Adam Howard at *The Nation*, and at Washington Post Live, Ivan Carter, Scott Taylor, and Manda Gross.

Then there are the folks at *Edge of Sports Radio*: Jeremiah Tittle on the wheels of steel, Boston Pete Koury, Ari B, Ivy Armstrong, Glen Younis,

Matt Fishman, COACH Kevin McNutt, and the folks at Left Jab: Mark Walsh, David and Mike Goodfriend.

And I would be remiss if I didn't shout to Mike Gentile, Sarah Meehan, and Aaron Bronester at Hardcore Sports Radio.

Thanks also to my agent, Scott Waxman, for making the deal. The best is yet to come.

There are current and former athletes who have kept me grounded in my thinking about sports: Etan Thomas, Scott Fujita, Dave Meggyesy, Jim Bouton, and last but miles from least, Dr. John Carlos.

There are sportswriters who have been beyond generous: Kevin Blackistone, Christine Brennan, Will Leitch, Jeremy Schaap, David Steele, Scoop Jackson, Jemele Hill, and Michael O'Keeffe.

But it's family, blood and otherwise, that endured the lunacy that goes into writing something like this: My partner Michele, my wonderful kids Sasha and Jacob. The dream team. Also my mother, Jane, my father, Jim, thanks for the ceaseless and unconditional support.

All my love to my sister, Annie, my brother-in-law, Jason, and their amazing children, Amira and Izzy. Also love to Marlene, Peter, Maggie, Michael, and Gus! And infinite thanks to Ed, Susan, Bryan, Denise, Chris, Meme, and Pop Pop. To my grandparents Alexander and Sylvia Rubin and Morris and Kate Zirin. We miss you every day.

And last, to every fan who spoke to me and helped shape my ideas around this book, all three thousand of you. You are the future owners of sports.

No, last, I want to thank Michele again. LLB.

Notes

INTRO: DIOGENES IN HIGH TOPS

1. Simon Critchley, "Cynicism We Can Believe In," *New York Times*, April 1, 2009.
2. Ed Snider, telephone correspondence, July 3, 2008.
3. Hunter S. Thompson, *Hey Rube: Blood Sport, the Bush Doctrine, and the Downward Spiral of Dumbness—Modern History from the Sports Desk* (New York: Simon & Schuster, 2004), 11.
4. Brad Schmidt, "Paulson: No Baseball Deal, No MLS in Portland," *Oregonian*, October 14, 2004, http://www.oregon.live.com/washingtoncounty/index.ssf/2009/10/paulson_no_baseball_deal_no_ms.html.
5. Mike Lupica, "Knicks Fans Deserve Much Better Than Recent History," http://www.prosportsdaily.com/comments/knicks-fans-deserve-much-better-than-recent-history-238346.html.
6. Jesse Barton, personal correspondence, August 30, 2009.
7. "Memorable Quotes from Miller's Crossing," http://www.imdb.com/title/tt0100150/quotes.

CHAPTER 1: WHEN DOMES ATTACK

1. Dave Zirin, "Football in L.A.: If There's No Team: It's Bonkers to Build a Stadium," *Los Angeles Times*, October 29, 2009, http://www.latimes.com/2009/oct/29/opinion/oe-zirin29.
2. Neil deMause, personal correspondence, April 13, 2007.
3. Neil deMause and Joanna Cagan, *Field of Schemes: How the Great Stadium Swindle Turns Public Money into Private Profit* (Lincoln, Neb.: Bison Books, 2008), 209.
4. Ibid., 36.
5. "New Orleans Mayor Orders Mandatory Evacuation as 'Catastrophic'

Hurricane Gustav Roars over Cuba," *London Evening Standard*, http://www.thisislondon.co.uk/news/article-23546267-new-orleans-mayor-orders-mandatory-evacuation-as-catastrophic-hurricane-gustav-roars-over-cuba.do.

6. Michael N. Danielson, *Home Team: Professional Sports and the American Metropolis* (Princeton, N.J.: Princeton University Press, 2001), 279.

7. Alecia P. Long, "Poverty Is the New Prostitution: Race, Poverty, and Public Housing in Post-Katrina New Orleans," *Journal of American History* (December 2007).

8. "Archie Manning: Saints Must be Wary of Winless Lions," *USA Today*, http://www.usatoday.com/sports/football/nfl/saints/2008-12-18-lions-saints_N.htm.

9. Saints fan, personal correspondence, August 31, 2009.

10. Richard Campanella, *New Orleans Then and Now* (Gretna, La.: Pelican Publishing, 1999), 26.

11. Arthur Q. Davis and J. Richard Gruber, *It Happened by Design: The Life and Work of Arthur Q. Davis* (Jackson: University of Mississippi Press, 2009), 50.

12. DeMause and Cagan, *Field of Schemes*, 62.

13. Ibid.

14. "StreetAdvisor: Houston, Texas," http://www.streetadvisor.com/texas/houston/demographics.

15. "Tulane—Louisiana Superdome," http://ncaafootball.com/index.php?s=&url_channel_id=34&url_article_id=12775&change_well_id=2.

16. "FEMA Public Assistance Division Still Busy One Year After Katrina," http://www.fema.gov/news/newsrelease.fema?id=29068.

17. ESPN's *Monday Night Football*, September 25, 2006.

18. Katy Reckdahl, "Hurricane Disaster Program Not Quite as Busy: Fewer Applying for Food-Stamp Aid," *Times-Picayune*, September 3, 2009, http://www.nola.com/hurricane/index.ssf/2009/09/disaster_program_not_quite_as.html.

19. Harry Shearer, "Obama to New Orleans: Drop Dead?," May 18, 2009, http://www.huffingtonpost.com/harry-shearer/obama-to-new-orleans-drop_b_204796.html.

20. Steven A. Riess, *Encyclopedia of Major League Baseball Clubs* (Westport, Conn.: Greenwood Publishing Group, 2006), vol. 1, 695.

21. Jonah Keri, "The Owners We Love to Hate," September 24, 2007, http://sports.espn.go.com/espn/page2/story?page=keri/owners/070924.

22. "Minnesota Twins Owner Pohlad Dies at 93," *USA Today*, January 6, 2009,

http://www.usatoday.com/sports/baseball/al/twins/2009-01-05-pohlad-obit_N.htm.

23. "Twins Owner Carl Pohlad Dies," *Minneapolis/St. Paul Business Journal*, January 5, 2009, http://twincities.bizjournals.com/twincities/stories/2009/01/05/daily8.html.

24. "Why Your Stadium Sucks: Hubert H. Humphrey Metrodome," http://newshaven.org/sports/why-your-stadium-sucks-hubert-h-humphrey-metrodome/.

25. Joe Christensen and Jim Souhan, "Legacy, Loyalty, Finances Defined Twins Owner," *Star Tribune*, January 5, 2009, http://www.startribune.com/sports/twins/37110909.html?elr=KArksLckD8EQDUoaEyqyP4O:DW3ckUiD3aPc:_Yyc:aUycaEacyU.

26. "Citizens Campaigning Against Renegade Legislators," http://www.ccarl.com/.

27. "Scott Miller's Bull Pennings: Carl Pohlad: 1915–2009," January 5, 2009, http://scott-miller.blogs.cbssports.com/mcc/blogs/entry/6270335/12742055.

28. DeMause and Cagan, *Field of Schemes*, 160.

29. Ibid., 169.

30. Ibid.

31. Peter Finley and Laura L. Finley, *The Sports Industry's War on Athletes* (Westpoint, Conn.: Praeger Security International, 2006), 133.

32. DeMause and Cagan, *Field of Schemes*, 170.

33. Ibid.

34. Jay Weiner, *Stadium Games: Fifty Years of Big League Greed and Bush League Boondoggles* (Minneapolis: University of Minnesota Press, 2000), 116.

35. Kenneth P. Vogel and Matthew Lindsey, "Sports Owners Fund McCain, Shun Obama," August 15, 2008, http://dyn.politico.com/printstory.cfm?uuid=C5A22B4A-18FE-70B2-A8B408A4049C60F3.

36. "Carl Pohlad: Political Campaign Contributions 2008 Election Cycle," http://www.campaignmoney.com/political/contributions/carl-pohlad.asp?cycle=08.

37. Dave Zirin, "Even in Minnesota," August 4, 2007, www.counterpunch.org/zirin08042007.html.

38. "Engineering Expert to Discuss I-35W Bridge Collapse," http://www.sdstate.edu/news/articles/khani-sahebjam.cfm.

39. Dennis Coates and Brad R. Humphrey, "The Stadium Gambit and Local Economic Development," *Cato Institute: Economic Development Policy* 23, no. 2.

40. Thomas G. Blomberg and Stanley Cohen, *Punishment and Social Control* (Hawthorne, N.Y.: Aldine de Gruyter, 2003), 404.
41. Richard Lapchick, "Do the Right Thing in D.C.," http://sports.espn .go.com/espn/page2/story?page=lapchick/060209&num=0.
42. Michael Neibauer, "Fenty Plans to Raid Ballpark Tax," *Washington Examiner*, July 26, 2009, http://www.washingtonexaminer.com/local/Fenty-plans-to-raid-ballpark-tax-51747192.html.
43. Tom Sullivan and Fred Lindecke, "What the Public Paid for the Cardinals' Stadium: The Media Never Told the Whole Story," *St. Louis Journalism Review*, June 2003, http://findarticles.com/p/articles/mi_hb6666/is_296_37/ai_n29355249/.
44. "Baseball Statistics: Comerica Park," http://www.baseball-statistics.com/Ballparks/Det/index.htm.
45. "Study: Publicly Funded Stadium in Washington, D.C., Amounts to Reverse Commuter Tax on Residents," November 8, 2004, http://www.ntu .org/main/press_release.php?PressID=668&org_name=NTUF.
46. "Reverse Robin Hood: D.C. Mayor Williams Mulcts from Taxpayers, to the Profit of Sports-Franchise Multimillionaires," November 30, 2004, http://www.nationalreview.com/comment/bandow200411300826.asp.
47. Roger G. Noll and Andrew S. Zimbalist, *Sports, Jobs, and Taxes: The Economic Impact of Sports Teams and Stadiums* (Washington, D.C.: Brookings Institute, 1997), 168.
48. Lori Montgomery, "Baseball Proposal Losing in D.C. Poll: Public Financing Plan Would Build Stadium," *Washington Post*, August 26, 2004, http://www .washingtonpost.com/wp-dyn/articles/A33715-2004Aug25.html.
49. Tom Boswell, "A Thing of Beauty," *Washington Post*, November 14, 2007, http://www.washingtonpost.com/wp-dyn/content/article/2007/11/13/AR2007111302361.html?nav=emailpage.
50. Rich Exner, "Data Central: Cleveland Ohio Statistics, Demographics & Census," September 29, 2009, http://www.cleveland.com/datacentral/index.ssf/2009/09/find_poverty_data_for_us_citie.html.
51. Sally Jenkins, "Badly Fooled by the Pitch," *Washington Post*, September 24, 2004, http://www.washingtonpost.com/wp-dyn/articles/A48793-2004Sep24.html.
52. David Nakamura, "Lapping Up a Major Victory, and Luxuries, at New Stadium; Fans Giddy After Storybook Ending (and the Occasional Cocktail)," *Washington Post*, March 31, 2008, http://www.washingtonpost .com/wp-dyn/content/article/2008/03/30/AR2008033001584.html.
53. Thomas Boswell, "Upon Inspection, New Home Has Some Sweet Aspects

to It," *Washington Post,* March 30, 2008, http://www.washingtonpost
.com/wp-dyn/content/article/2008/03/29/AR2008032902217.html.

54. Ibid.

55. Marc Fisher, "What Do You Get for Your $611 Million?," *Washington Post,*
http://voices.washingtonpost.com/rawfisher/2008/03/what_do_you_get_
for_your_611_m.html.

56. Sally Jenkins, "Is the District Being Sold a Bill of Goods?," *Washington
Post,* September 30, 2004, http://www.washingtonpost.com/wp-dyn/
articles/A60832-2004Sep29.html.

57. "The Business of Baseball: #14 Washington Nationals," *Forbes,* April
22, 2009, http://www.forbes.com/lists/2009/33/baseball-values-09_
Washington-Nationals_337401.html.

58. Thomas Heath and David Nakamura, "After 17 Months, Baseball Introduces Nats' Owner: Lerner Group Pledges to Work Closely on Stadium,"
Washington Post, May 4, 2006, http://www.washingtonpost.com/wp-dyn/
content/article/2006/05/03/AR2006050301121.html.

59. Tierney Plumb, "Washington Nationals to Pay Overdue Rent," *Washington Business Journal,* October 28, 2008, http://washington.bizjournals
.com/washington/stories/2008/10/20/daily8.html.

60. Ibid.

61. Dave McKenna, "Unsportsmen of the Year: In 2008, the Lerners Taught
Us the Meaning of Ingratitude," *Washington City Paper,* December 17,
2008, http://www.washingtoncitypaper.com/display.php?id=36612.

62. Steve Guzowski, personal correspondence, August 29, 2009.

63. Lena H. Sun and Lyndsey Laytner, "Red Line Train Operator Used Brakes
in Failed Bid to Stop Six-Car Train," *Washington Post,* June 24, 2009,
http://www.washingtonpost.com/wp-dyn/content/article/2009/06/23/
AR2009062300653.html.

64. Jim Bouton, personal correspondence, January 9, 2007.

65. Ibid.

CHAPTER 2: BUSINESS, NEVER PERSONAL

1. James Barron and Anna Quindlen, *The* New York Times *Book of New
York: 549 Stories of the People, the Events, and the Life of the City—Past and
Present* (New York: Black Dog and Leventhal Publishing, Inc., 2009), 379.

2. Tom Fornelli, "Citi Field Is Already Falling Apart," September 6, 2009,
http://mlb.fanhouse.com/2009/09/06/citi-field-is-already-falling-apart/.

3. "In a League of Its Own: America's National Football League Offers a

Business Lesson to Other Sports," *Economist,* April 27, 2006, http://www
.economist.com/businessfinance/displaystory.cfm?story_id=6859210.

4. Mark Sando, "Blackout Watch: Report from the NFC West," http://espn.
go.com/blog/nflnation/post/_/id/7088/blackout-watch-report-from-the-
nfc-west.

5. Ibid.

6. Daniel Okrent, "Detroit: The Death—and Possible Life—of a Great
City," *Time,* September 24, 2009, http://www.time.com/time/nation/
article/0,8599,1925796,00.html.

7. Michael David Smith, "Local Blackout in Detroit," October 29, 2009,
http://profootballtalk.nbcsports.com/2009/10/29/local-blackout-in-
detroit/.

8. "Study: Economy Lessens Super Bowl Economic Impact," *Tampa Bay
Business Journal,* January 21, 2009, http://tampabay.bizjournals.com/
tampabay/stories/2009/01/19/daily32.html.

9. Jay Cridlin, "Super Bowl Parties Are Victim of Economy," *St. Petersburg
Times,* November 25, 2008, http://www.tampabay.com/sports/article
916210.ece.

10. "Super Bowl Ads Deliver Cars, Movies, Animals," February 1, 2009, http://
cbs5.com/entertainment/Super.Bowl.Commercials.2.924158.html.

11. Ibid.

12. Harvey Araton, "At the Half, It's B-r-u-u-u-u-u-u-u-c-e," *New York Times,*
January 29, 2009, http://www.nytimes.com/2009/01/30/sports/football/
30araton.html?_r=1.

13. Ronald Blum, "Slider in the Seats: Major League Baseball Attendance
Drops for Second Straight Season," *Washington Examiner,* October 2,
2009, http://www.washingtonexaminer.com/sports/ap/mlb-attendance-
drops-for-second-straight-season-63300312.html.

14. "Global Recession Puts Golf Industry Deep in the Rough," February 24,
2009, http://www.dailymarkets.com/stocks/2009/02/23/global-recession-
puts-golf-industry-deep-in-the-rough/.

15. Associated Press, "Economic Meltdown Finally Hits NFL—Layoffs: More
Than 10 Percent of League's Headquarters Staff Will Lose Their Jobs," December 9, 2008, http://nbcsports.msnbc.com/id/28141796/.

16. Associated Press, "League to Lay Off About 80 Amid Economic Slow-
down, Stern Says," October 13, 2008, http://sports.espn.go.com/nba/
news/story?id=3640507.

17. Tom Lemke, "NBA Gets a Loan," *Washington Times,* February 26,

2009, http://www.washingtontimes.com/news/2009/feb/26/nba-set-to-acquire-175-million-line-of-credit/.

18. Bill Simmons, "Welcome to the No Benjamins Association," February 27, 2009, http://sports.espn.go.com/espn/page2/story?page=simmons/090227.

19. Ibid.

20. William C. Rhoden, "Sports of the Times: Recession Is a Relative Term in Baseball," *New York Times,* November 17, 2008m http://query.nytimes.com/gst/fullpage.html?res=990CE4D9123BF934A25752C1A96E9C8B63.

21. Todd Lighty and Kathryn Bergen, "Olympic Opposition Getting Second Wind as Support in Chicago Fades," *Chicago Tribune,* September 3, 2009, http://archives.chicagotribune.com/2009/sep/03/local/chi-olympics-poll-03-sep03.

22. Richard Sandomir, "City Approves $370.9 Million to Complete Yankee Stadium," *New York Times,* January 16, 2009, http://www.nytimes.com/2009/01/17/nyregion/17bonds.html.

23. Dustin Dow, "Bengal COA Values Plummet," January 14, 2008, http://www.seasonticketrights.com/PressBoxArticle.aspx?cid=38.

24. Wallace Matthews, "For Playoffs, Yankees Hold or Cut Ticket Prices," *Newsday,* September 1, 2009, http://www.newsday.com/sports/baseball/yankees/for-playoffs-yankees-hold-or-cut-ticket-prices-1.1415272.

25. Ryan Sutton, "Cowboys' $1.15 Billion Stadium Serves Frito Pies, Bad Burgers," http://www.bloomberg.com/apps/news?pid=20601088&sid=a1giqjLTWxcg.

26. Jason Notte, "Cowboys Stadium Goes Upscale: Big Spender: The New $933 Million Cowboys Stadium Puts Football Second to Kobe Beef and Private Lounges," September 24, 2009, http://www.entrepreneur.com/thestreet/pf/10594798.html.

27. Jeff Mosier, "New Dallas Cowboys Stadium May Not Have Naming Deal for '09," *Dallas Morning News,* February 16, 2009, http://www.dallasnews.com/sharedcontent/dws/dn/latestnews/stories/021609dnmetnamingrights.3db415d.html.

28. Harper Caron, personal correspondence, November 2, 2009.

29. Peter King, "Monday Morning Quarterback," September 7, 2009, http://sportsillustrated.cnn.com/2009/writers/peter_king/09/06/mmqb/index.html?eref=sihp.

30. Jeff Mosier, "Dallas Cowboys Fans Wrestle with $100K Price Tag on Seat

Rights," *Dallas Morning News,* November 29, 2007, http://www.dallas news. com/sharedcontent/dws/news/localnews/stories/112907dnmetseason tickets.2bd58bf.html.

31. "Jerry Jones Party Pass Leaves Cowboys Fans Pissed; You Been Blinded," September 22, 2009, http://youbeenblinded.com/jerry-jones-party-pass-leaves-cowboys-fans-pissed/4061.
32. Allan Classen, personal correspondence. August 30, 2009.
33. Randy, "NY Giants Fan," personal correspondence, August 29, 2009.
34. Jayson Stark, "Welcome to the New Moneyball: Less Talk About the Economy and More About the Money Players of 2009," March 30, 2009, http://sports.espn.go.com/mlb/preview09/columns/story?columnist=stark_jayson&id=4025962.
35. Roger Hanigan, personal correspondence, August 31, 2009.

CHAPTER 3: THE KEYSER SOZE PRINCIPLE

1. Howard Cosell and Peter Bonventre, *I Never Played the Game* (New York: HarperCollins, 1985).
2. "The 400 Richest Americans: #31 Philip F. Anschutz," *Forbes,* September 21, 2006, http://www.forbes.com/lists/2006/54/biz_06rich400_Philip-F-Anschutz_DSAK.html.
3. Dick Smillies, "The Stealth Media Mogul," *Forbes,* June 29, 2009, http://www.forbes.com/2009/06/28/anschutz-weekly-standard-business-media-examiner.html.
4. Ibid.
5. Ibid.
6. Ibid.
7. Michael Calderone, "Phil Anschutz's Conservative Agenda," October 16, 2009, http://www.politico.com/news/stories/1009/28355.html.
8. Matt Haber, "Who Is Philip Anschutz? (and Why Is He in Business with Michael Jackson and the *Weekly Standard*?," August 7, 2009, http://www.portfolio.com/companies-executives/2009/08/07/who-is-philip-anschutz-and-why-is-he-in-business-with-michael-jackson-and-the-weekly-standard/.
9. Justin Clark, "Citizen Anschutz: How the Conservative Christian Head of Regal Cinemas Is Trying to Change How You See Movies," March 23, 2006, http://www.nerve.com/dispatches/clark/citizenanschutz/printcopy.asp.
10. Kenneth P. Vogel and Matthew Lindsey, "Sports Owners Fund McCain,

Shun Obama," August 15, 2008, http://www.politico.com/news/stories/0808/12548.html.

11. Ed Snider, personal correspondence, July 3, 2008.

12. Edward L. Hudgins, "Ayn Rand's Stamp on American Culture," http://www.objectivistcenter.org/cth--1696-ARstamp.aspx.

13. Mike Allen, "Pro-war Group Launches $15 Million Ad Blitz," August 22, 2007, http://www.politico.com/news/stories/0807/5479.html.

14. Ibid.

15. Will Branch, "Sarah Palin and Ed Snider's Game Misconduct," October 8, 2008, http://www.philly.com/philly/blogs/attytood/This_Saturday_turn_your_back_on_the_pucker.html.

16. Lynn Zinser, "Palin Met with Boos at Flyers Opener," *New York Times*, October 11, 2008, http://slapshot.blogs.nytimes.com/2008/10/11/a-misplaced-hockey-mom-moment/.

17. Janet Pickel, "Palin Drops Puck at Flyers Game," *Patriot-News*, October 11, 2008, http://www.pennlive.com/midstate/index.ssf/2008/10/palin_drops_puck_at_flyers_gam.html.

18. Greg Wynshynski, "If Only This Were the End of Election-Year Politics in Hockey," October 13, 2008, http://sports.yahoo.com/nhl/blog/puck_daddy/post/If-only-this-were-the-end-of-election-year-polit?urn=nhl,114538&cp=3.

19. "Flyers Get VP Candidate Palin for Ceremonial Faceoff in Season Opener," http://blogs.phillyburbs.com/news/bcct/flyers-get-vp-candidate-palin-for-ceremonial-faceoff-in-season-opener/.

20. Dave Zirin, "Palin Drops the Puck," October 13, 2008, http://www.huffingtonpost.com/dave-zirin/palin-drops-the-puck_b_134215.html.

21. Will Bunch, "Palin's Slap Shots from the Right," *Philadelphia Daily News*, October 20, 2008, http://www.philly.com/philly/news/20081020_Ed_Snider_s_slap_shots_from_the_right.html?text=reg&c=y.

22. Ed Snider, telephone correspondence, July 3, 2008.

23. Bryan Burwell, "NFL Should Think Twice on Rush Limbaugh," *St. Louis Post-Dispatch*, October 7, 2009, http://www.stltoday.com/stltoday/sports/columnists.nsf/bryanburwell/story/E196145D80764B2F86257648000EF26B?OpenDocument.

24. Ibid.

25. Ibid.

26. Media Matters, http://mediamatters.org/mmtv/200909150017.

27. Media Matters. http://mediamatters.org/research/200909250030.

28. Ohm Youngmisuk, "Black NFL Players Crush Prospect of Playing for a Rush Limbaugh–Owned St. Louis Rams," *New York Daily News,* October 9, 2009, http://www.nydailynews.com/sports/football/ 2009/10/09/2009-10-09_black_nfl_players_crush_prospect_of_playing_for_a_rush_limbaughowned_st_louis_ra.html#ixzz0XPepjD24.

29. Ibid.

30. Ibid.

31. Roman Oben, "From Bad to Worse," *Washington Post,* October 7, 2009, http://views.washingtonpost.com/theleague/panelists/2009/10/rush-limbaugh-st-louis-rams-oben.html.

32. Judy Battista, "Goodell Voices Concern over Limbaugh," *New York Times,* October 13, 2009, http://fifthdown.blogs.nytimes.com/2009/10/13/goodell-voices-concern-over-limbaugh/.

33. Ibid.

34. Kenneth Vogel and Matthew Lindsay, "Sports Owners Fund McCain, Shun Obama," August 15, 2008, http://www.politico.com/news/stories/0808/12548.html.

35. Ibid.

36. Ibid.

37. Ibid.

38. "Battin' 1.000: Building America's Campaign for Life," http://www.all.org/battin1000/index.htm.

39. Ibid.

40. Max Blumenthal, "The Christian Right's Humble Servant," http://www.alternet.org/election04/20499/.

41. Ibid.

42. "Baseball's Owners Go to Bat for Bush," Associated Press, September 14, 2004, http://nbcsports.msnbc.com/id/5991983/.

43. Eric Pooley with S. C. Gwynne, "How George Got His Groove," *Time,* June 21, 1999, http://www.time.com/time/magazine/article/0,9171,991286-9,00.html.

44. Lee Russ, "A League of His Own," August 22, 2005, http://watchingthewatchers.org/news/88/league-his-own.

45. Julian Borger, "The Brains," *Guardian,* March 9, 2004, http://www.guardian.co.uk/world/2004/mar/09/uselections2004.usa1.

46. Charles Lewis, *The Buying of the President* (New York: Avon Books, 2000), 204–8.

47. "Road to Politics Ran through a Texas Ballpark," *New York Times,* Sep-

tember 24, 2000, http://www.nytimes.com/2000/09/24/politics/24BASE
.html.

48. Lewis, *Buying of the President,* 204–8.

49. Ibid.

50. Ibid.

51. Ibid.

52. Ibid.

53. Joe Conason, "Bush, Inc.: Understanding the Political Dynasty That's Made Crony Capitalism a Way of Life, *Salon,* August 21, 2003.

54. Ibid.

55. Brooks Jackson, "Bush as Businessman: How the Texas Governor Made His Millions," May 13, 1999, http://www.cnn.com/ALLPOLITICS/stories /1999/05/13/president.2000/jackson.bush/.

56. "Baseball's Owners Go to Bat for Bush," Associated Press.

57. Ibid.

CHAPTER 4: THE BOSS: GEORGE STEINBRENNER AS THROWBACK AND ROLE MODEL

1. Kenneth Lovett, "Yanks Beaned Taxpayers, Stadium Report Says," *New York Daily News,* September 16, 2008, http://www.nydailynews.com/ ny_local/bronx/2008/09/15/2008-09-15_yanks_beaned_taxpayers_ stadium_report_sa-3.html.

2. Dick Schapp, *Steinbrenner!* (New York: Avon Books, 1983).

3. John Romano, "George Steinbrenner's Legacy Still Evident in These New York Yankees," *St. Petersburg Times,* October 28, 2009, http://www.tampa bay.com/sports/baseball/rays/george-steinbrenners-legacy-still-evident-in-these-new-york-yankees/1047506.

4. "Yankee Stadium," http://www.baseball-statistics.com/Ballparks/NYY/ index.htm.

5. Ed Eagle, "Steinbrenner Sued over YES Idea," August 29, 2009, http:// mlb.mlb.com/news/article.jsp?ymd=20090829&content_id=6679224 &vkey=news_mlb&fext=.jsp&c_id=mlb.

6. Robert Elias, *The Empire Strikes Out: How Baseball Sold U.S. Foreign Policy and Promoted the American Way Abroad* (New York: New Press, 2010), 250.

7. "Yankees Force 'God Bless America' on Fans: Lawsuit," April 15, 2009. http:// www.reuters.com/article/domesticNews/idUSTRE53E66F20090415.

8. "NYCLU Sues NYPD on Behalf of Baseball Fan Ejected from Yankees Sta-

dium During 'God Bless America,'" April 15, 2009, http://www.nyclu.org/node/2342.

9. Ibid.

10. Thom Weidlich, "New York Man Sues Yankees, Police over Ejection from Ballgame," April 16, 2009, http://www.bloomberg.com/apps/news?pid=2 0601079&sid=awp5zvUvkwYE&refer=home.

11. Gay Talese, "There Are Fans—And Yankee Fans," *New York Times*, June 29, 1958.

12. Patrick Saunders, "Bronx Cheer for Bombers," *Denver Post*, December 16, 2008, http://www.denverpost.com/psaunders/ci_11240652.

13. Schapp, *Steinbrenner!*, 35.

14. Jeff Mahler, *Ladies and Gentlemen, the Bronx Is Burning: 1977, Baseball, Politics, and the Battle for the Soul of a City* (New York: Picador, 2006), 29–31.

15. Jim Gerard, *Yankees Suck! The Unofficial Guide for Fans Who Hate, Despise, Loathe, and Detest Those Bums from the Bronx* (New York: Chamberlain Bros., 2005), 49.

16. Phil Pepe, *The Ballad of Billy and George* (Guildford, Conn.: Lyons Press, 2008), 14.

17. Ibid., 43.

18. George Vesey, "Sports of the Times: Dick Young, in His Time," *New York Times*, September 2, 1987, http://www.nytimes.com/1987/09/02/sports/sports-of-the-times-dick-young-in-his-time.html.

19. Schapp, *Steinbrenner!*, 39.

20. Mark Puma, "'The Boss' Made Yankees a Dictatorship," http://espn.go.com/classic/biography/s/Steinbrenner_George.html.

21. "Sports World Specials: A Yankee in First," http://www.nytimes.com/1981/09/21/sports/sports-world-specials-a-yankee-in-first.html.

22. Schapp, *Steinbrenner!*, 84–85.

23. Ibid., 117–18.

24. Ibid., 48.

25. Gerard, *Yankees Suck!*, 56.

26. Dick Heller, "Steinbrenner's Alliance with Gambler Backfired," *Washington Times*, August 1, 2006, http://www.washingtontimes.com/news/2006/aug/01/20060801-120017-1911r/.

27. John Harper, "Yankees Reach Preliminary Agreement on Eight-Year Deal with Mark Teixeira," *New York Daily News*, December 26, 2008, http://www.nydailynews.com/sports/baseball/yankees/2008/12/23/2008-12-23_yankees_reach_preliminary_agreement_on_e.html.

28. Michael Gormley, "NY Lawmaker: Yankee Subsidies Hit Taxpayers, Fans," *USA Today*, September 16, 2008, http://www.usa today.com/sports/baseball/2008-09-16-3141026797_x.htm; "Congressional Panel Rips Yanks, NYC Over New Stadium Financing," September 18, 2008, Associated Press, http://sports.espn.go.com/mlb/news/story?id=3595265.

29. See Naomi Klein, *The Shock Doctrine: The Rise of Disaster Capitalism* (New York: Metropolitan Books, 2007), 155.

30. "Congressional Panel Rips Yanks," Associated Press; Greg B. Smith, "Dennis Kucinich Says Yankee Stadium Tax Deals Smell Bad," *New York Daily News*, September 18, 2008, http://www.nydailynews.com/ny_local/bronx/2008/09/18/2008-09-18_dennis_kucinich_says_yankee_stadium_tax_.html.

31. "Congressional Panel Rips Yanks," Associated Press.

32. Ibid.

33. Tom Robbins, "Five Reasons Why Bronx Beep Adolfo Carrión Will Be a Great HUD Secretary," *Village Voice*, December 8, 2008, http://blogs.villagevoice.com/runninscared/archives/2008/12/five_reasons_wh.php

34. Mike Lupica, "George Steinbrenner Gets All-Star Treatment from Fans at Yankee Stadium," *New York Daily News*, July 16, 2008, http://www.nydailynews.com/sports/baseball/yankees/2008/07/15/2008-07-15_george_steinbrenner_gets_allstar_treatme-2.html.

35. Jack Curry, "Steinbrenner, 78, Appears to Hugs, Kisses and Cheers," *New York Times*, July 16, 2008, http://query.nytimes.com/gst/fullpage.html?res=9E00E0D81E3EF935A25754C0A96E9C8B63

36. Schapp, *Steinbrenner!*, 200.

CHAPTER 5: CLAY BENNETT, THE SEATTLE SUPERSONICS, AND THE QUESTION OF OWNERSHIP

1. http://www.ihateclay.com/why-hoops-matter/.

2. Walter O'Malley's official website, http://www.walteromalley.com/biog_short_page4.php?lang=eng.

3. "Baseball Quotes and Sayings," http://www.sayingsnquotes.com/quotations-by-subject/baseball-quotes-and-sayings/.

4. Don Norman, *Chavez Ravine: 1949* (San Francisco: Chronicle Books, 2003), 7.

5. Ibid., 17.

6. Katrina vanden Heuvel, "Frank Wilkinson's Legacy," *Nation*, January 10, 2006.

7. Mark Ramirez, "Documentary Gives Life to a Community Erased," *Seattle Times,* July 1, 2005, http://seattletimes.nwsource.com/html/television/2002353626_chavez01.html.

8. *Chavez Ravine: A Los Angeles Story,* Independent Lens, http://www.pbs.org/independentlens/chavezravine/cr.html.

9. Ibid.

10. Michael D'Antonio, *Forever Blue* (New York: Riverhead Books, 2009), 273–74.

11. E. M. Swift, "Now You See Him, Now You Don't," *Sports Illustrated,* December 15, 1986.

12. Neil deMause and Joanna Cagan, *Field of Schemes: How the Great Stadium Swindle Turns Public Money into Private Profit* (Lincoln, Neb.: Bison Books, 2008), 1.

13. Ibid., 6.

14. Swift, "Now You See Him."

15. "The Great Families of Indianapolis," *Indianapolis Monthly,* http://www.indianapolismonthly.com/articleNew.aspx?id=77262&page=08.

16. DeMause and Cagan, *Field of Schemes,* 407.

17. Evan Weiner, "Seattle Move Shows That Fans Just Don't Matter," *New York Sun,* July 10, 2008, http://www.nysun.com/sports/seattle-move-shows-that-fans-just-dont-matter/81593/.

18. Bruce Schoenfeld, "Where the Thunder Comes Dribbling Down the Plain," *New York Times,* October 24, 2008.

19. Ibid.

20. *Sonicsgate,* http://www.sonicsgate.org/.

21. Schoenfeld, "Where the Thunder."

22. Jesse Hagopian, interview, December 3, 2008.

23. Pete Redington, "Freesport," *Valley Advocate,* August 14, 2008.

24. Jim Brunner, "E-mails Reveal Sonics Owners Intended to Bolt from Seattle," *Seattle Times,* April 10, 2008, http://seattletimes.nwsource.com/html/localnews/2004339103_sonicsheds.html.

25. Frank Hughes, "The Man Who Will Take Over the SuperSonics Franchise Reluctantly Puts Himself in the Spotlight," *Tacoma News Tribune,* October 1, 2006.

26. Ibid.

27. Ibid.

28. Henry Abbott, "Not Averse to Controversy: Meet Aubrey McClendon," Truehoop, http://espn.go.com/blog/truehoop/post/_/id/3787/not-averse-to-controversy-meet-aubrey-mcclendon.

29. Ibid.
30. Nico Pitney, "McCain Co-Chair Calls Obama 'A Guy of the Street,' Raises Drug Use," October 9, 2008, http://www.huffingtonpost.com/2008/10/09/mccain-co-chair-calls-oba_n_133369.html.
31. Marc J. Spears, "Not Buying It," *Boston Globe*, November 5, 2007.
32. Schoenfeld, "Where the Thunder."
33. Ibid.
34. Percy Allen, "Howard Schultz Drops Sonics Suit," *Seattle Times*, August 30, 2008.
35. Hughes, "The Man Who."
36. Jim Caple, "Can't Seattle Keep the Storm?," August 27, 2007, http://sports.espn.go.com/espn/page2/story?page=caple/070827.
37. Art Thel, "Stern and Bennett: Scoundrels Must Be Held Accountable," *Seattle Post-Intelligencer*, April 20, 2008, http://www.seattlepi.com/thiel/359886_thielbar21.html.
38. Percy Allen, "An Interview with Clay Bennett, Owner of Sonics," *Seattle Times*, May 20, 2007, http://seattletimes.nwsource.com/html/sports/2003714508_soni20.html.
39. J. A. Adande, "Sonics' Excitement Tempered by Departure Talk," October 12, 2007, http://sports.espn.go.com/nba/columns/story?columnist=adande_ja&page=BigPicture-Sonics.
40. Percy Allen, "Sonics Co-Owner McClendon Fined $250K," *Seattle Times*, June 13, 2008.
41. Espn.com news services, "NBA Owners Approve Sonics' Move, Pending Litigation," April 19, 2008, http://sports.espn.go.com/nba/news/story?id=3353270.
42. Jim Brunner, "E-mails Reveal."
43. Schoenfeld, "Where the Thunder."
44. Ibid.
45. Ibid.
46. Jack McCallum, interview, April 5, 2009.
47. Percy Allen, "NBA Approves Sonics' Move to Oklahoma City," *Seattle Times*, April 18, 2008, http://seattletimes.nwsource.com/html/sports/2004358405_websonivote18.html.
48. Schoenfeld, "Where the Thunder."
49. Espn.com news services, "SuperSonics, Seattle Reach Last-Minute Settlement," http://sports.espn.go.com/nba/news/story?id=3471503.
50. Ibid.
51. Ibid.

52. Dean Paton, interview, December 3, 2008.
53. Todd Klempner, interview, August 30, 2009.
54. Associated Press, "NBA Team Off to OKC as Sonics, Seattle Settle," July 2, 2008 http://nbcsports.msnbc.com/id/25502466/.
55. Espn.com news services, "NBA Owners Approve."
56. Sam Bernstein, interview, December 3, 2008.
57. Josh Peter, "Trail of Tears Follows Sonics to Oklahoma," February 12, 2008, http://sports.yahoo.com/nba/news?slug=jo-seattlethunder021209 &prov=yhoo&type=lgns.
58. Ibid.
59. William L. Hamilton, "Investing in Wine: Now May Be the Time," *New York Times*, May 20, 2009, http://www.nytimes.com/2009/05/21/business/businessspecial3/21wine.html.
60. Etan Thomas, interview, July 31, 2009.

CHAPTER 6: MONEY LAUNDERING FOR THE LORD: CHARLIE MONFORT AND DICK DEVOS KEEP THE FAITH

1. Tom Krattenmaker, *Onward Christian Athletes* (Lanham, Md.: Rowman & Littlefield, 2010), 108.
2. Aaron N. Wise and Bruce S. Meyer, *International Sports Law and Business*, vol. 1 (Cambridge, Mass.: Kluwer Law International, 1997), 274–75.
3. Krattenmaker, *Onward Christian Athletes*, 107.
4. Ibid.
5. Ibid., 108.
6. Ibid., 109.
7. Outreach of Hope website, http://www.outreachofhope.org/index.cfm/PageID/362.
8. Ira Berkow, cited in Krattenmaker, *Onward Christian Athletes*, 108.
9. Ibid.
10. Tom Krattenmaker, e-mail interview, June 2009.
11. Krattenmaker, *Onward Christian Athletes*, 111.
12. Ibid., 180.
13. Bob Nightengale, "Baseball's Rockies Seek Revival on Two Levels," *USA Today*, June 1, 2006, http://www.usatoday.com/sports/baseball/nl/rockies/2006-05-30-rockies-cover_x.htm.
14. Ibid.
15. Ibid.
16. Ibid.

17. Ibid.

18. Ibid.

19. Andrew Nuschler, "Jim Tracy and the Colorado Rockies Beg the Question: Is Satan the Answer?," June 24, 2009, http://bleacherreport.com/articles/205660-the-colorado-rockies-and-jim-tracy-prove-satan-is-the-answer.

20. Nightengale, "Baseball's Rockies."

21. Eric Weiner, "The Craziest F'n Baseball Story You'll Read This Year," June 8, 2006, http://www.huffingtonpost.com/eric-j-weiner/the-craziest-fn-baseball_b_22521.html.

22. Russ Bellant, The Coors Connection: How Coors Family Philanthropy Undermines Democratic Pluralism (Cambridge, Mass.: South End Press, 1991), 66.

23. M. E. Sprengelmeyer, "Tancredo Stands Ground on Mecca," Rocky Mountain News, August 6, 2008.

24. Max Blumenthal, "Rick Santorum's Beastly Politics," Nation, November 1, 2006.

25. Eric Schlosser, Fast Food Nation: The Dark Side of the All-American Meal (New York: Perennial, 2002), 157–58.

26. Ibid., 160.

27. Ibid.

28. Ibid.

29. Ibid.

30. Ibid., 149.

31. Tom Krattenmaker, interview, November 9, 2008.

32. Nightengale, "Baseball's Rockies."

33. Paul Ott, Outside the Lines, August 13, 2006, ESPN.

34. Warren St. John, "Sports and Salvation on Faith Night at the Stadium," New York Times, June 2, 2006.

35. Paul Newberry, "Mixed Signals as Gays Try to Find Their Place in the Sports World," Associated Press, July 2, 2004.

36. Krattenmaker, Onward Christian Athletes, 120.

37. http://www.thirdcoastsports.com/.

38. Patrik Jonsson, "At Thursday's Braves Game, Bring a Glove—and a Bible?," Christian Science Monitor, July 27, 2006.

39. Third Coast Sports website, http://www.thirdcoastsports.com/.

40. "The Sexual Development Stages," http://www.troubledwith.com/ParentingTeens/A000000315.cfm?topic=parenting%20teens%3A%20homosexuality.

41. Ibid.

42. http://www.sovo.com/2006/8-4/news/localnews/braves.cfm.

43. "Focus on the Family," http://www.rightwingwatch.org/content/focus-family.

44. Max Blumenthal, "Justice Sunday Preachers," *Nation,* April 26, 2005.

45. Media Matters for America, August 3, 2005, http://mediamatters.org/mmtv/200508030007.

46. Blumenthal, "Justice."

47. Ibid.

48. Rob Boston, "The Alliance Defense Fund Agenda," *Church & State,* June 2004.

49. Interview, Barry Lynn, January 29, 2009.

50. Ibid.

51. Ben Shpigel, "Rockies Place Their Faith in God, and One Another," *New York Times,* October 23, 2007.

52. Jim Bullington, interview, April 5, 2009.

53. Ibid.

54. Associated Press, "FBI Investigates Rockies' Claims," *New York Times,* October 27, 2007.

55. Chris Rock, DVD, *Never Scared* (HBO, 2004).

56. "The World's Billionaires," http://www.forbes.com/lists/2007/10/07 billionaires_The-Worlds-Billionaires_Rank_10.html.

57. Neil deMause, www.fieldofschemes.com, October 2, 2006, http://www .fieldofschemes.com/news/archives/2006/10/magic_offer_50m.html.

58. "Few Hundred People Attend Groundbreaking for New Orlando Magic Arena," *Orlando Sentinel,* September 4, 2008.

59. Ibid.

60. Pat Williams, *How to Be like Rich DeVos: Succeeding with Integrity in Business and Life* (Deerfield Beach, Fla.: Health Communications, 2004).

61. Rachel Burstein and Kerry Lauerman, "She Did It Amway," *Mother Jones,* September/October 1996.

62. Ibid.

63. Ibid.

64. Ibid.

65. Ibid.

66. Ibid.

67. Charles R. Babcock, "Amway's $2.5 Million Gift to GOP the Largest Ever," *Washington Post,* January 11, 1995, A01.

68. Bill Berkowitz, "Amway's Domestic Revival," *Z Magazine,* March 2009, http://www.zmag.org/zmag/viewArticle/20742.

69. Ibid.

70. Free Congress Foundation website, http://www.freecongress.org/about
fcf.aspx.

71. Bob Moser, "The Crusaders," *Rolling Stone,* April 7, 2005.

72. White House, "President and Mrs. Bush Deeply Saddened by the Death
of Dr. D. James Kennedy," September 6, 2007, http://georgewbush-
whitehouse.archives.gov/news/releases/2007/09/20070906-7.html.

73. Moser, "The Crusaders."

74. Bellant, *The Coors Connection,* 26.

75. Ibid., 27.

76. Jeremy Scahill, interview, October 7, 2009.

77. Jeremy Scahill, *Blackwater* (New York: Nation Books, 2008).

78. Chris Cillizza, "The Fix," *Washington Post,* November 7, 2006, http://
voices.washingtonpost.com/thefix/house/northup-loses-democrats-
rejoic.html; Micheline Maynard, "Race Profile," *New York Times,* http://
www.nytimes.com/ref/washington/raceprofile_MICHIGANGOV.html.

79. Paul Vigna, "Writers Disagree on Faith and Family Promotion," March
2, 2009, http://blog.pennlive.com/fanbox/2009/03/writers_disagree_on_
faith_and.html.

80. Ibid.

81. Jeff Kunerth, "Orlando Protesters Target Magic Owner for Support of Gay
Marriage Ban," *Orlando Sentinel,* September 29, 2009.

82. http://en.wikipedia.org/wiki/Florida_Amendment_2.

83. Kunerth, "Orlando Protesters."

84. Jeffery M. Jones, "More Independents Lean GOP," Gallup, September 30,
2009, http://www.gallup.com/poll/123362/independents-lean-gop-party-
gap-smallest-since-05.aspx.

CHAPTER 7: PETER ANGELOS AND THE SHREDDING
OF THE ORIOLE WAY

1. Mark Maske, "Angelos: A Maverick Who Wants to Deal; He Aims to End
Strike, Not Befriend Fellow Owners," *Washington Post,* February 6, 1995.

2. Ibid.

3. Law offices of Peter G. Angelos, http://www.angeloslaw.com/pga.htm.

4. Elliott Almond, "Angelos' Orioles: Simply Labor of Love—'Guy from Baltimore' Puts His Money Where Loyalties Are," *Seattle Times,* October 4, 1997.

5. Mark Hyman, Milton Kent, Don Markus, and Peter Schmuck, "The Ori-

oles' New Owners," *Baltimore Sun,* October 5, 1993, http://www.baltimore sun.com/sports/horse-racing/bal-mckay100593,0,2839979.story.

6. Jack Curry, "Baseball Set to Continue Fighting Ban of Cuba from Tournament," *New York Times,* December 16, 2005, http://query.nytimes.com/ gst/fullpage.html?res=9A02E5DD1630F935A25751C1A9639C8B63&sec =&spon=&pagewanted=all.

7. Ibid.

8. "Angelos Named Marylander of the Year," *Baltimore Sun,* December 1998.

9. *The Novak Zone,* interview with Cal Ripken, August 30, 2003, http:// transcripts.cnn.com/TRANSCRIPTS/0308/30/smn.16.html.

10. Jerry Crasnick, "Orioles Mired in a Full-Blown Identity Crisis," September 14, 2006, http://sports.espn.go.com/mlb/columns/story?columnist= crasnick_jerry&id=2587235.

11. *The Red Zone with Clayton Ferraro and Adam Mendelson,* http://fox sportsradio1200.com/The-Red-Zone-with-Clayton-Ferraro-and-Adam-Mendels/3015255.

12. Hal Bodley, "Palmeiro Suspended for Steroids Policy Violation," *USA Today,* August 1, 2005, http://www.usatoday.com/sports/baseball/al/ orioles/2005-08-01-palmeiro-suspension_x.htm.

13. Roch Kubatko, "Palmeiro Suspended," *Baltimore Sun,* August 2, 2005, http://www.baltimoresun.com/sports/orioles/bal-te.palmeiro02aug02, 1,4324519.story.

14. Transcript, "House Committee on Oversight and Government Reform Hearing on Illegal Steroid Use by Major League Baseball Athletes," *Washington Post,* January 15, 2008, http://www.washingtonpost.com/wp-srv/ sports/articles/steroidhearing_011508.html.

15. Thomas Boswell, "A Big Star Plays a Bad Hand," *Washington Post,* August 2, 2005, http://www.washingtonpost.com/wp-dyn/content/article/ 2005/08/01/AR2005080101532.html.

16. ESPN news services, "Hall of Famer Suspicious of Oriole's Output," http:// sports.espn.go.com/mlb/news/story?id=1760890.

17. Kubatko, "Palmeiro Suspended."

18. David Steele, interview, April 3, 2009.

19. Jorge Arangure Jr., "O's Angelos Dishes on All Things Baseball," *Washington Post,* March 19, 2007, http://www.washingtonpost.com/wp-dyn/ content/article/2007/03/18/AR2007031801262.html.

20. Associated Press, " 'Free the Birds': Orioles Fans Walk Out in Protest," http://sports.espn.go.com/mlb/news/story?id=2597721.

21. Ibid.
22. Steele interview.
23. Ray Suarez interview with Angelos, "Baseball Strike," *PBS Online News Hour*, August 16, 2002, http://www.pbs.org/newshour/bb/sports/july-dec02/strike_8–16.html.
24. Roger G. Noll and Andrew S. Zimbalist, eds., *Sports, Jobs, and Taxes: The Economic Impact of Sports Teams and Stadiums* (Washington, D.C.: Brookings Institution, 1997), 245.
25. Dennis Coates and Brad R. Humphreys, *Professional Sports Facilities, Franchises and Urban Economic Development*, University of Maryland at Baltimore County Department of Economics, working paper, 03-103, 2003.
26. Dave Zirin, "Cleaning Up After the Orioles," *Nation*, September 4, 2007, http://www.thenation.com/doc/20070910/zirin.
27. Ibid.
28. Ibid.
29. Ibid.
30. Ron Cassie, interview, April 2, 2009.
31. Crasnick, "Orioles Mired."

CHAPTER 8: DAN SNYDER: WHEN COSTANZA GOT HAIR

1. Steve Coll, "Monday Night Football," *New Yorker*, October 26, 2009, http://www.newyorker.com/online/blogs/stevecoll/2009/10/monday-night-football.html.
2. Dan Steinberg, "Notes from the Burgundy Revolution," *Washington Post*, October 28, 2009, http://www.washingtonpost.com/wp-dyn/content/article/2009/10/27/AR2009102703571.html?sub=AR.
3. James V. Grimaldi, "For Redskins Fans, Hard Luck Runs into Team's Hard Line," *Washington Post*, September 3, 2009, http://www.washingtonpost.com/wp-dyn/content/article/2009/09/02/AR2009090203887.html.
4. Dan Steinberg, "Riggins Says Snyder Is 'a Bad Guy,'" *Washington Post*, November 4, 2009, http://voices.washingtonpost.com/dcsportsbog/2009/11/john_riggins_says_daniel_snyde.html.
5. "NFL Fan Value Experience," November 7, 2007, http://sportsillustrated.cnn.com/2007/football/nfl/10/29/fvi.redskins/.
6. James V. Grimaldi, "Redskins Fans Waited While Brokers Got Tickets," *Washington Post*, September 2, 2009, http://www.washingtonpost

.com/wp-dyn/content/article/2009/09/01/AR2009090103984.html?
hpid=topnews.

7. Jason C. from Arlington, comments, http://www.yelp.com/biz/fedex-field-
hyattsville.

8. Dave McKenna, "Breaking News: Fans Say Redskins Selling Beer in FedEx
Field Bathrooms!," *Washington City Paper,* October 17, 2009, http://www
.washingtoncitypaper.com/blogs/citydesk/2009/10/17/cheap-seats-
daily-breaking-news-fans-say-redskins-now-selling-beer-in-fedexfield-
bathrooms/.

9. Dave McKenna, "Fee for All Parking at FedExField," *Washington City
Paper,* August 12, 2009, http://www.washingtoncitypaper.com/display
.php?id=37660.

10. Dave McKenna, "Patriot Games: Redskins Put a Price Tag on Commem-
orating 9/11," *Washington City Paper,* September 22, 2006, http://www
.washingtoncitypaper.com/cheap/2006/cheap0922.html.

11. Bathroom Readers Institute, *Uncle John's Third Bathroom Reader* (New
York: St. Martin's Press, 1990).

12. McKenna, "Fee for All Parking."

13. Ibid.

14. Drew Magary, "The Most Hopeless Franchise in Football. Jamboroo,
Week 5," October 8, 2009, http://deadspin.com/5377099/the-most-
hopeless-franchise-in-football—jamboroo-week-5.

15. "Dan Snyder Should Be on *The Office,*" *Sporting News,* October 1, 2008,
http://www.sportingnews.com/blog/leeh2003/tag/WashingtonRedskins.

16. Paul Attner, "In Your Face," *Sporting News,* August 28, 2000.

17. Ibid.

18. Ibid.

19. Ibid.

20. Mehul Nariyawala, "Dan Snyder—From a College Dropout to Billionaire Owner of Washington Redskins," *Chicago Business Weekly,* October 28, 2004, http://media.www.chibus.com/media/storage/paper408/
news/2004/10/28/GsbNews/Evc-Lines.Up.Dan.Snyder.As.Luncheon
.Keynote.For.November.12.Conference-785894.shtml.

21. David Brooks, "A Money Player in a Power Town," *New York Times,* December 26, 1999, http://www.nytimes.com/1999/12/26/magazine/a-money-
player-in-a-power-town.html?scp=1&sq=david%20brooks%20daniel%20s
nyder&st=cse&pagewanted=all.

22. Nariyawala, "Dan Snyder."

23. Ibid.

24. Jewish Virtual Library, "Daniel Snyder, 1965–," http://www.jewishvirtual
    library.org/jsource/biography/DanSnyder.html.
25. Magary, "The Most Hopeless."
26. NFL Fanhouse, "Redskins GM Vinny Cerrato Now a Radio Host, New
    Co-Workers Wish He'd Stay Away," September 18, 2008, http://nfl
    .fanhouse.com/2008/09/18/redskins-gm-vinny-cerrato-now-a-radio-
    host-new-co-workers-wish/.
27. Dave McKenna, "Radio Violence: Redskins Keep Using New Media to Go
    After Old Media," *Washington City Paper,* October 1, 2008, http://www
    .washingtoncitypaper.com/display.php?id=36275.
28. Ibid.
29. Jack Shafer, "Snyder Broadcasting," *Slate,* January 20, 2006, http://www
    .slate.com/id/2134605/.
30. Dave McKenna, "The Anti-Media Media," *Washington City Papers,*
    October 21–27, 2005, http://www.washingtoncitypaper.com/cheap/2005/
    cheap1021.html.
31. Mike Wise, interview, April 5, 2009.
32. Leonard Shapiro, "WTOP Won't Say 'Redskins'; Radio Station Heeds Na-
    tive Americans' Distaste," *Washington Post,* March 15, 1992.
33. Thom Loverro, "*Sporting News* Redskins Survey Has Interesting Re-
    sponses," *Washington Times,* September 23, 2009, http://www.washington
    times.com/weblogs/lovey-land/2009/sep/23/sporting-news-redskins-
    survey-has-interesting-resp/.
34. BBC News, "Redskins Under Fire for 'Racist' Name," January 10, 2002,
    http://news.bbc.co.uk/2/hi/americas/1753321.stm.
35. Mike Wise, "Questionable Naming Rights," *Washington Post,* Septem-
    ber 17, 2005, http://www.washingtonpost.com/wp-dyn/content/article/
    2005/09/16/AR2005091601640.html.
36. Shirley Povich, *All Those Mornings . . . At the Post* (New York: PublicAf-
    fairs, 2005), 145.
37. Wise, "Questionable Naming Rights."
38. Charles K. Ross, *Outside the Lines: African Americans and the Integration
    of the National Football League* (New York: New York University Press,
    1999).
39. Ibid.
40. Ibid.
41. Ibid.
42. Attner, "In Your Face."
43. Sally Jenkins, "Bruce Allen's First Task with the Redskins: Repair the Fis-

sures of Vinny Cerrato's Making," *Washington Post,* December 18, 2009, http://www.washingtonpost.com/wp-dyn/content/article/2009/12/17/AR2009121702283.html.

CHAPTER 9: DONALD STERLING: SLUMLORD BILLIONAIRE

1. Page 2 staff, "The List: Worst Owners," http://espn.go.com/page2/s/list/owners/010710.html.
2. Frank Lidz, "The Worst Franchise in Sports History (and the Man Responsible)," *Sports Illustrated,* April 17, 2000, http://sportsillustrated.cnn.com/vault/cover/featured/9737/index.htm.
3. Tom Bradley, "Quote Abyss," http://www.quoteabyss.com/author.php?a=3371&au=Tom_Bradley_quotes.
4. Lidz, "The Worst Franchise."
5. Ibid.
6. Ibid.
7. Bruce Newman, "Can the NBA Save Itself?," *Sports Illustrated,* November 1, 1982, http://sportsillustrated.cnn.com/vault/article/magazine/MAG1126059/2/index.htm.
8. Ibid.
9. Lidz, "The Worst Franchise."
10. Ibid.
11. Ibid.
12. Ibid.
13. Ibid.
14. Ibid.
15. Ibid.
16. Nick Bakay, "Jerry Buss vs. Donald T. Sterling," February 9, 2001, http://www.nickbakay.com/archives/jerry_buss_vs_donald_t_sterling.
17. Lidz, "The Worst Franchise."
18. Ibid.
19. Peter Keating, "Uncontested: The Life of Donald Sterling," *ESPN the Magazine,* June 1, 2009.
20. Kevin Arnovitz, "Pound Sterling," Truehoop, March 7, 2009, http://espn.go.com/blog/truehoop/post/_/id/6053/pound-sterling.
21. Associated Press, "Sterling Settles Housing Bias Lawsuit," November 3, 2009.
22. Patrick Range McDonald, "Donald T. Sterling's Skid Row Mirage," *L.A. Weekly,* March 20, 2008, http://www.laweekly.com/2008-03-20/news/donald-t-sterling-8217-s-skid-row-mirage/1.

23. Ibid.
24. Ibid.
25. Ibid.
26. Keating, "Uncontested."
27. Ibid.
28. Bomani Jones, "Sterling's Racism Should Be News," August 10, 2006, http://sports.espn.go.com/espn/page2/story?page=jones/060810.
29. Marcel Mutoni, "Baylor: Sterling Is Running a 'Southern Plantation-Type' Structure," February 12, 2009, http://www.slamonline.com/online/nba/2009/02/donald-sterling-is-running-a-southern-plantation-type-structure-says-elgin-baylor/.
30. Ibid.
31. "NBA Owner in Sex Scandal," *Smoking Gun*, http://www.thesmokinggun.com/archive/0812041sterling1.html.
32. Ibid.
33. Ibid.
34. Ibid.
35. McDonald, "Donald T. Sterling's."
36. Ibid.
37. Ibid.

CHAPTER 10: THE WAL-MART WAY: DAVID GLASS AND THE KANSAS CITY ROYALS

1. Louis Dimas, interview, October 15, 2009.
2. "Dying Boy Brought in to Cheer Up Kansas City Royals," *Onion*, September 29, 2005, http://www.theonion.com/content/node/41193.
3. Bob Dutton, "Royals' Brass Still Focused on This Season," *Kansas City Star*, July 15, 2009, http://www.kansascity.com/164/story/1327535-p2.html.
4. Ronald Blum, "Large-Market Teams Dominate MLB Playoffs," Associated Press, http://www.heraldtribune.com/article/20091101/article/911011045?Title=Large-market-teams-dominate-MLB-playoffs.
5. Jason Whitlock, "This Glass Is Empty," http://sports.espn.go.com/espn/page2/story?page=whitlock/060615.
6. "The Wal-Martization of America," *New York Times*, November 15, 2003, http://www.nytimes.com/2003/11/15/opinion/the-wal-martization-of-america.html.
7. Lee Drutman, "Value and Values at Wal-Mart—Behind That Implacable Smiley Face," *Providence News-Journal*, http://www.commondreams.org/views05/0825-22.htm.

8. Ibid.
9. Steven Greenhouse, "In-House Audit Says Wal-Mart Violated Labor Laws," *New York Times,* January 13, 2004, http://www.nytimes.com/2004/01/13/business/13WALM.html.
10. Tamara Straus, "When Wal-Mart Comes to Town," May 24, 2001, http://www.alternet.org/story/10919.
11. "Wake Up, Walmart," http://wakeupwalmart.com/facts/.
12. Ibid.
13. Lee Sustar, interview, October 5, 2009.
14. Sam Mellinger, "Strike of '94 Was 'Strike Three' for the Winning Royals," *Kansas City Star,* http://www.kansascity.com/sports/royals/story/1380112.html.
15. Neil A. Lewis, "On a Supreme Court Prospect's Résumé: 'Baseball Savior,'" *New York Times,* May 14, 2009, http://www.nytimes.com/2009/05/15/us/15sotomayor.html.
16. Mellinger, "Strike of '94."
17. Ibid.
18. Whitlock, "This Glass Is Empty."
19. Neil deMause, "Royals, Chiefs Get Their Boodle," April 5, 2006, http://www.fieldofschemes.com/news/archives/2006/04/royals_chiefs_g.html.
20. Mellinger, "Strike of '94."
21. Ann Zimmerman and Kris Maher, "Wal-Mart Warns of Democratic Win," *Wall Street Journal,* http://online.wsj.com/article/SB121755649066303381.html.
22. Ibid.
23. Allen Palmeri, "Royals' Hillman Holds on to Faith," *Baptist Press,* May 8, 2008, http://www.sbcbaptistpress.org/BPnews.asp?ID=28008.

CHAPTER 11: JAMES DOLAN: SERPENT IN EDEN

1. S. L. Price, "Lord Jim," *Sports Illustrated,* February 6, 2007, http://sports illustrated.cnn.com/2007/writers/the_bonus/02/06/price.knicks0212/1.html.
2. Associated Press, "David Stern Criticizes Knicks Management," October 31, 2007.
3. Joel Siegel, "Oedipus at the Garden," *New York,* May 21, 2005, http://nymag.com/nymetro/news/people/features/11545.
4. Price, "Lord Jim."
5. Ibid.

6. Espn.com news services, "Dolan: No Firings, Strategy Is Right," http://sports.espn.go.com/nba/news/story?id=2351222.

7. Russ Bengtson, "A Couple Knicks Lists," http://www.slamonline.com/online/nba/2007/12/a-couple-knicks-lists/.

8. Chris Mannix, "Dubious History: Knicks Repeat Others Mistakes with James Contract," *Sports Illustrated,* January 6, 2006, http://sportsillustrated.cnn.com/vault/article/web/COM1052876/index.htm.

9. Mike McGraw, "Del Negro Calm After the Storm of 42-Point Loss," *Daily Herald,* November 20 2008, http://www.dailyherald.com/story/?id=252592&src=150.

10. Brian Joura, "Top 10 Worst Moves by New York Knicks GM Isiah Thomas," December 1, 2007, http://sportales.com/basketball/top-10-worst-moves-by-new-york-knicks-gm-isiah-thomas/.

11. Bill Simmons, "The Rest of the West," November 4, 2004, http://sports.espn.go.com/espn/page2/story?page=simmons/041104.

12. Thomas Neumann, "The Worst Contracts in NBA History," February 12, 2009, http://sports.espn.go.com/espn/page2/story?page=contracts/090212&sportCat=nba.

13. "After Beating Old Boys Club, Anucha Browne Sanders Is Coming Up Roses," *New York Daily News,* September 27, 2008, http://www.nydailynews.com/sports/basketball/knicks/2008/09/27/2008-09-27_after_beating_old_boys_club_anucha_brown.html.

14. Richard Sandomir, "Jury Finds Knicks and Coach Harassed a Former Executive," *New York Times,* October 3, 2007, http://www.nytimes.com/2007/10/03/sports/basketball/03garden.html.

15. Thomas Zambito, "Isiah Explains Double Standard on Slurs in Garden Trial," *New York Daily News,* September 18, 2007, http://www.nydailynews.com/sports/basketball/knicks/2007/09/18/2007-09-18_isiah_explains_double_standard_on_slurs_.html#ixzz0XXkS77Ng.

16. Jane Ridley, "James Dolan's Indifference Shows Anything Goes at MSG," *New York Daily News,* September 19, 2007, http://www.nydailynews.com/sports/basketball/knicks/2007/09/19/2007-09-19_james_dolans_indifference_shows_anything.html#ixzz0XXkwaYIO.

17. Orlando Patterson, "Jena, O.J., and the Jailing of Black America," *New York Times,* September 30, 2007.

CHAPTER 12: THE NHL: SKATING ON SLUSH?

1. Tripp Mickle, "NHL's Attendance, TV Ratings Both Showing Increases," *Street and Smith's Sports Business Journal*, January 19, 2009, http://www.sportsbusinessjournal.com/article/6117.
2. Richard Garner, interview, April 3, 2009.
3. Scott Burnside, "Union Disputes Claim, No Progress Made," August 27, 2004, http://sports.espn.go.com/nhl/columns/story?id=1868685.
4. Rudy Martzke, "NHL's Woes Could Worsen if ESPN Opts Out of TV Deal," *USA Today*, February 18 2005, http://www.usatoday.com/sports/hockey/nhl/2005-02-18-tv-deal_x.htm.
5. Travis Sedore, interview, April 3, 2009.
6. Mickle, "NHL's Attendance."
7. Dan Wetzel, "And So It Ends," Yahoo! Sports, February 16, 2005.
8. King Kaufman, "King Kaufman's Sports Daily," *Salon*, December 14, 2004, http://www.salon.com/news/sports/col/kaufman/2004/12/14/tuesday/index.html.
9. Associated Press, "NHL Gets Offer to Sell the League," March 4, 2005, http://www.sptimes.com/2005/03/04/Sports/NHL_gets_offer_to_sel.shtml.
10. Espn.com news services, "League Dislikes NHLPA's Replacement Player Stance," March 27, 2005, http://sports.espn.go.com/nhl/news/story?id=2022161.
11. Al Strachan, "Bettman Backs Himself into Plan B Corner," *Toronto Sun*, March 3, 2005, http://slam.canoe.ca/Slam/Hockey/NHL/2005/03/03/pf-948640.html.

CHAPTER 13: THE UNHOLY GALL OF THE PAULSONS

1. Sarah Friesen, "Sam Adams, Randy Leonard and Merritt Paulson Strike Deal to Revamp PGE Park," *Oregonian*, July 9, 2009, http://www.oregonlive.com/portland/index.ssf/2009/07/city_paulson_strike_deal_to_re.html.
2. Portland General Electric Co /OR/ 10-K (Annual Reports), 2009-02-25, http://www.scribd.com/doc/12937296/PORTLAND-GENERAL-ELECTRIC-CO-OR-10K-Annual-Reports-20090225.
3. Maury Brown, "Interview Merritt Paulson: Owner Portland Beavers," August 14, 2007, http://www.bizofbaseball.com/index.php?Itemid=81&id=1433&option=%20com_content&task=view.

4. Adam Sanchez, "Why Bail Out Merritt Paulson?," *Oregonian*, February 26, 2009, http://www.oregonlive.com/opinion/index.ssf/2009/02/why_bail_out_merritt_paulson.html.
5. Anna Griffin, "Merritt Paulson: A Man to Play Ball With," *Oregonian*, March 10, 2009, http://www.oregonlive.com/news/oregonian/anna_griffin/index.ssf/2009/03/merritt_paulson_a_man_to_play.html.
6. Sanchez, "Why Bail Out."

CHAPTER 14: FOR A FEW STEROIDS MORE

1. Stew Winkel, "Bud Selig: When Will He Finally Be Held Accountable for the Steroid Era?," February 9, 2009, http://bleacherreport.com/articles/121977-bud-selig-when-will-he-be-held-accountable-for-his-role-in-the-steroid-era.
2. D. K. Wilson, "The Mitchell Investigation Aftermath: It's Time to Get Religion," December 18, 2007, http://sportsonmymind.com/2007/12/18/the-mitchell-investigation-aftermath-its-time-to-get-religion/.
3. Ibid.
4. Ibid.
5. Winkel, "Bud Selig."
6. Anonymous, interview, September 15, 2005.
7. Howard Bryant, *Juicing the Game: Drugs, Power, and the Fight for the Soul of Major League Baseball* (New York: Plume, 2006), 77.
8. Dan Wetzel, "Clemens Is No Different Than Bonds," December 13, 2007, http://sports.yahoo.com/mlb/news?slug=dw-clemenssteroidsearly121307.
9. Bryant, *Juicing the Game*, 150.
10. Dorsey White, interview, August 30, 2009.
11. Jayson Stark, "A-Rod Has Destroyed Game's History," February 8, 2009, http://sports.espn.go.com/mlb/columns/story?columnist=stark_jayson&id=3892788.
12. Ibid.
13. Bryant, *Juicing the Game*, 293.
14. Ibid., 86.
15. Ibid., 225.

CHAPTER 15: "WHAT'S A SCOUSER?"
TOM HICKS GOES EUROPEAN

1. Tony Barrett, "Tom Hicks Jnr: How Visit to the Sandon Turned Nasty," *Liverpool Echo,* February 25, 2008, http://www.liverpoolecho.co.uk/liverpool-news/local-news/2008/02/25/tom-hicks-jnr-how-visit-to-the-sandon-turned-nasty-100252-20520749/.
2. Ibid.
3. Ibid.
4. CND, "Tom Hicks Jr. Has a Pint with the Locals. What Could Possibly Go Wrong?," February 25, 2008, http://liverpool.theoffside.com/team-news/tom-hicks-jr-has-a-pint-with-the-locals-what-could-possibly-go-wrong.html.
5. Dave Renton, interview, May 22, 2008.
6. Tony Barrett, "Gillett & Hicks, One Year On: From Hope to Despair," *Liverpool Echo,* February 6, 2008, http://www.liverpoolecho.co.uk/liverpool-fc/liverpool-fc-news/2008/02/06/gillett-hicks-one-year-on-from-hope-to-despair-100252-20441485/.
7. Shaun Harkin, interview, December 1, 2008.
8. Chris Noon, "U.S. Tycoons Buy Liverpool Soccer Club," *Forbes,* February 6, 2007, http://www.forbes.com/2007/02/06/liverpool-gillet-update-markets-equity-cx_cn_0206markets16.html.
9. Dr. Grant Farred, interview, June 6, 2008.
10. Ibid.
11. "Red Calm: Warring Gillett and Hicks Call a Ceasefire at Liverpool," *London Evening Standard,* June 20, 2008, http://www.thisislondon.co.uk/sport/article-23497147-red-calm-warring-gillett-and-hicks-call-a-ceasefire-at-liverpool.do.
12. "History of Liverpool FC," http://www.liverpoolmania.com/early-history.php.
13. Tetteh Otuteye, "The True Spirit of Shankly," June 18, 2009, http://www.thisisanfield.com/2009/06/18/the-true-spirit-of-shankly/.
14. Dave Renton, interview, May 22, 2008.
15. John Reid, "The Death of the People's Game: The Great Premier League Swindle," *Socialist Party U.K. Press,* http://www.socialistparty.org.uk/ReclaimTheGame/reclaimthegame1.htm.
16. Ewing Grahame, "Scotland's Scott Brown: Playing in a World Cup Is the Pinnacle," *London Telegraph,* October 10, 2006, http://www.telegraph.co.uk/

sport/football/international/scotland/3168585/Scott-Brown-Playing-in-a-World-Cup-is-the-pinnacle-Football.html.

17. "Football Trivia," http://footballtrivia.wordpress.com/page/3/.

18. "The Heysel Stadium Tragedy, 1985," BBC restrospective, http://www.bbc .co.uk/dna/h2g2/alabaster/A713909.

19. Phil Scraton, "Hillsborough Football Stadium Disaster: A Fight for Justice and Wounds That Never Heal," *London Telegraph*, March 27, 2009, http://www.telegraph.co.uk/sport/football/leagues/premierleague/liverpool/5056427/Hillsborough-football-stadium-disaster-a-fight-for-justice-and-wounds-that-never-heal.html.

20. Ibid.

21. Jim White, "Liverpool Fans Turn on Andy Burnham at Hillsborough Memorial, *London Telegraph*, April 19, 2009, http://www.telegraph.co.uk/sport/football/leagues/premierleague/liverpool/5160448/Liverpool-fans-turn-on-Andy-Burnham-at-Hillsborough-memorial.html.

22. Ibid.

23. Nick Harris, "Footballer Falls Foul of the Rules as He Shows His Political Colours," *Independent*, March 22, 1997, http://www.independent.co.uk/news/footballer-falls-foul-of-the-rules-as-he-shows-his-political-colours-1274203.html.

24. Richard Aikman, "Rafa v. the Americans: A Timeline of Open Warfare," June 17, 2006, http://www.mirrorfootball.co.uk/opinion/blogs/mirror-football-blog/Rafa-v-the-Americans-A-timeline-of-open-warfare-article181053.html.

25. Tim Rich, "Tom Hicks Tells Benitez to Shut Up and Coach," *London Telegraph*, November 24, 2007, http://www.telegraph.co.uk/sport/football/2326532/Tom-Hicks-tells-Benitez-to-shut-up-and-coach .html.

26. Tony Barrett, "Tom Hicks: Jurgen Klinsmann 'Only an Insurance,'" *Liverpool Echo*, January 14, 2008, http://www.liverpoolecho.co.uk/liverpool-fc/liverpool-fc-news/2008/01/14/tom-hicks-jurgen-klinsmann-only-an-insurance-100252–20347645/.

27. The Gaffer, "Why Hicks & Gillette Are Giving Americans a Bad Name," January 15, 2008, http://www.epltalk.com/why-hicks-gillette-are-giving-americans-a-bad-name/1287.

28. Ibid.

29. Antony Kastrinakis, "Rafalution," *Sun*, March 24, 2009, http://www.the sun.co.uk/sol/homepage/sport/football/article2336788.ece.

30. Associated Press, "Hicks Says Teams Won't Be Affected," April 4, 2009, http://sports.espn.go.com/mlb/news/story?id=4041596.
31. Tony Barrett, "Liverpool FC Co-owner Tom Hicks Hit by Credit Crunch Blow," *Liverpool Echo,* May 15, 2008, http://www.liverpoolecho.co.uk/liverpool-fc/liverpool-fc-news/2008/05/15/liverpool-fc-co-owner-tom-hicks-hit-by-credit-crunch-blow-100252-20914232/.
32. Associated Press, "Liverpool's Gillett Reveals 'Unworkable' Ties with Hicks," March 28, 2008, CBC, http://www.cbc.ca/sports/soccer/story/2008/03/28/liverpool-owners.html.
33. Anonymous, interview, June 22, 2008.
34. James Pearce, "Share Liverpool FC Tell George Gillett and Tom Hicks: Sell Our Club to Us," *Liverpool Echo,* November 6, 2008, http://www.liverpoolecho.co.uk/liverpool-fc/liverpool-fc-news/2008/11/06/share-liverpool-fc-tell-george-gillett-and-tom-hicks-sell-our-club-to-us-100252-22196546/.
35. Ibid.
36. http://www.spiritofshankly.com/.
37. Robert Wilonsky, "Tom Hicks' Liverpool FC Partner Meets with Detractors, Who Still Want Duo to Shut Up and 'Sell Up,'" *Dallas Observer,* September 15, 2008, http://blogs.dallasobserver.com/unfairpark/2008/09/tom_hicks_liverpool_fc_partner.php.
38. Ibid.
39. Dr. Grant Farred, interview, June 6, 2008.

OUTRO: LOOKING TOWARD GREEN BAY

1. Sue Halpern, "Home Field Advantage," *Mother Jones,* November–December 2002, http://www.motherjones.com/politics/2002/11/home-field-advantage.
2. Ibid.
3. Ibid.
4. Jesse Zarley, interview, August 15, 2009.
5. David Meggyesy, interview, October 30, 2009.
6. David Morris and Daniel Kraker, "Rooting the Home Team: Why the Packers Won't Leave—and Why the Browns Did," *American Prospect,* September–October 1998, http://www.newrules.org/governance/article/rooting-home-team-why-packers-wont-leave-and-why-browns-did.
7. Yuseph, interview, August 29, 2009.
8. Halpern, "Home Field Advantage."

9. Ibid.
10. Rick Chernick, interview, April 11, 2009.
11. Dave Zirin, "Nader Tackles Sports," *Nation,* June 30, 2008, http://www.the nation.com/doc/20080714/zirin.
12. Christopher L. Gasper, "Adalius Thomas Sounds Off on the NFL," *Boston Globe,* April 3, 2009, http://www.boston.com/sports/football/patriots/reiss_pieces/2009/04/adalius_thomas_1.html.
13. Robert McChesney, interview, November 6, 2009.